Praise

'Mathew Frith offers a masterful recovery of the protectionist school of political economy that shaped nineteenth-century America, restoring its analytical power and revealing its enduring relevance to contemporary debates over trade and development. This book will stand as the authoritative reference on the subject for years to come.'

Carlos Eduardo Suprinyak, Associate Professor of Economics, American University of Paris, France.

'Frith's book fills a significant gap in the scholarly literature by offering what is to date the most comprehensive review of the theoretical underpinnings of America's central contribution to the history of economic thought. An engaging and accessible read, *America's Neglected Protectionist Tradition* reveals that protectionism is about much more than just tariffs.'

Christopher W. Calvo, Florida International University, USA; Author of The Emergence of Capitalism in Early America.

'This book is essential reading for those who still don't acknowledge USA's deep protectionist heritage which has returned with such a force today.'

Lars Magnusson, Emeritus Chair Professor of Economic History, Uppsala University, Sweden; Author of Mercantilism: The Shaping of an Economic Language.

'A well-written and clearly organized exploration of the neglected and timely topic of American protectionist thought from the founding era to the twentieth century.'

Lawrence Peskin, Professor of History and Geography, Morgan State University, USA; Author of Manufacturing Revolution: The Intellectual Origins of Early American Industry.

'Mathew Frith has provided an interesting and lucid examination of the philosophy and economic theory of a group of early American economists, a group neglected by modern mainstream economics with its bias toward free trade. Frith correctly argues the protectionist policy promoted by the group was well-suited to the historical conditions of the early American nation. There is much food for thought, both for those interested in early American economic history and its leading thinkers, and for those who see merit in fitting tariff and industrial policy to the current economic and social conditions of a country.'

Harry Bloch, John Curtin Distinguished Emeritus Professor, Curtin University, Australia.

America's Neglected Protectionist Tradition

America's Neglected Protectionist Tradition

The Economics That Forged a Nation

Mathew A. Frith

ANTHEM PRESS

Anthem Press
An imprint of Wimbledon Publishing Company
www.anthempress.com

This edition first published in UK and USA 2026
by ANTHEM PRESS
75–76 Blackfriars Road, London SE1 8HA, UK
or PO Box 9779, London SW19 7ZG, UK
and
244 Madison Ave #116, New York, NY 10016, USA

British Library Cataloguing-in-Publication Data
A catalogue record for this book is available from the British Library.

Library of Congress Cataloging-in-Publication Data: 2026935832

ISBN-13: 978-1-83999-926-0 (Hbk)
ISBN-10: 1-83999-926-8 (Hbk)

Cover Credit: Public Domain, Creative Commons Zero

This title is also available as an eBook.

COVER IMAGE DESCRIPTION

The economists and statesmen pictured on the cover are:

First row (left to right): Alexander Hamilton; Tench Coxe; Mathew Carey; Henry Clay.

Second row (left to right): Friedrich List; Henry Charles Carey; E. Peshine Smith; William Elder.

Third row (left to right): Ellis H. Roberts; David Hall Rice; Robert Ellis Thompson; Van Buren Denslow.

In loving memory of Punchie, my loyal companion who sat beside me through every chapter.

America has no reason to be ashamed of the long series of writers and orators that have upheld that policy [of protection] which has been that of the Republic through more than two-thirds of its history—Hamilton, Tench Coxe, List, the Careys, Dr. Jackson, John Rae, Raymond, Calvin Colton, Phillips, Choate, Webster, Clay, Everett, Stephen Colwell, Greeley, the Elders, Bigelow, Dixwell, and others still living[1]

— Robert Ellis Thompson

[It is my] hope that some able minds may be led to review their conclusions, and to read or read again, with candid spirit, what has been urged by Rae, Phillips, Carey, List, Bowen, Seaman, Thompson, Greeley, E. P. Smith, Kelley, Elder, and many others who have written in favor of protection.[2]

— George B. Dixwell

Notes

1. Thompson, "Protection Versus Free Trade," 234.
2. Dixwell, *Free Trade Examined*, 3.

CONTENTS

LIST OF TABLES

PREFACE

Alexander Hamilton, Henry Charles Carey, and a score of other protectionist thinkers once commanded the attention of presidents and shaped the economic destiny of America. Today, their theoretical contributions have been so thoroughly expunged from economic discourse that even mentioning "American Protectionism" in academic circles provokes either blank stares or reflexive dismissal. How did an intellectual tradition that was responsible for forging the world's largest economy become virtually extinct in economic scholarship?

This scholarly neglect takes on a whole other dimension when one considers the degree to which protectionism has returned to the forefront of contemporary policy debates. If one wants to seriously understand and debate protectionist policies, it is necessary to understand the economic system of its most sophisticated champions. I thus undertook this study to provide an explication and clarification of the economic philosophy and theory of this important, but neglected, school of economic thought. In doing so, I have tried to maintain a sympathetic yet critical perspective. By immersing myself in the writings of the American Protectionists, it has increasingly confirmed my view that their theories do not require validation from external authorities and contemporary systems of thought, but should be judged from their own standpoint. Whilst counter-arguments certainly exist, and their ideas were vigorously contested by their nineteenth-century opponents, cataloguing these debates falls outside the scope of this work. The purpose here is to provide a systematic reconstruction of the American Protectionists' own theoretical framework. Because the American Protectionists have been routinely dismissed in the secondary literature, such an account is well overdue.

Indeed, the dismissal of the American Protectionists in the secondary literature no doubt stems, in no small part, from the tendency of judging past or alternative theories through the prism of the prevailing thought of the time. I have therefore attempted to lay down the principles and theories of the American Protectionists in a way that is accessible for the modern reader while remaining true to the original meaning intended in their writings. The economics discipline can learn a lot from these thinkers. I therefore ask my fellow economists to put aside any negative preconceptions they may have towards protectionism, and read this work with an open mind. I believe that many will be very surprised at what they will find.

Despite the underlying motivation behind this book, it remains true that it is, at its core, a work on the history of economic thought. The original aim of this research project was to produce an intellectual history of the American Protectionist School by examining each writer within the tradition. Yet, due to the vast number of thinkers uncovered, combined with the remarkable degree of theoretical consistency among them, a systematic reconstruction of the School's theoretical framework proved to be a more interesting and valuable contribution. This should not imply, however, that the research was carried out without reference to the biographical background of these individual thinkers. The initial project involved a significant amount of biographical work, and what was produced has since been condensed into a collection of small biographies. Those who are seeking to get the most out of the present volume would therefore benefit from having these biographical sketches as a companion. These biographies are available for download at www.americanprotectionists.org/biographies and provide valuable context for understanding each thinker's contribution to the School. The more comprehensive intellectual history of the American Protectionist School remains a future project.

I should also stress that although this book is based upon my PhD research, it differs considerably from the PhD dissertation. New evidence has been uncovered, and every chapter of the book has been refined and rewritten. This book, therefore, provides a far stronger and more definitive analysis than that found in the PhD dissertation. That said, the dissertation contains a standalone literature review and more comprehensive footnotes and citations than are practical for a book of this nature. Researchers who are seeking additional primary and secondary source material, and a more substantive list of citations for their own work, may find the comprehensive footnotes featured in the dissertation useful as a bibliographic resource.

Finally, before diving into the book, it is perhaps necessary to make explicit a few points. First, it is important to reiterate that what is to come is not an intellectual history (i.e., it is not a retelling of the development of ideas in their factually precise sequence), but a general treatment of the principles and ideas widely held by the American Protectionist School. This naturally presents limitations. The views ascribed to the School, for instance, will inevitably be generalizations. Indeed, like every other school of economic thought, there will always be points of divergence and disagreement among individual thinkers within the School. Readers seeking exceptions and alternate viewpoints not covered here, may wish to consult the companion material as well as the footnotes contained in the dissertation. The other limitation surrounds the matter of contextualizing and historicizing the evolution of the ideas of the American Protectionists across the full scope of the School's existence. Because this work represents a general reconstruction of their system of economic thought, it necessarily means that the ideas of individual thinkers involved cannot be situated perfectly within their historical circumstances. Whilst this concern is valid, such an approach is better suited for an intellectual history, which remains a future project.

Another point to bring to the reader's attention is that this study draws almost exclusively upon, and thus quotes heavily from, the primary literature of the American Protectionists. The heavy use of quotations is a deliberate act of the author, and whilst this is not uncommon in the history of economic thought, it warrants explanation for the general reader. Too often ideas or beliefs have been ascribed to a particular economist or a group of economists when they held no such belief at all. Such distortions are especially problematic with the rise of pseudo-references and pseudo-citations for it is impossible to verify the validity of every citation which appears in a work. By demonstrating what the American Protectionists said in their own words, this should hopefully avoid the errors of the past and give the reader confidence in the findings of this research.

Whilst this book is written primarily for economists and historians of economic thought, I trust that it will also interest policymakers, political theorists, and anyone interested in contemporary debates about trade, industrial policy, and economic development. No specialized knowledge is required beyond basic economic concepts, though readers should expect engagement with deep theoretical arguments. Readers whose primary interest lies in the protectionist case for tariffs and trade policy may wish to begin with Chapters 10 and 11, before returning to the earlier chapters for the theoretical foundations that underpin those arguments. It is my hope that by the end of the book, the reader will be left with a fair and just rendering of the system of thought developed by the American Protectionists—a system that deserves serious reconsideration.

ACKNOWLEDGMENTS

The intellectual debts accumulated in preparing this work are considerable. First and foremost, I owe an enormous debt of gratitude to Jerry Courvisanos who read over and offered invaluable feedback on countless drafts of the book. I likewise acknowledge the invaluable support and assistance provided by Alex Millmow, Jeremy Smith, and the late John Pullen. The insights offered by Carlos Eduardo Suprinyak and Harry Bloch also proved valuable in refining the book. My thanks also go to Scott Scheall for generously reviewing the Introduction and Chapter 3, and to Simon Burgess for his comments on an early draft of the Introduction. Tim Battin and Tony Ramsay also have my enduring appreciation for their consistent support throughout my academic career.

Many others have also supported me through the completion of this work, whether via helpful advice, suggestions, comments, and encouragement. These include: Tony Aspromourgos, Miriam Bankovsky, William S. Belko, Richard van den Berg, Rebeca Gomez Betancourt, Sheldon Brown, Ross Emmett, Jeff Ferry, Ian Fletcher, David Gilchrist, Scott Harrison, David Hart, Steven Kates, John King, Michael Kortt, Shin Kubo, Julia Marchevsky, Michael McClure, Stephen Meardon, Rod O'Donnell, Paul Oslington, Scott Paul, Lawrence Peskin, Carlos Alberto Rivera Carreño, Matthew Ryan, Dan Ryan, Matthew Smith, Riko Stevens, Thomas Thurner, Keith Tribe, Sofia Valeonti, Ryan Walter, and James Wible. My colleagues at the University of New England deserve recognition for their encouragement, including George Chen, Subas Dhakal, Brian Dollery, David Hadley, Nam Hoang, Shawn Leu, Emilio Morales, Jonathon Moss, Stuart Mounter, Lucie Newsome, Rene Villano, Andrea Wallace, and Subba Reddy Yarram.

The assistance of library and archive staff has been indispensable to this research. My sincere appreciation goes to personnel at the following institutions: Huntington Library, Historical Society of Pennsylvania, Library Company of Philadelphia, Massachusetts Historical Society, Princeton University Library, Hagley Museum and Library, University of Delaware Archives, Friends Historical Library at Swarthmore College, University of Wisconsin Archives, University of Chicago Archives, Houghton Library and Harvard Archives, Kislak Manuscript Center and University Archives and Records Center at the University of Pennsylvania, and Peter Harrington Booksellers. I would also like to thank the five anonymous peer-reviewers who evaluated the original book proposal, and the three anonymous peer-reviewers who reviewed the completed manuscript, for their thoughtful feedback and encouraging words. I am also grateful to everyone at Anthem Press for their guidance and assistance.

Last but certainly not least, my family deserves profound recognition for their patience and support. Above all, my wife Maddy has been a constant source of love, support, and patience throughout this journey. My parents also merit special acknowledgment. Even during difficult times, they made countless sacrifices to ensure that my brothers and I received the best possible education and upbringing, for which I remain immensely grateful. Chris and Cam, my brothers, have shown remarkable patience and provided immense support throughout this period.

INTRODUCTION

The classical period of economics, a period from roughly 1776 to the early twentieth century, is an important epoch in the development of the economics discipline. This fact is readily acknowledged by historians of economic thought. Yet too often the classical period is treated with almost an exclusive focus on developments in Britain, and to a lesser extent, developments in continental Europe. Such scholarship is not to be discouraged, but it is important not to lose sight of developments elsewhere. One such example is the American Protectionist School of economic thought which originated with the ideas of Alexander Hamilton and his contemporaries. These American Protectionist writers were active in the economic debates in the United States, and, contrary to popular belief, it was their ideas, not the free trade theory of the British Classical School, which formed the basis of Republican economic policy in the United States during the classical period. These were the economic ideas that built America.

This book represents a general treatment of the economic philosophy and theory of the American Protectionist School, which spanned from the late eighteenth to the twentieth century. In particular, it is concerned with those American Protectionist writers who aligned themselves with the American System of private enterprise, protective tariffs, and internal improvements. Together, these writers would forge a distinctively American approach to political economy. For simplicity, they shall be referred to hereafter as the American Protectionists. In providing a general treatment of this school of economic thought, the book rediscovers and reconstructs the system of economic philosophy and theory developed by the American Protectionists. The book is thus an intellectual exercise in recovery, and the recovery of this lost system of thought represents the main contribution of the book.

In reconstructing American Protectionist thought, it should be stressed that the study is not one which focuses only on the ideas of Alexander Hamilton, Friedrich List, and Henry Charles Carey, with other writers being shunted aside. Focusing on a few great names, it seems, has created a distortion of the historical record, with American Protectionist thought supposedly reaching its climax and dying out with Henry Carey. Not only did American Protectionist thought not die out with Carey, the general conclusion arrived at, from a broad survey of the primary literature, is that American Protectionist thought came to a full flowering in the writings of the period post-Carey. This is not to say that the post-Carey writers are the main focus in the book, which would imply an inevitable downgrading of their antecedents. It merely underscores the need to provide a general account which draws upon the full breadth of American Protectionist literature.

This book is also not intended to be an intellectual history of the School in the strict and literal sense, but it does attempt to cover all the major aspects of their economic system. Whilst there is, of course, an internal diversity of thought within the American Protectionist School, the degree of consensus which emerged amongst the writers of the School is quite remarkable. The general trajectory of their thought was, for the most part, cumulative, as opposed to competitive. Rather than significant disagreements arising among the authors, the different authors within the School tended to elaborate upon earlier ideas or emphasize different features within the system of thought. The American Protectionists thus appeared to be far more unified than most other schools of economic thought at the time and even most schools of thought in the modern era—a position which will emerge from this study.

The Argument of the Book in the Context of the History of Economic Thought

The main contribution of this work is the rediscovery and reconstruction of the economic system of the American Protectionists. There is, however, an underlying motivation behind this contribution. The argument advanced in this book is that this system constitutes a sophisticated and coherent doctrine of economics that rivals and—in the view of the author—surpasses their classical contemporaries, and even modern schools of economic analysis. The ideas of the American Protectionists should not simply be studied out of mere academic curiosity, but as a source of insight for modern economic thinking. Whilst many excellent studies have documented the success of protectionist policies throughout history, often they only point to free trade theory being at odds with practice.[1] Recovering the system of the American Protectionists moves us beyond the typical "theory versus practice" debate concerning free trade. Not only does their system provide a direct theoretical challenge to free trade theory, it also explains exactly why nations have and can successfully develop using protectionist policies.

Yet, in spite of their sophisticated and comprehensive approach to economic theory the American Protectionists are all but forgotten today.[2] This neglect reflects a broader tendency within mainstream economics. It is an established view in mainstream economics that only the theories contained in the most recent articles of the leading academic journals are valid for understanding the economy. The presumption is that the latest theories have distilled all that is valuable from the past, while discarding its errors. It thus implies that there is nothing to be gained from re-examining the ideas of past economists. Yet this understanding, often designated as the Whig theory of intellectual history, betrays a limited knowledge of how economic thought actually progresses. The development of economic ideas does not simply proceed in an onward and upward march, whereby inferior theories are continually being discarded in favor of more scientifically correct ones. Mark Blaug, the prominent historian of economic thought, observes this point well, noting that "the development of economic thought has not taken the form of a linear path towards present truths. It has progressed, but many have been the detours imposed by the exigencies of time and place."[3]

The Whig theory of intellectual history can be contrasted with the "paradigmatic approach" associated with Thomas Kuhn.[4] Kuhn demonstrates that science, and in our case, economics, does not simply progress in a linear movement towards ever-increasing correctness. There is instead a tendency for a prevailing paradigm or school of thought to become locked-in. Once locked-in, the paradigm will only give way to a competing doctrine through an accumulation of anomalies and contradictions that the theory is incapable of explaining. Granted, these "scientific revolutions" are viewed by Kuhn as correcting the course of intellectual history, allowing it to eventually proceed in the onward and upward march depicted in the Whig theory. But there are added dimensions to this process which casts doubt on whether the history of economics is truly self-correcting.

The works of philosophers Imre Lakatos and Paul Feyerabend extend Kuhn's analysis by arguing that the acceptance and rejection of paradigms is more complex than simply applying rigorous scientific testing or an objective criterion to the theory. This is especially true for economics since economists are unable to conduct large-scale controlled experiments and nor are they able to replicate trials, as this would entail re-running historical events. According to Lakatos, paradigms often employ a "protective belt" of auxiliary assumptions, hypotheses, and modifications to explain away the various anomalies and contradictions that arise.[5] In other words, economic paradigms can adapt and defend themselves, sometimes for decades after their flaws have been exposed.

The prevailing paradigm will therefore prove far more resistant to change than assumed by Kuhn. Often there is a complex and even psychological process involved in bringing about a paradigm shift, with scholars persisting with the existing paradigm even in the face of growing anomalies, and only abandoning it once it is deemed to be a waste of time to continue any further. Feyerabend goes even further, however, arguing that there really exists no criterion or fixed rule at all for evaluating paradigms. Instead, academic research programs almost always persist by adding an ever-growing list of *ad-hoc* postulates to the paradigm to make it temporarily compatible with the various anomalies and contradictions that arise.[6] In short, economic paradigms can persist not because they are correct, but because they are entrenched.

This paradigmatic approach is complemented in the field of economics by the writings of Deirdre McCloskey. According to McCloskey, the acceptance or rejection of a theoretical paradigm in economics is just as much rhetorical and literary as it is rational and scientific. Or to put it differently, in economics, being persuasive can matter just as much as being correct. The rhetorical power of a theory is thus an essential element for maintaining existing paradigms or bringing about a paradigm shift.[7] It is therefore difficult to discern between a paradigm consisting of credible economic theory and one of simple rhetoric. By implication, it does not necessarily follow that a newly accepted paradigm will be more correct than the one it displaces, or that there are not alternate theories of equal or even greater value. Economics will therefore tend to move in a zig-zag pattern whereby superior theories may be supplanted by inferior ones, rather than following a linear progression in the onward and upward march of history.[8] This is why economic knowledge can be lost and forgotten over time. If superior theories can therefore be displaced by inferior ones, it means that the American Protectionists may have simply been casualties of ebbs and flows of the history of economic thought.

One need not adopt the nihilistic implications of the above analysis, nor does it provide a free pass to blindly dismiss mainstream economics as devoid of any redeeming qualities. Instead, it underscores the need for an open-minded and pluralist approach to the study of economics. This paradigmatic approach also does not in itself demonstrate that the ideas of the American Protectionists are superior to that taught in mainstream textbooks. What it demonstrates is that there can be no presumption that contemporary economic thought is superior to earlier thought, or that more well-known economists or more well-known schools of thought are more worthy than lesser-known ones. For if it holds true that the overall trajectory of economics is just as much a matter of rhetorical persuasion as it is objective truth, it stands to reason that fallacious and erroneous theories may elbow aside sounder ones. Indeed, it would not be too much of a stretch to say that the ideas of the American Protectionists would be especially prone to this sort of treatment due to the general aversion which mainstream economics, both historical and contemporary, has towards protectionism. Ideas can easily be dismissed if they are at variance with the views of the prevailing paradigm. Likewise, it is easy to see how revisionist studies in the history of economic thought can fail to recognize and recover lost knowledge, especially if the researcher carrying out the study is approaching it from the standpoint of the prevailing paradigm.

The above analysis holds important implications for the present study as well as its relevance for modern scholarship. Among other things, protectionism, a pillar central to the policy program of the American Protectionists, continues to be widely dismissed as unsound and economically illiterate within mainstream economics. Yet, few economists have actually been acquainted with the ideas and arguments of the American Protectionists. The critics of protectionism typically employ the theory of comparative advantage, or some modern equivalent, in defense of free trade. This was a theory that was widely discredited within American Protectionist circles over a century ago. By ignoring such developments in the history of economic thought and simply dismissing these economists as archaic scribblers from a bygone era, we risk making economics a shallower and less rigorous discipline than it otherwise could be. Valuable insights can be discovered in the writings of long dead thinkers, and the rediscovery of these insights constitutes the creation of new economic knowledge for the present.

This theoretical discussion is not a mere ivory-tower exercise. It has profound practical implications. The contemporary relevance of American Protectionist thought is underscored by the resurgence of protectionist policies in the United States and elsewhere. Such developments have emerged without engagement with America's own historic and theoretically-rich tradition of protectionist political economy. By offering a sophisticated and informed case for protection, the American Protectionists provide valuable insights for contemporary policy debates. Thus, to restate the central argument of the book, the system of the American Protectionists represents a sophisticated and systematic school of economic thought that deserves recovery and merits our consideration. The chapters that follow will demonstrate this claim.

Structure of the Book

To foreshadow what to expect from this book, the following provides an outline of the contents of this work. Chapter 1 involves setting the scene for this study. Its purpose is to equip the reader with relevant background information and context concerning the School. It is very easy to start off with a discussion of economic theory without explaining the thinkers and institutions involved, but this often results in confusion. Thus, in order to make the book more comprehensible, the chapter introduces the different economists and statesmen who formed the American Protectionist School. It then explores the nexus between nineteenth century American economics and politics, and particularly how the School aligned itself with the Federalist, Whig, and Republican parties throughout the period in question. The chapter then situates the American Protectionists within the broader landscape of nineteenth century economic thought. In doing so, particular emphasis is placed on the American Protectionists' evolving relationship with the different strands of Classical thought, as well as the German Historical and Progressive Schools. The chapter ends with a discussion of how the School organized themselves as an intellectual movement, and details how the American Protectionists mobilized themselves through a network of industry associations, think tanks, and protectionist advocacy groups.

Chapter 2 provides an overview of the general policy framework advocated by the American Protectionists. To a large extent, the School is defined by its policy program, namely the American System. An analysis of their policy program will therefore enable the reader to better appreciate and understand exactly what the School is about, hence why this chapter precedes the theoretical chapters of the book. In providing an overview of their policy framework, a conscious attempt is made to highlight the remarkably nuanced position of the American Protectionists. In particular, the name "protectionist" may give the misconception that these writers were anti-market and fervent champions of state activism. In actual fact, the American Protectionists generally only endorsed state intervention in the form of protective tariffs, with the proceeds being used to finance the development of infrastructure. In other matters of public policy, the American Protectionists were more often on the side of less government intervention, preferring instead for the State to play a passive nightwatchman role within the internal market. By laying this groundwork early on, this chapter seeks to pre-emptively dissuade any misconceptions about the School.

Chapters 3 through 11 constitute the main theoretical chapters of the book. Chapter 3 discusses the moral and social philosophy of the School. The chapter begins with a discussion of the underlying vision of the School, before proceeding with a discussion of the philosophy, methodology, and even the theology underpinning American Protectionist thought. In particular, the chapter demonstrates how American Protectionist thought is predicated on natural law, the inductive method, and a rejection of the Classical "economic man." The chapter finishes with a discussion of the nature of wealth as conceived by the American Protectionists, and highlights their distinction they made between individual and national wealth. By providing an overview of these philosophical foundations, the chapter establishes the conceptual base upon which the theoretical system of the American Protectionists was built.

Chapter 4 focuses on the theoretical foundations of the School, or to put it differently, what can be considered as the building blocks of their theoretical system. This is perhaps one of the most important chapters in the book since the latter chapters cannot be properly understood without these foundations. These foundations also represent some of the more profound insights of the American Protectionist School, as they often contrast sharply with those that underpin Classical, Marxist, and modern schools of economic thought.

Chapter 5 sets out the value tradition of the American Protectionists. This chapter, in particular, discusses the reproduction cost theory of value which represents a distinctly American Protectionist approach to value theory. In doing so, this chapter clears away many misconceptions about the reproduction cost theory of value and contrasts it with the more static approach to value theory of the Classical economists. In clearing away these misconceptions, the chapter demonstrates how the American Protectionists saw declining prices as a sign of economic prosperity, which connects with their analysis of national wealth.

Chapter 6 concerns the theories of the American Protectionists pertaining to growth, development, and entrepreneurship. In a sense, the entire school of thought is one of growth and development, and as such, every chapter contained within this book concerns growth and development in some way. There is enough material, however, to provide a separate treatment of the topic, even though every other chapter is necessary to fully understand their views on the matter of growth and development. What is made clear within this chapter, and throughout the book more broadly, is that the American Protectionists were dynamic thinkers who stressed the importance of human ingenuity and invention.

Chapter 7 explores the theory of distribution developed by the American Protectionists. In contrast to Ricardian and Marxist economics, the American Protectionists were champions of what they saw as a harmony of interests between workers and capitalists. In discussing their theory of distribution, the chapter highlights the interplay between productivity and wage growth in American Protectionist thought. Moreover, against the tendency in the Classical and Marxist traditions of treating class structures as fixed and permanent, the American Protectionists stressed the ability for individuals to better themselves and to move between economic classes. This theory of social or class mobility was central to the American Protectionist system of thought, and represents the other key area of focus of the chapter.

Chapter 8 concerns the interconnected theories of population, association, and agglomeration, or what the American Protectionists termed "concentration." The American Protectionist theory of population can be seen as the antithesis of Malthusian economics. In contrast to Malthusian economics, their theory espouses the view that population growth promotes abundance, as opposed to scarcity. This question of population also connects with the American Protectionists' distinctive concept of association, which at its core, depicts individuals as social creatures. These ideas on population and association then go on to form the foundations of their analysis of population density and their theory of agglomeration.

Chapter 9 discusses the theory of the business cycle. In particular, this chapter concerns their analysis of recessions and depressions. Although the concept of macroeconomics is largely foreign to nineteenth-century economic thought, the American Protectionists proceeded to construct a theory of the business cycle predicated on technological developments at the microeconomic level. For all practical purposes, this chapter can thus be considered as their contribution to what is now considered macroeconomics.

Chapter 10 discusses the theory of international trade developed by the American Protectionists and provides a comprehensive coverage of their key arguments for protectionism. In doing so, the chapter provides a complete overview of their argument for protectionism. This includes the more well-known arguments, such as those for infant-industry protection, as well as the lesser-known and more generalized arguments for permanent protection. By the end of this chapter, the reader should have a thorough understanding of the key arguments espoused by the School in defense of tariff protection.

The study then proceeds to Chapter 11, which addresses the views of the American Protectionists concerning taxation. Contrary to what one might expect, the American Protectionists can be considered as adhering to a philosophy of low taxation and would even anticipate many of the ideas now associated with supply-side economics. This chapter also complements the previous chapter on international trade. There is a tendency in modern economics to treat protection and taxation in isolation to one another, but this obfuscates many important insights offered by the American Protectionists. The American Protectionists never viewed tariff protection as independent from the subject of taxation, but rather as two elements of the one system. Thus, in order to provide a complete picture of the American Protectionist system of thought, an examination of their theory of taxation is thus necessary.

The concluding chapter draws together the findings of the earlier chapters to explain exactly what the American Protectionist School is. In doing so, there is a conscious attempt to demonstrate how the different components of their economic theory integrate into a coherent and systematic whole. The discussion then proceeds with an examination of the American Protectionists' place in the history of economic thought, before returning to the question of economic paradigms and mounting an argument for resurrecting this lost tradition. The book concludes by drawing out the broader implications of American Protectionist thought for economic analysis and public policy in the modern era.

At the end of all this, you should be left with a coherent understanding of what American Protectionist thought was all about and will be able to appreciate this unique and original system of economic thought. For those readers who are motivated by this book to pursue further research in the area, there will no doubt be areas of disagreement, but if the book encourages individuals to look at the economics of the American Protectionists for themselves and to take their ideas seriously, it will have succeeded in its objective of restoring them to their rightful place in the history of economic thought.

Notes

1. Chang, *Kicking Away the Ladder*; Bairoch, *Economics*; Reinert, *Rich Countries Got Rich*; Fasteau and Fletcher, *Industrial Policy*; Fletcher, *Free Trade Doesn't Work*. Reinert, Fasteau, and Fletcher also provide theoretical frameworks.
2. For valuable general scholarship on American economic thought, see Calvo, *Capitalism in Early America*, and Dorfman, *Economic Mind*. For an alternate account of American protectionist thought, see Hudson, *Protectionist Take-off*. For a comparative international perspective, see Helleiner, *Neomercantilists*. For an exhaustive economic history of the period, see Irwin, *Clashing Over Commerce*. For recent specialized studies, see Meardon, "Reciprocity"; "Yankee Ingenuity"; Valeonti, "Carey's Monetary Thought"; Rossi, "Protecting America"; Frith, "Outline". For an influential popular treatment, see Lind, *Land of Promise*. A more comprehensive literature review appears in the author's doctoral thesis.
3. Blaug, *Theory in Retrospect*, 8.
4. Kuhn, *Scientific Revolutions*, 45.
5. Lakatos, *Research Programmes*, 179.
6. Feyerabend, *Against Method*.
7. McCloskey, *Rhetoric*. Though McCloskey uses 'rhetoric' not as pejorative, but to highlight the conversational nature of scientific argumentation.
8. This zig-zag depiction of the history of economic thought is advanced by Rothbard, *Classical Economics*, ix–x; and implied in Roncaglia, *Wealth of Ideas*, 5–11.

Chapter One

SETTING THE SCENE

The American Protectionists

Not long after the American Revolution came to a close, a second struggle for independence was emerging. This time, it was not for political independence, but economic independence, and it would not be fought with muskets. It would be fought with ideas. Whilst not a literal war, the implications were no less important. In the *Report on Manufactures*, Hamilton declared, for instance, that the development of industry was necessary for "not only the wealth, but the independence and security" of the United States. If this war were to be fought with ideas, its generals were those who committed these ideas to paper. Nearly 70 economists, from Hamilton's *Report on Manufactures* to the turn of the twentieth century, shaped American protectionist thinking. What began as a small circle of economic thinkers in Hamilton's orbit would evolve through four generations into a movement encompassing academics, industrialists, journalists, and even presidents. Indeed, whilst some sources have attempted to distance Hamilton from the later generations of American Protectionists that followed, these later protectionists clearly saw themselves as heirs to Hamilton's economic philosophy, with Mathew Carey going so far as to label their tradition of American protectionism as the "Hamiltonian school of political economy."[1]

The first and smallest group of American Protectionists roughly spans from the late eighteenth century (c. 1780) to the period prior to the Panic of 1819. These "gladiators of the quill" include William Bingham, William Barton, Tench Coxe, and Alexander Hamilton himself.[2] The most notable of these thinkers were, of course, Hamilton and Coxe, who together penned what could be considered America's declaration of economic independence—the *Report on the Subject of Manufactures*. Both figures should, as the Boston-based Home Market Club explains, be "recognized as … father[s] of the protective system in America."[3] Latecomers would also join the ranks of this first group, including the geographer and mapmaker John Melish and the statesman Alexander J. Dallas.

The second group spans roughly from the Panic of 1819 to the publication of Henry Carey's *The Past, The Present, and the Future* in 1848. The dominant figure was Mathew Carey, the protectionist publisher who became the de facto leader of the School following Hamilton's death. His circle included the lawyer Daniel Raymond, whose *Thoughts on Political Economy* represented the first systematic American treatise on the subject. The New England contingent of the movement was led by the diplomat Alexander Hill Everett, and also included the prominent lawyer Willard Phillips, and clergyman Calvin Colton, who held the Chair of Political Economy at Trinity College. The movement also drew from diverse professions including publishers (Hezekiah Niles), clergy (Lyman Beecher), physicians (Samuel Jackson), merchants (David Stirrat), military men (William Jennison), and politicians (George Tibbits, William Charles Jarvis).

The political speeches and reports of key American Protectionist statesmen were also central to the movement during this period. These statesmen include the Kentuckian Henry Clay, who is often recognized as the father of the American System, and the New Englanders Daniel Webster and Rufus Choate. Whilst not always thought of when discussing American economic thought, the German émigré Friedrich List is also included in this study, since his protectionist views were a direct result of his residence in Pennsylvania and his connection with Mathew Carey.[4] This also applies to the Canadian economist John Rae, whose major work was sponsored by the Boston protectionists, and who was perhaps the most sophisticated thinker in the School since Hamilton and Coxe.[5] The movement also extended beyond the Northern states, and penetrated into the more traditional free-trade stronghold of the South through the writings of Nathaniel A. Ware and William Gregg.

The third group formed around Henry Charles Carey, the son of Mathew Carey, and spans from 1848 to around 1875. Henry Carey was undoubtedly the most influential American Protectionist thinker since Alexander Hamilton. His inner circle included the publisher Horace Greeley, who founded the *New York Tribune*, the physician William Elder, who assisted Carey in the preparation of his *Principles of Social Science*, and the lawyer E. Peshine Smith, who advised prominent Whig statesman William Seward. The academic presence included Francis Bowen at Harvard, William Dexter Wilson at Cornell, and Robert Ellis Thompson of the University of Pennsylvania, who was also a close friend of Carey. The movement also drew financial and intellectual backing from the ironmasters Stephen Colwell and Joseph Wharton, founder of the Wharton School of Business. Other members of this group include Ezra Seaman, who was a treasury official during the Taylor and Fillmore Administrations, and the journalist and newspaper proprietor Andrew W. Young. The Pennsylvania statesmen William D. Kelley and Andrew Stewart also provided political leadership through their Congressional speeches and writings.

The fourth and largest group overlaps with the previous generation and spans from the postbellum period through the turn of the twentieth century. Despite being the largest of the four groups and—in the author's view—the most refined, these writers are by far the most neglected in the secondary literature. The intellectual leadership of the School passed to Robert Ellis Thompson and William Elder from the previous generation, joined by Van Buren Denslow, who together represent the thought leaders of post-Carey protectionism. Indeed, even Alfred Marshall observed, during his trip to the United States in 1875, that "Thompson's *Social Science*" was regarded by American Protectionists "as to a large extent superseding Carey."[6]

The journalistic wing of this generation was particularly strong. This included John L. Hayes, Albert Clarke, Giles B. Stebbins, John W. Hinton, John Philip Young, David H. Mason, George Gunton, and Cyrus Elder, the younger brother of William Elder.

The movement also drew support from industrialists and merchants, most notably Erastus B. Bigelow, who founded the National Association of Wool Manufacturers, along with George B. Dixwell and John Welsh. Likewise, the movement also attracted a diverse range of professionals, including lawyers (David H. Rice, George B. Curtiss, Orrin Skinner), educators (Jacob Harris Patton, George M. Steele), and the publisher Henry Carey Baird, the nephew of Henry Carey. Like the previous generations, political support also reached the highest levels, and included President William McKinley, Presidential Candidate James G. Blaine, Speaker Thomas Brackett Reed, and Representatives Roswell G. Horr and Justin Smith Morrill. There were also government officials, including US Treasurer Ellis H. Roberts, Secretary of the Navy Richard W. Thompson, Pennsylvania Governor Henry M. Hoyt, Census official Robert P. Porter, and diplomat and spy Thomas H. Dudley. These are the thinkers who made up the American Protectionist School.

Before proceeding further, however, there are two misconceptions about the School that require correction. The first relates to the supposed hostilities between the New England and Pennsylvanian protectionists. It has been argued, for instance, that "the Boston protectionists" stood "in sharp contrast to the theories of [Pennsylvania] economists."[7] By implication, this suggests that the two were separate and distinct traditions. This claim, however, is more mythology than actual history, and rests entirely on a recycled quote allegedly from John Rae. The quote in question suggests that Alexander Everett, and by extension, the New England Protectionists, were supposedly "scared of Mathew Carey's work," with Mathew Carey representing the leader of the Pennsylvanians.[8] The problem is that no quote of the kind exists in any of Rae's writings, nor in any of his recorded letters.

Far from being hostile toward one another, the two considered themselves as part of one tradition.[9] Indeed, the claim that the Bostonians were scared of the Pennsylvanians does not stand up to the slightest scrutiny. If Everett was so "scared" of Mathew Carey, he would not have united with Carey at both the 1827 Harrisburg Tariff Convention and 1831 New York Friends of Domestic Industry Convention.[10] The kinship between the two groups is perhaps best illustrated by Robert Ellis Thompson's praise for his New England counterparts:

> We [the Protectionists] of Pennsylvania rejoice in the prosperity of our sister state as though it were our own … No state has done more to make that policy [of protection] the American law than has Massachusetts … by the able advocacy of protection by men like Daniel Webster, [Willard] Phillips, Oliver Putnam, Francis Bowen, John L. Hayes, George B. Dixwell, and a score of others.[11]

Such expressions of mutual admiration were typical of the relationship between the two groups, belying any notion of rivalry or fear.

The second misconception concerns the economist Simon Patten. Although nominally protectionist, Patten can hardly be considered as a member of the School. Whilst there is, of course, an internal diversity of ideas among the traditional American Protectionists, these differences are one of emphasis and degree. When it comes to Patten, the difference is fundamentally one of kind. Patten was a Progressive, whose ideas were drawn primarily from the German Historical School.[12] Patten was thus an advocate of the so-called "socialism of the chair," a system which included price and wage controls, progressive income tax, and state monopolization. This has very little in common with the American System of Capitalism which descended from Hamilton and Coxe.

The Nexus Between American Economic Thought and Politics

For over a century and a half, the Federalists, Whigs, and Republicans served as the political arm in the struggle for American economic independence, translating protectionist doctrine into national policy. The relationship between American Protectionist thought and political development was not merely a correlation, but a compact. Unlike European economic schools that developed primarily in academic circles, American Protectionist thought emerged within the political sphere itself. The seminal texts of the tradition—Hamilton and Coxe's *Report on Manufactures*, Dallas' *Report*, Clay's American System speeches, and the Congressional addresses of Webster and Choate—were not academic treatises but political documents, written by statesmen and their advisers for immediate legislative purposes. These origins meant that politics and economics would co-evolve and shape one other throughout nineteenth-century America. An examination of this nexus is therefore essential for understanding how American Protectionist doctrine evolved from Hamilton's initial formulation through its various party incarnations.

Whilst some popular sources have tried to explain away party differences by depicting the Federalists, Whigs, and Republicans as champions of big government, and the Democrats as bastions of the free market, for all this to somehow culminate in the two parties' switching sides with Woodrow Wilson's New Freedom and later Franklin D. Roosevelt's New Deal, the reality is far more complex. The underlying philosophy of the Democratic Party was not so much one of free markets and limited government, but militant egalitarianism (at least among whites) and democracy based on majoritarian rule. This contrasts sharply with the Federalist-Whig-Republican tradition, the latter of which emphasized an older-style republican order predicated on meritocracy, industrial capitalism and private property.

The ideology of the Federalists, Whigs, and Republicans remained more-or-less consistent throughout the nineteenth and early twentieth centuries. As historian John Gerring puts it:

> Notwithstanding the organizational death of one party and its replacement by another, a civil war … and several realignments of partisan voting allegiances, the evidence … suggests that a fairly consistent view of the political world was carried over from the party of [Henry] Clay to the party of Lincoln to the party of Calvin Coolidge, the last bearer of American Whiggism.[13]

This political lineage from the Federalists to the Republican party was also avowed by the leading Republicans of the time. Calvin Coolidge himself acknowledged this, declaring that the Republican Party "through its present declaration of principles, through the traditions which it inherited from its predecessors, the Federalists and the Whigs … is representative of those policies … adopted under the lead of Alexander Hamilton."[14] The tariff plank, in particular, was the cornerstone of this tradition, as observed by a contemporary editorial:

> The Republican party … from its birth has been the party of protection. From Hamilton to McKinley, whether under the name Federalist, Whig or Republican … protection is about the only political tenet for which the Republican party distinctively and traditionally stands.[15]

Whereas the evolution of the Federalist–Whig–Republican side of politics is relatively easy to account for, the complexity comes when tracking the evolution of the Democratic Party and how their egalitarian and democratic principles manifested as public policy and how these principles intersected with economic thought.

A useful way of understanding this nexus between politics and economic thought is to look at the party systems of the United States. The first-party system, which operated from about 1790 to 1828, came about as the result of fractures within the Washington Administration. The two emerging factions formed into the parties known as the Federalists and the Democratic–Republicans. Federalists were the forerunners of the Whig Party and eventually the Republicans, whereas the Democratic–Republicans can be seen as the forerunner of the modern-day Democrats. The Federalists were the party of Washington's Treasury Secretary and the founder of the American Protectionist School, Alexander Hamilton. The Federalists believed in fostering a strong industrial economy, and championed Hamilton's program of a national bank and state-sponsored industrial development, as elaborated in Hamilton's *Report on Manufactures* and his other state papers. Other protectionist thinkers within the Federalist ranks included William Bingham, Tench Coxe, and William Barton.[16] The Federalists were thus aligned with what may be considered the embryonic stages of the American Protectionist School.

The other party, the Democratic–Republicans, rallied around the then Secretary of State, Thomas Jefferson. In contrast to the Hamiltonian Federalists, the Democratic–Republicans embodied much of the egalitarianism of the later Democratic party, but were more restrained and tempered in their approach. Jefferson accepted capitalist society and generally favored limited government as a safeguard against the remnants of feudalism and aristocracy. His vision of American capitalism differed from Hamilton's, however, in that he envisioned a preindustrial and classless republic of yeoman farmers. Like Hamilton, the ideas of Jefferson became associated with a school of economic thought that has since been labeled the "Jeffersonian School." Although not exactly a coherent body of thought, the Jeffersonian School represented a synthesis of sorts between local agrarian doctrines, the ideas of the French Physiocrats, Adam Smith, and the French Liberal School.[17]

The Physiocrats, including Jefferson's friend Dupont de Nemours, emphasized the notion that agriculture was the only productive form of economic activity, which goes some ways to explaining the pre-industrial philosophy of the Jeffersonians and their aversion to Hamilton's *Report*. This was also complemented by the French Liberal School, commonly associated with the writings of Jean-Baptiste Say. These thinkers were ardent defenders of *laissez-faire* and free trade. In fact, Jefferson even considered Say's *Treatise on Political Economy* to be "shorter, clearer, and sounder" than Adam Smith's *Wealth of Nations*.[18] Yet, the biggest influence on Jefferson was the French Liberal Destutt de Tracy, whose work Jefferson translated into English.[19] De Tracy was highly scathing of special privileges granted to particular classes by the State, and this naturally tied in well with Jefferson's aversion to protective tariffs.[20]

This Jeffersonian physiocratic-liberal tradition likewise found domestic intellectual support in thinkers, such as John Taylor of Caroline, and Jefferson's protege, Thomas Cooper, who later broke away and founded his own School, known as the Southern Doctrine. In spite of the general commitment to free markets extolled by the Jeffersonians, the egalitarian underpinnings of their philosophy are highlighted by Jefferson's own favorable views on progressive taxation. In the words of Jefferson:

> I am conscious that an equal division of property is impracticable … [But a] means of silently lessening the inequality of property is to exempt all from taxation below a certain point, and to tax the higher portions of property in geometrical progression as they rise. Whenever there is in any country, uncultivated lands and unemployed poor, it is clear that the laws of property have been so far extended as to violate natural right.[21]

In short, Jeffersonian ideology was egalitarian at its core, but this egalitarianism was intimately connected with free markets and limited government due to the skepticism held toward the State as a mechanism for monopoly, special privilege, and aristocracy.

Of course, it should be acknowledged that this is a simplification of a complex period of American political history, as the economic policies enacted by each party were not always consistent with each party's professed ideology, and nor were both parties divided squarely along economic lines. Democratic–Republicans, for instance, particularly under the more nationalist James Madison and his Treasury Secretary Alexander Dallas, proved quite willing to utilize Hamiltonian-style policies during their terms in office, even though they were the policies which the party had previously criticized.[22] What is clear, however, is that the economic ideology of the Whigs and Republicans can be traced to Hamilton's Federalist Party, and the ideology of the Democratic Party can be seen as an ideological continuation of Jefferson's Democratic–Republicans. Unlike the first-party system, the alignment of politico-economic creed would become more clearly cemented in the later party systems.

As the Federalists faded as a political force in the 1810s, the United States reverted to a one-party system. The Democratic–Republicans now represented a broad church, as many former Federalists flocked to the party. One-party rule proved unable to reconcile Hamiltonian nationalism with Jeffersonian liberal-agrarianism, however, leading to schism in the 1820s. This schism would bring forth the second-party system, which spanned from roughly 1829 to 1854.

The industrial and nationalistic faction of the Democratic–Republicans, led by protectionists Henry Clay and Daniel Webster, eventually broke away to form the

Whig Party. The Whigs assumed the mantle of the Federalists, establishing themselves as the party of Henry Clay's American System of protective tariffs and internal improvements. As the party of protection, numerous American Protectionist writers and orators would occupy Whig ranks. The emergence of the Whigs was also marked by a notable evolution in American Protectionist thought. Whereas Hamilton had advocated for the temporary use of bounties and subsidies for infant industries, the new generation of American Protectionists abandoned subsidies for the exclusive use of tariffs. This reflected the careful distinction made by American Protectionists between "protectionism" and "paternalism."[23]

The remaining faction of the Democratic–Republicans formed into the Democratic Party. Largely continuing in the Jeffersonian tradition, the Democrats, under the leadership of Andrew Jackson and his successors, were roughly the party of libertarianism and *laissez-faire* economics, but with a more populist and militant egalitarianism. As historian William S. Belko explains:

> The core concepts underlying Jacksonian Democracy [were] equal protection of the laws; an aversion to a moneyed aristocracy, exclusive privileges, and monopolies, and a predilection for the common man; majority rule; and the welfare of the community over the individual.[24]

The Jacksonian Democrats maintained the Jeffersonian commitment to French Liberalism, whilst also supplementing these ideas with Ricardian theory. Often, these ideas were popularized in the American political scene by a group of radical free market activists, known as the "Loco-Focos," who expounded their arguments counterintuitively on collectivist and anti-elitist grounds.[25]

The Democratic Administrations, which dominated federal politics until the Civil War, were advised by both Loco-Focos and more mainline free traders. Among these were the likes of Clinton Roosevelt, Jacob Cardozo, Amasa Walker, and Treasury Secretary Robert J. Walker, who was responsible for the controversial and highly free-trade-oriented 1846 *Treasury Report*. Indeed, the Walker *Treasury Report* offers a clear case of the egalitarian orientation of the Democrats, with passages describing tariffs as "discrimination against the poor and in favor of the rich" and emphasizing how "to the poor this tax operates most oppressively."[26] This even led the more labor-oriented Whig and Protectionist Horace Greeley to declare that the Democrats were "impelled rather by jealousy or hatred of wealth than by dislike to Protection *per se*."[27] American Protectionists, on the other hand, espoused a harmony of interests between workers and capitalists. They were also willing to tolerate inequality, focusing instead on maximizing social mobility, so that workers could become capitalists themselves.

The *laissez-faire* orientation of the Democratic Party only goes so far, however, in explaining their philosophy, as there was a substantial interventionist element which exerted influence within the party. This deviation from *laissez-faire* (which is not wholly inconsistent with Classical economics) can be seen through the implementation of labor legislation and a 10-hour workday by the Van Buren Administration.[28] Horace Greeley, again, questioned this policy, writing that "we do not regard this measure as promising any great benefit," preferring the negotiation of labor hours to be left to "mutual agreement."[29] The American Protectionists were, of course, champions of high wages and better conditions for workers, but they argued that sustained improvements in these conditions could only be achieved through productivity growth and sound industrial conditions rather than by legislative decree.

The divergence between the Whigs and Democrats is perhaps best summarized by historian Arthur M. Schlesinger, who explains that "the real issue between the Whigs and Jackson[ian Democrats] was, thus, not freedom of enterprise. Both parties would concede that enterprise should be free, [and] would claim always to be acting to protect this freedom" but each would "intervene in business … in the name of freedom." Jeffersonians would intervene on behalf of the commoner "and institute a ten-hour day, while the Hamiltonian [Whigs] would flourish free-trade principles when questions of trade unionism or corporation control were brought up," whilst "establishing protective tariffs" in the next instance.[30] The position is also evidenced by Democratic politician and social thinker George Bancroft, who observed that:

> The [free trade] system of political economy may solve the question of the commercial intercourse of nations … but its abandonment of labor to the unmitigated effects of … competition can never be accepted … [whilst] no practicable system of social equality has been brought forward … it does not follow that none can be devised.[31]

This is not to suggest that either party's commitment to free enterprise was disingenuous. Both essentially affirmed free market principles, but neither adopted a fundamentalist position that viewed the free market in a purely literal sense and without important policy qualifications.

Meanwhile, the Northern Democrats were accompanied by their Southern counterparts. Under the leadership of John C. Calhoun, the Southern Democrats subscribed to an Americanized version of Ricardian and Malthusian economics, which they combined with novel developments of their own. This "Southern Doctrine" aligned with the free market policies of the Northern Democrats, but with an added defense of slavery and the plantation system, which they justified on Ricardian and Malthusian grounds.[32] The Southern Doctrine can also be seen as a throwback to the ideas of the Physiocrats since it was fashioned with an appeal to agrarianism.

Intellectually, there was a cadre of Southern thinkers under the leadership of the South Carolinian economist Thomas Cooper. These economists provided theoretical support for this doctrine, and were even responsible for advising the Democratic Party.[33] Of course, it should be acknowledged that not all Democrats were in lockstep on the issue of slavery. By the late 1840s, the abolitionist faction of Northern Democrats, known as the Barnburners, grew increasingly dissatisfied with the party's leadership for refusing to denounce slavery, and subsequently broke away to form the Free-Soil Party. These Free Soilers were heavily influenced by the free trade ideas of both Richard Cobden and John Bright of the Manchester School, believing that free labor and free trade were intimately connected.[34] These Free Soilers would have a significant influence on the political realignment in the third-party system.

The third-party system (1854–1896) maintained the previous ideological divisions. The key difference was that the Republicans replaced the Whigs as the champions of the American System, and that the ideas of Richard Cobden would exert more force within Democratic politics. The deaths of Henry Clay and Daniel Webster proved to be the death knell of the Whig Party, with the Whigs collapsing in the mid-1850s. In 1854, former Whigs established the Republican Party in coalition with former Free-Soil Democrats, with Free Soilers as the junior partner.[35] Although the Republican Party formed in opposition to the expansion of slavery, former Whigs, as the party majority, soon proved successful in establishing the American System as Republican policy. The most influential protectionist during this period was Henry Charles Carey. As Vice President of the Pennsylvania branch of the Republicans and an advisor to Abraham Lincoln, Carey represented a towering intellectual in Republican politics.[36] Carey's influence was epitomized by the passage of the Morrill Tariff of 1861, which raised tariff rates to unprecedented heights.[37] Toward the end of the third-party system, a newer generation of Carey-inspired writers would emerge to update and formalize Carey's economic system.

Democrats maintained their support for French Liberalism, with the writings of Say being updated by those of Frederic Bastiat.[38] The Republican embrace of protectionism also led Free Soilers to either abandon the Republicans for the Democratic Party, or remain part of an ever-dwindling minority of disaffected Republicans, known as Mugwumps, who for all intents and purposes supported Democratic economic policy. The existing orientation of the Democratic Party toward French Liberalism also made it a natural home for Cobdenism, and this was only reinforced by former barnburners and Free-Soilers returning to the fold.[39] Cobdenism, or the Manchester School, stressed the radical adoption of free trade and nonintervention in international economic affairs. This was not only seen as economically expedient, it was deemed necessary for achieving global peace. Although this did not represent a radical departure from their existing position, it reinforced their commitment to free trade. For one thing, whereas free trade had previously meant "tariffs for revenue only," Democrats would now entertain the substitution of tariffs for progressive income tax to achieve greater freedom of trade, which coincided with their broader egalitarian goals.[40] The rise of Cobdenism also prompted American Protectionists to redirect their energy away from the English Classical School and more toward Richard Cobden and the Manchester School.

The fourth-party system, which operated from 1896 to around 1932, represents the most radical transformation of the American political landscape. Whilst it did not see the introduction of any new major party, there was an internal transformation of the existing political order. This involved the transformation of the Democrats from roughly the party of *laissez-faire* and free markets to a progressive and statist party. This transformation began with the nomination of William Jennings Bryan to the Democratic ticket in 1896. This new Democratic Party increasingly backed heavy government intervention with an emphasis on social welfare legislation. Its new ideology was along the lines of the emerging Progressive School associated with the likes of Edwin E. R. Seligman, Thorsten Veblen, and Richard T. Ely, who mentored Woodrow Wilson.

These Progressives were disciples of the social welfare and economic planning doctrines of the German Historical School. The internal transformation of the Democrats was significant but remained consistent with the party's egalitarian roots. This is again well captured by John Gerring who notes that "William Jennings Bryan is the rightful father of the Progressive-New Deal Democratic party, bringing to it a regulatory style and redistributive purpose found hitherto only outside the mainstream of American party politics." Starting with Bryan, "the focus of this newfound sense of political direction" of the Democratic Party "was the welfare state and its associated public philosophy—pragmatism, statism, scientific expertise, [proto-]Keynesian economic policies, and redistributive social policies." In short, "Democratic ideology in the Bryan-Wilson-Roosevelt era was, to state the obvious, strongly egalitarian."[41]

The Republicans, for their part, underwent limited change in economic philosophy with the introduction of the fourth-party system, as illustrated by the nomination of William McKinley. As a staunch advocate of the American System, McKinley went on to successfully contest the 1896 election against Bryan. The Republicans remained broadly consistent on economic policy, reaffirming their commitment to protectionism, infrastructure development, and low taxation. The American System continued to represent orthodox Republican Party policy for the next several decades. Even President Warren G. Harding, who historians have tended to regard as an advocate of *laissez-faire* capitalism, was in fact an advocate of the American System. This is seen plainly in Harding's inaugural address to Congress:

> It has been proved again and again that we cannot, while throwing our markets open to the world, maintain American standards of living and opportunity, and hold our industrial eminence in such unequal competition. There is a luring fallacy in the theory of banished barriers of trade, but preserved American standards require our higher production costs to be reflected in our tariffs on imports.[42]

Following the standard prescription of the American Protectionists, Harding oversaw drastic cuts in income tax, an increase in tariff protection, and the expansion of highways and other internal improvements during his presidential term. Indeed, the inveterate protectionist economist Robert Ellis Thompson was an avid supporter of Harding, praising "Mr. Harding['s] ... nationalist convictions" and "protectionist sentiments."[43] Overall, the main change in terms of protectionist theory, and its corollary, Republican economic policy, was its greater emphasis on attacking progressive and big government programs.

Relationship with Other Schools of Thought

The story of the American Protectionists is not only one of economic independence, it is one of intellectual independence. Their economic thought did not consist of a mere handful of exceptions to Classical economics, nor was it a stepping stone to Progressivism. It was an independent and distinctly American school of economic thought that deserves to be understood on its own terms. The relationship between American Protectionists and other schools of economic thought may appear complicated when viewed across the full scope of the School's existence (c. 1790–1930). Yet, this is more a matter of optics than of substance. The American Protectionists' core beliefs remained remarkably consistent throughout their existence, and they were steadfast in maintaining their independence from foreign economic doctrines—whether it be English, French, or German. What changed, however, was their rhetorical strategy in the contest of ideas. Before Socialist or Progressive ideas were considered a serious threat, contending with the Classicals and other free market schools occupied the foreground of American Protectionist thought. Yet, despite their differences, the American Protectionists had more in common with these writers than with the Socialists and Progressives who emerged later. It was only once Progressive ideas became a powerful political and intellectual force in the United States that the American Protectionists recalibrated their arguments and elevated their more market-oriented views to the foreground.

Until the late nineteenth century, American Protectionists confronted a relatively stable constellation of free-trade schools. Since there were no serious alternatives to the economic philosophies of protectionist and free-trade capitalism in the United States, they naturally only needed to contend with the different strands of free trade economics. Beginning in the Hamiltonian period, the rival ideology consisted of latent Physiocracy, Smithian economics, and French Liberalism in the form of Jeffersonian economics. The first of these, Physiocracy, held agriculture as the sole possessor of productiveness. The other two, Smithian and French liberalism, extolled the virtues of free trade, with the latter particularly hostile to special governmental privilege. Hamilton, Coxe, and their allies therefore needed to dismantle the Physiocratic notion that agriculture was the sole possessor of productiveness, as well as Smith's notion of agriculture's superior productiveness. Once physiocracy became increasingly discredited as an ideology, the emerging protectionist movement increasingly directed their efforts to confronting Smithian and French Liberalism.

By the 1820s, however, the ideas of the English Classical School appeared on the scene through the works of Thomas Robert Malthus and David Ricardo. While still taking aim at Smith and Say, the American Protectionists gradually shifted their focus to these newer doctrines. In fact, the transformation of Classical economics at the hands of Malthus and Ricardo aided protectionism as an intellectual movement. Whereas the optimistic doctrines of Smith and Say received relatively wide acceptance among American policy makers and the educated public, Americans were far less receptive to the gloomy doctrines of Ricardo and Malthus.[44] In what would be labeled as the "dismal science," Ricardo and Malthus had transformed the sanguine system of Smith to one predicated on iron laws of subsistence.

Roughly coinciding with the emergence of Malthusian and Ricardian economics were the economic crises following the War of 1812 and the Panic of 1819, which generated widespread calls to shield American industry from foreign competition. These economic conditions, combined with this less palatable form of Classical economics, created an opening for American Protectionism to emerge as a credible intellectual alternative.[45] Indeed, it would prove far easier for the American Protectionists to dismantle the doctrines of Malthus and Ricardo, and by doing so, supplant them with their own doctrine—one which, unlike Ricardo and Malthus, was predicated on optimism and class harmony. At first, Ricardian economics did not dominate academic economics in the United States. It would not be until the success of John Stuart Mill's *Principles of Political Economy* in 1848 that Mill's refurbished neo-Ricardian economics would go on to conquer the American intellectual scene. Prior to this, the textbook, *The Elements of Political Economy*, written by the American free trader Francis Wayland would be orthodoxy in American universities, particularly those in the North.[46] Wayland's approach to economics was Classical, though non-Ricardian, and was largely predicated on moral reasoning.

Ricardian and Malthusian economics did establish a foothold, however, in the Southern States through the Southern Doctrine. This distinctly Americanized version of Ricardian and Malthusian economics would be employed in defense of the plantation system and against calls for industrialization.[47] As a result, it was naturally pitted against the American Protectionists. After the Civil War, however, the Southern doctrine would fade as an intellectual force. It was during this time that John Stuart Mill's brand of Ricardian economics was sweeping through academic circles. Thus, from its conception, academic economics in the United States was dominated by Classical economics in one form or another. The American Protectionists made some inroads in academia, but as we shall see in the next section, these were on an isolated basis and often short lived. Yet, in spite of their rather limited academic presence, American Protectionism still represented a potent intellectual force in the United States, especially after the writings of Henry Charles Carey.

In the latter half of the nineteenth century, a greater plurality of economic schools began emerging in the American intellectual scene. In addition to Mill's brand of Ricardian Classicism, another Americanized take on Ricardian economics emerged with the ideas of Henry George and the single tax movement. Not only was Georgism staunch in its advocacy of a single tax on land, it was also staunch in its advocacy of free trade. Likewise, the ideas of the Manchester and French Liberal Schools found American disciples and converts, the most notable of these being Arthur Latham Perry and David Ames Wells. Marginalist and proto-Neoclassical ideas also entered into the American scene with the ideas of John Bates Clark. Finally, there were a number of Social Darwinist thinkers, such as William Graham Sumner, who published *Protectionism, the Ism That Teaches That Waste Makes Wealth* and who defended free trade on the grounds of survival of the fittest. The ideas of the American Protectionists were thus broadened to not only combat the increasingly antiquated ideas of Malthus and Ricardo, but also these newer and, in many ways more militant free trade ideologies as well.

On the more interventionist side, the ideas of the German Historical School began to make their mark on the American intellectual scene. At first, the American Protectionists considered the Germans as potential allies, united by their shared critique of Classical economics. However, once these works began to be translated into English, the enthusiasm which the American Protectionists held for the German Historical School started to dissipate. In 1878, the work of the prominent German economist Wilhelm Roscher appeared in the United States under the title *Principles of*

Political Economy. Not only did this translation reveal that the Germans supported both the Ricardian theory of rent and Malthusian theory of population—theories which were an anathema to the American Protectionists—it also only provided a lukewarm defense of protectionism under specific circumstances and considered free trade to be the norm. To add insult to injury, Roscher also castigates Henry Carey for his advocacy of a perpetual protective tariff and admonishes him for his apparent "absolute inability to conceive the Malthusian law of population."[48] It became increasingly clear that the Germans were no friend of the American Protectionist. This attitude is perhaps best demonstrated by Van Buren Denslow, who notes that "Roscher runs over Carey like an industrious ant over the pyramid of Gizeh, carefully noting all exterior inequalities but mutely powerless to comprehend any one sublime meaning."[49] Indeed, the aversion toward the German Historical School is also well captured by Robert Ellis Thompson, who explains that

> The school of the *Kathedersocialsten* [socialism of the chair] … sometimes [known as] the Historical School. To this last title they have no proper right … They are cosmopolitan, like the economists they criticise, and, in the absence of any stable principle of economic science, they often carry their destructive criticisms of the older doctrines to an unwarrantable length, assigning to law, custom, and individual idiosyncrasy a reach of influence which leaves no room for any genuine economic science.[50]

The Germans not only exported writings to the United States, they also exported thinkers, or more precisely, they trained American graduates who would transpose German economics to the United States. Upon returning to the United States, these German trained Americans would be referred to as the "New School," known today as Progressives. The virtual founder and leading figure of the Progressive School was Richard T. Ely, who was responsible for teaching most of the later members of the School. Ely completed his doctorate in 1879 under the supervision of Karl Knies, a key figure in the German Historical School. When Ely returned to the United States, he spent several decades teaching at John Hopkins University and then the University of Wisconsin; during which time Ely built an intellectual empire, churning out numerous influential students who went on to become economists and social reformers. This was a novel development in American economics. Whereas the American Protectionists saw a significant, but carefully defined, role for the State, the Progressives, like their German forebears, saw themselves as scientific technocrats, who with the right knowledge and the use of state power could fine tune the economy to reach social goals.[51] This was known as *Kathedersozialism* or the "socialism of the chair."

Not all Progressives were free traders, but the vast majority were, and they generally approached the issue from a different angle from that of the traditional free trade schools. This meant that the Protectionists now occupied the unique and delicate position of defending internal free markets against the Progressives whilst simultaneously defending the Protectionist position against an onslaught from both free traders and Progressives. The inveterate protectionist Robert Ellis Thompson, in two of his critical reviews of Ely's work, perhaps best exemplifies the Protectionist attitude towards the

Progressives whilst also indicating the key differences between the two schools. In the words of Thompson:

> We would call Prof. Ely an unprincipled Free Trader. The fundamental difference between Protectionists and Free Traders is that with reference to the sphere of the State's activity. Prof. Ely not only rejects the Free Trade theory of State passivity with regard to the industrial life of the country, but he goes far beyond Protectionists in his willingness to extend the sphere of State action. Yet he opposes Protection on the ground of the practical inconveniences and abuses which attend that policy … Ely's book disappoints us.[52]

And:

> Defects … result from Prof. Ely's position as a member of the new [progressive] or "historical" school of economists … the common fault of this school that it refuses to distinguish between socialistic and economic movements, and that they give the former an importance which is not their due. This comes from [them] being engaged in a mere negative revolt against the Political Economy of *Laissez-faire,* without having a positive doctrine to combat its follies … Their failure to define the extent and measure of their revolt against the doctrine of the "orthodox" economists … [creates] the danger of running into modified socialism themselves. Indeed, they never have done justice to the truth [which] there is in the *Laissez-faire* doctrine.[53]

Concerned with the meteoric rise of the Progressives as an intellectual force, the American Protectionists became more aggressive and explicit in their criticisms of socialism and the soft socialism of the Progressives. After all, the American Protectionists were largely on the same page as the Classicals in their support of the private enterprise system, and their Republican allies were no longer competing in the political sphere against free trade capitalists, but progressive reformers, particularly after William Jennings Bryan secured the 1896 Democratic nomination. It must be said, however, that the American Protectionists were undeterred in defending their distinctly American approach to political economy against both the old and emerging doctrines of foreign economics. They continued to advocate the same American System which they always adhered to, and were still largely operating on the theoretical foundations established by Alexander Hamilton and Tench Coxe. What changed toward the end of the nineteenth century and into the twentieth century was the context and climate in which they presented their arguments. As opposed to only confronting one chief rival in the contest of ideas, the American Protectionists were now caught in the middle ground among a plurality of competing ideologies.

Institutional Infrastructure and Organization of the School

With the halls of academia dominated by the doctrines of the English and French economists, the American Protectionists were largely seen as outsiders. Some American Protectionists secured academic posts, of course, but they represented a few small islands in the sea of Classical, and by the late nineteenth century, Progressive economics.

This marginalization was well observed by the prominent Whig Rufus Griswold, who noted how the ideas of American Protectionists were denied admission "at the University in the street next door to that in which [Henry Carey] has his residence." Their economics departments were instead "composed of ideas from … nearly obsolete systems: Say and Ricardo are regarded as expositors of the last and ultimate doctrine."[54] Indeed, despite his popularity among the broader public and political circles, Carey was, in the words of Robert Ellis Thompson, "pointed out to [economics] students … as the author whom, before all others, they were to refute in their prize essays."[55] John L. Hayes perhaps said it best, declaring that:

> It cannot be denied that a tendency to free-trade doctrine largely prevails in our great cities, in fashionable circles, and among literary and professional men, and, what is more than all to be regretted, in our colleges.[56]

In response, the American Protectionists would cultivate their own private institutional network to spread their philosophy. There were attempts to establish an academic presence. As early as 1822, Mathew Carey offered the University of Maryland an endowment to establish a chair of political economy for Daniel Raymond, but this offer was turned down.[57] Attempts were also made in 1828 to establish a chair for Friedrich List at Lafayette College in Pennsylvania, but this also proved unsuccessful.[58] However, perhaps the boldest, and ultimately the most tragic, of these attempts was the establishment of the Wharton School of Finance and Political Economy at the University of Pennsylvania in 1881.[59] The iron magnate Joseph Wharton, a Protectionist writer himself, founded the Wharton School with the explicit intent of spreading the American Protectionist doctrine. In the charter of the School, Wharton stipulated that teaching should "inculcate and impress upon the students … the necessity for each nation to care for its own and maintain by all suitable means its industrial and financial independence." He even stressed that "no apologetic or merely defensive style of instruction must be tolerated" on the issue of protection. Instead, "the right and duty of national self-protection must be firmly asserted and demonstrated."[60]

In establishing the School, Wharton handpicked Robert Ellis Thompson to serve as Professor of Social Science (Political Economy) and the Dean. Albert S. Bolles, another protectionist, was also picked as the Professor of Mercantile Law and Practice. The School's standing as leader of protectionist economics was reinforced by Henry Carey and Stephen Colwell, who endowed the institution with a library containing over six thousand works on political economy—the largest such library in North America at the time.[61] It finally seemed as if American Protectionist thought had found a permanent home within academia. However, changing currents within academic culture would eventually thwart these efforts. By the late nineteenth century, there was an increasing trend toward credentialism. Previously, instruction in the United States did not require a doctorate, but this was increasingly giving way to the German model. Compounding the problem was the rarity of doctoral studies in the United States, so most graduate students in the social sciences went to Germany, the home of the PhD. To boost its reputation, the University of Pennsylvania, like many others, sought out these more credentialed graduates from the German seminaries.

In 1883, Edmund J. James, an economist who had studied alongside Simon Patten and Richard T. Ely at the University of Halle under the German Historicist Joannes Conrad, became the first of these German graduates to join the Wharton School. This would eventually prove fatal for the American Protectionists. James was appointed as director of the Wharton School, and from here, James sought to recreate the Wharton School in the image of the German seminaries and stack it with likeminded Progressives. In 1887, James recruited Simon Patten and appointed him as Professor of Political Economy, and demoted Robert Ellis Thompson to the Welsh Chair of History. Both James and Patten considered the American Protectionist doctrines which descended from Hamilton through Carey as too unsophisticated for university education and sought to replace it with their own Germanic-inspired economic thought. Indeed, the Protectionist and associate of Joseph Wharton, Lorin Blodgett noted that "the movement in the University is deliberately planned and intended to effect the reversal of the [protectionist] economic teaching which has been characteristic of [the] institution" and that "several pretended friends of the protectionist doctrine," no doubt referring to James and Patten, "are secretly their active enemies."[62] The Wharton School fell increasingly under the ideological capture of the Progressives, and Thompson became ostracized within the very institution which he helped found.

By 1892, James sought to oust Thompson from the university completely. In a letter written to the Provost of the University recommending Thompson's termination, James charged that Thompson spent too much time lecturing and conducting independent research, and not enough time on one-on-one consultation with students; that he was unwilling to adopt new historical methods and higher standards of education; and that he failed to collaborate with the rest of the staff. Finally, James took issue with Thompson running his own classes on political economy.[63] Yet, in doing so, Thompson was the only faculty member upholding the original intentions of the Wharton School. Indeed, Thompson himself warned that with no one else teaching the American Protectionist political economy, "if [he] had stopped teaching it, this would have abolished it from the University, and suspended the operations of the Wharton School."[64]

A closer examination of James's charges against Thompson reveals their true purpose. The first of the charges levelled against Thompson is peculiar. Running too many lectures is like punishing a worker for being too productive. Thompson's students also did not seem to mind the apparent lack of consultation, as a group of his undergraduate students organized a petition and received 314 student signatures praising Thompson's teaching abilities.[65] Regarding the second charge, it appears that Thompson merely refused to adopt the so-called "new historic methods" of the German Historical School, choosing instead to maintain the traditional approach of the American Protectionists. As to the refusal to collaborate, by this point, Thompson was the only remaining American Protectionist at the Wharton School, and given that James and Patton sought to purge traditional protectionist thought from the university, it is no wonder that Thompson would refuse to collaborate with those who were seeking to hijack the Wharton School.

Thompson responded that attempts to oust him were purely ideological in nature. Indeed, the two latter charges levelled against him are merely symptoms of a larger ideological rift. Writing to Joseph Wharton, Thompson explained that his "work is on the line of teaching of Mr. Carey, Mr. Colwell, and the other representatives of the Philadelphia School" of Protectionists. By now he was "the only representative of the school" at Wharton. "The rest were graduates under either [the Social Darwinist] Professor [William Graham] Sumner of Yale or Professor Conrad" of the German Historical School.[66] Meanwhile, regarding "the fear that, if [Thompson] should resign, the doctrine of protection would be in danger," Edmund James assured the University Provost this would not violate the Wharton School charter, as "Dr. Patten [was] an even more radical and thorough-going protectionist than Prof. Thompson himself."[67] The Provost's background, however, was in anatomy, and he was in no position to understand the nuances of economic thought. In this case, "more radical and thorough-going" translates into the heavy-handed "socialism of the chair" which the American Protectionists rejected. Thompson's position was ultimately terminated in 1892. So too were the original intentions of the Wharton School.

The tragedy of the Wharton School typifies the struggle faced by the American Protectionists in penetrating the halls of academia, and, as a result, the Protectionists sought out alternative arrangements for spreading their doctrine. Earlier protectionists like Tench Coxe and Mathew Carey had attempted similar organizations, but these remained small and localized.[68] By the late nineteenth century, however, the American Protectionists had built an alternate network parallel to academia through industrial associations, think tanks, and protectionist advocacy groups. The most notable of these were the Industrial League, the American Iron and Steel Association, the National Wool Manufacturers Association, the Home Market Club, and the American Protective Tariff League.

The Industrial League represented an umbrella organization. Its membership comprised other agricultural, mining, and industrial associations. Founded in 1868, it served as a protectionist lobby group that brought together the sometimes disparate protectionist causes into a consolidated and unified movement. The objectives of the League were explicitly protectionist with its constitution asserting that its purpose was (1) "the cultivation of a spirit of mutual confidence between all industrial organizations of the United States, for the purpose of securing harmonious action in regard to any tariff revision"; (2) "the exercise of such influence as it may possess to prevent unfriendly tariff legislation by Congress"; (3) "the publication and distribution of tracts and other printed statements which shall advocate the policy of Protection to Home Industry"; and (4) "the employment of competent persons to advocate the Protective policy in public addresses."[69]

The Industrial League was the brainchild of Joseph Wharton, who was one of the founders alongside the Pennsylvanian industrialist and Republican Congressmen Daniel J. Morrell, the iron manufacturers Morton McMichael and William Sellers, and Henry Carey's nephew, Henry Carey Lea.[70] The educational work of the Industrial League was of a broad nature. It produced the *Industrial Bulletin*, which was edited by the protectionist Cyrus Elder, who also served as secretary of the League. It also printed and distributed various treatises, tracts, and Congressional speeches in favor of protection, exceeding a million copies for the year 1888. This included the distribution of protectionist textbooks to universities and colleges. The League also sponsored lectures and funded newspapers of a protectionist orientation, including the *Chicago Inter-Ocean* (which employed Van Buren Denslow and David H. Mason).

Of all the organizations, the American Iron and Steel Association (AISA) was undoubtedly the most well-resourced. AISA predates the Industrial League, having been founded in 1864 by a group of American iron and steel manufacturers. The wealthy industrialist Eber Brock Ward served as the Association's first president, and as early as 1866, Giles B. Stebbins would serve as the Association's Secretary. Since its inception, AISA was an explicitly protectionist organization. The clearest statement of its intellectual allegiance was the awarding of honorary memberships to Henry Carey, Stephen Colwell, Andrew Stewart, and Horace Greeley in the year following its establishment.

Similar to the Industrial League, the Association produced its own bulletin, known as the *Bulletin of the American Iron and Steel Association*. The Bulletin covered a broad range of topics relating to the iron and steel industry, but it was staunchly protectionist in character. It would be edited by the Protectionist James M. Swank, who would eventually take over as secretary. It was through AISA that the writings of the American Protectionists were most heavily distributed. Indeed, the Association's *Bulletin* attested that they knew "of no agency during the last dozen years that has systematically distributed treatises on Protection in popular form."[71] In addition to distributing existing literature, the Association also oversaw and published new protectionist literature including Joseph Wharton's *National Self-Protection,* and Giles B. Stebbins' *A Tariff is Not a Tax*, among other tracts.

The National Association of Wool Manufacturers (NAWM) was founded in 1864 by the carpet manufacturer and American Protectionist writer Erastus B. Bigelow who served as its President for a great many years. From its inception, the association was explicitly protectionist. Its founding document praised "The Morrill Tariff" which it "gratefully acknowledged as a most important step in the progress of American manufactures."[72] Indeed, to show their appreciation, the NAWM bestowed Justin Smith Morrill, the Congressman who produced the bill, with an honorary membership. *The Bulletin of the National Association of Wool Manufacturers* was also established in 1869, and it was through this publication that the NAWM was able to spread protectionist doctrine and promote protectionist writings. John L. Hayes, ever the admirer of Henry Carey and a Protectionist writer himself, would serve as secretary of the Association from 1864 until his death in 1887. During this time, Hayes served as editor of the *Bulletin* where he maintained its protectionist character.

Beyond industry associations, the American Protectionists established dedicated think tanks. The two most important of these were the Home Market Club and the American Protective Tariff League. The Boston-based Home Market Club was founded in 1886 by the textile manufacturer George Draper, who was converted to the cause of protection by the ideas of Henry Clay, Daniel Webster, and Horace Greeley. While more of an advocate than a theorist, Draper did produce his own work entitled *Some Views on the Tariff Question* as well as various smaller articles on the topic. It is difficult to ascertain the full scope of the early operations of the Home Market Club. But, like the other organizations, the Home Market Club did produce their own publication, known as the *Home Market Bulletin*. It was in 1889, however, with the appointment of Albert Clarke as the Club's Secretary, that the activities of the Club became significantly broadened, morphing into more of a protectionist think tank. Clarke, himself a Protectionist writer, took over as editor of the *Home Market Bulletin,* renaming it *The Protectionist. The Protectionist* became one of the leading journals of American Protectionist thought, as well as a marketing arm and disseminator of the treatises and writings of the American Protectionist thinkers.

The American Protective Tariff League represented the sister organization of the Home Market Club, performing many of the same functions. The organization was founded by the businessman Edward H. Ammidown and the Protectionist writer Robert P. Porter in 1885, and it was intended as a counter organization to the staunchly free-trade Cobden Club. The principles adopted by the League included making "known in every practical way the principles and advantages of the American Protective System."[73] Among the League's executives were various American Protectionist writers, such as Thomas Haines Dudley (the first Vice President), Robert P. Porter (the second Vice President), and Henry M. Hoyt (General Secretary). Others, such as Ellis H. Roberts (Vice President of the New York branch), also filled the ranks of the League. Similar to the other organizations, the Tariff League published their own journal, *The American Economist*, which regularly featured articles from the key American Protectionist writers. *The American Economist*, along with the Home Market Club's *The Protectionist*, represented the two foremost protectionist journals in the United States. In addition to the above, the Tariff League also published and distributed their own literature, organized essay competitions, and hosted lectures and seminars.

The American Protectionists thus largely operated in exile from formal academic institutions. It was through their affinity with the Republican Party, industry associations, and protectionist advocacy groups and think tanks, that the American Protectionists sustained and spread their doctrine. Indeed, this outsider status perhaps explains why the School has gone unnoticed by so many historians of economic thought, and why academic economists have routinely ignored the contributions of the American Protectionists, despite their doctrines flourishing within political and industrial circles in their own time. The close connection with industrial circles will, of course, raise questions of motive and vested interests. Nevertheless, the ideas of the American Protectionists cannot simply be dismissed by appealing to the financial motivations of the theorists or their associates. Their ideas must be judged on their own merit.

Notes

1. Carey, *Common Sense,* 3–4; Meardon, "*Reciprocity,*" 454, similarly posits a coherent tradition of US protectionism stemming from Hamilton through his nineteenth-century followers. For opposing arguments, see Irwin, "Aftermath," 820; and Elkins and McKitrick, *Federalism,* 261.
2. Maclay, *Sketches,* 205.
3. Lodge, intro. *Hamilton's Report,* n.p.

4. List resided in Pennsylvania from 1825 to 1832. In his *Outlines* (5–6), List explicitly aligned himself with the protectionist tradition, declaring "war" against "the system of Adam Smith and Co [...] on the part of the American System." See companion material on List.
5. Rae's *Statement* (365–366) quotes from Hamilton's *Report*, and cites the American System as validating his principles. Rae was recognized as a member of the School by at least eight American Protectionists. See companion material on Rae.
6. Marshall, *Correspondence*, 3:160.
7. Hudson, *Protectionist Take-off*, 18.
8. O'Connor (*Economics*, 45) and Hudson (*Protectionist Take-off*, 18) cite Mixter's 1901 edition of Rae's *Sociological Theory* as the source of the alleged quote.
9. Frith, "Protectionist Thought," 38f.
10. Niles, *Journal*, 1–11; Dorfman, *Economic Mind*, 2:780.
11. Thompson, "Pennsylvania Protectionists," 649.
12. Patten credits the German Historical School, Mill, Marx, and Henry George as influences, making no mention of American Protectionist writers, see Patten, *Reconstruction*, 2.
13. Gerring, *Ideologies*, 57.
14. Coolidge, "Heritage," 109.
15. Gunton, "Tariff an Issue?," 479–486.
16. Coxe and Barton eventually became Democratic-Republicans but maintained support for Hamilton's program. Cooke, *Coxe*, 338–347.
17. Dorfman, "Jefferson," 98–121.
18. Jefferson quoted in Skousen, *Modern Economics*, 51.
19. Dorfman, *Economic Mind*, 1:434; Rothbard, *Economic Thought*, 2:7; Salerno, "French Liberal School," 133.
20. O'Connor, *Economics* 25; Salerno, "French School," 133.
21. Jefferson, *Papers*, 8:682.
22. Alexander Dallas oversaw the introduction of the Tariff of 1816, see Walters, *Dallas*, 189.
23. See also Peskin, "Republicans," 235–262, 239.
24. Belko, "Tax on the Many," 277.
25. Dorfman *Economic Mind*, 2:652–661, 731–743; Byrdsall, *Loco-Foco*.
26. Walker, "Report," 226, 222.
27. Greeley, "Tariff Question," 113.
28. Schlesinger, *Jackson*, 265.
29. Greeley quoted in Schlesinger, *Jackson*, 266.
30. Schlesinger, *Jackson*, 514–515.
31. Bancroft, *Progress*, 34.
32. Colston, "Free Society," 12–13; Hodgson, "Malthus' Essay," 742–770; O'Connor, *Economics*, 49–56.
33. Dorfman, *Economic Mind*, 2:527–539, 844–848; O'Connor, *Economics*, 49.
34. Meardon, "Cobden's Quandary," 210–212.
35. Foner, *Free Soil*, 19; Holt, *Whig*, 980.
36. Thompson, "Carey," [1883], 721.
37. For Carey's influence on the Morrill Tariff, see Lee, "Carey," 280–302.
38. Salerno, "French School," 113.
39. Curtiss, *Industrial Development*, 3: 35, 254; Lui, *Smith's America*, 135.
40. This came to fruition during the Cleveland Administration, but was struck down as unconstitutional, see Joseph, *Income Tax*, 86.
41. Gerring, *Ideologies*, 188, 180, 204.
42. Harding, "Inaugural Address," (March 4, 1921).
43. Thompson, "Tariff a Live Issue," 269.
44. Even after Ricardo's *Principles* appeared, Say's *Treatise* remained the "most popular of the European treatises" in the US. Dorfman, *Economic Mind*, 2:513–514.

45. For the surge in protectionist writings following the Panic of 1819, see Browning, *Panic of 1819*, 351–352.
46. Dorfman, *Economic Mind*, 2:770, 3:49–50; O'Connor, *Economics*, 5–6.
47. O'Connor, *Economics*, 49–56; Hodgson, "Malthus' Essay," 742–770.
48. Roscher, *Principles*, 1878, 446f.
49. Denslow, "American Economics," 17–18.
50. Thompson, *Elements*, 26.
51. For important thinking on this technocratic bias, see Leonard, *Illiberal Reformers*, 10; Furner, *Advocacy and Objectivity*.
52. Thompson, "Economic Literature," [1888], 214–215.
53. Thompson, "Economic Literature," [1886], 9–10.
54. Griswold, "Carey," 79.
55. Thompson, "Carey," [1879], 827.
56. Hayes, *Protective Question*, 3.
57. Carey, *Autobiographical*, 93–96; O'Connor, *Economics*, 32.
58. O'Connor, *Economics*, 35.
59. Sass, *Pragmatic Imagination*, 33.
60. Wharton, "Deed of Trust," June 22, 1881, box 52, Wharton School Deeds and Indentures folder, *JWP*.
61. Sass, *Pragmatic Imagination*, 33.
62. Blodgett to Wharton, April 16, 1892, Robert Ellis Thompson folder, *GACP1*.
63. James to Pepper, undated, The Case of Robert Ellis Thompson folder 1, *GACP1*.
64. Thompson to Board of Trustees, June 13, 1892, Case of Robert Ellis Thompson, folder 2, *GACP1*.
65. "Student Petition to the Board of Trustees," Robert Ellis Thompson folder, *GACP1*.
66. Thompson to Wharton, April 2. 1892, Wharton School 1892 folder, *GACP1*.
67. James to Pepper, Undated, Robert Ellis Thompson Folder, *GACP1*.
68. Bishop, *American Manufactures*, 238; Peskin, *Manufacturing Revolution*, 216, 93–118.
69. "Constitution," Industrial League Record Book, n. p., box 232, folder 9, *AISIR*.
70. Industrial League Record Book, 4, box 232, folder 9, record Book, *AISIR*.
71. Iron and Steel Association, "New Campaign for Protection," 4.
72. Association of Wool Manufacturers, *Objects*, 4.
73. Protective Tariff League, "Principles," 80.

Chapter Two

THE AMERICAN SYSTEM OF CAPITALISM

In 1832, Abraham Lincoln declared that "my politics are short and sweet … I am in favor of the internal improvement system, and a high protective tariff."[1] In these short few lines, Lincoln articulated the American System of Capitalism. This system, embraced by Lincoln decades prior to saving the Union, encapsulated the economic philosophy responsible for transforming the United States from an economy dwarfed by the industrial might of Britain to one that surpassed the entire industrial capacity of the British Empire by the early twentieth century. Yet this "American System" that Lincoln championed has been largely erased from our economic memory, replaced by a popular narrative that America was built on *laissez-faire*. This idea that America's economic heritage is one of *laissez-faire* and free trade resonates with both free market advocates who applaud it, and socialists who condemn it. Yet this narrative would be an anathema to the true architects who forged American economic development. For one thing, American Protectionists, from Alexander Hamilton to William McKinley, saw protective tariffs and market freedom as intimately connected. For them, tariffs did not restrict economic liberty but expanded it through what would be termed "industrial freedom."

Beyond the *Laissez-Faire* Mythos

To understand how protection could enhance rather than restrict economic freedom requires moving beyond the laissez-faire mythos that dominates modern economic discourse. Against the simplified narrative of free markets versus government intervention, an alternative approach recognizes that there is always some kind of embedded institutional, legal, and policy framework within the capitalist system. Markets must operate within a framework of restrictions and regulations, and such parameters allow the market to function properly. This is how the American Protectionists approached the subject of public policy. Indeed, as David Rice explains in his *Protective Philosophy*, "unrestricted commercial intercourse between its citizens, within certain broadly defined limits, is advantageous." Yet, "I say within certain broadly defined limits, because it cannot escape notice that even in this national field of commerce we have had, and always shall have, certain laws regulating matters pertaining to it."[2]

The above necessarily implies that the market system can be shaped through the direction of some authority which usually takes the form of a government. The American Protectionists can be best understood in this manner, as writers on how the market system is, or rather should, be structured—with this structure taking the form of their American System of Capitalism. This view, of course, should not be understood to mean that the American Protectionists were opposed to economic freedom. On the contrary, they were eager champions of freedom. However, they were realistic that economic freedom can only be secured through a system of laws and restrictions, with protective tariffs representing one such restriction. As George M. Steele explains:

> Freedom must be real and practical, not merely theoretical… To assure and preserve this freedom, is one of the functions of government. It should protect each member of society against fraud and violence. It cannot furnish labor, or create capital; it cannot repeal the laws of nature, or enact new ones. But it may… take any available means to thwart any movement of interested foreign parties to overwhelm and destroy nascent industries of its own citizens, as they come into competition with the former.[3]

The view that markets must exist within a framework of regulations and restrictions is not unique to the American Protectionist writers. Although they would have detested the particular system of restrictions espoused by the American Protectionists, the Classical economists, popularly depicted as extreme and dogmatic disciples of *laissez-faire*, themselves subscribed to this view. Indeed, "the Classical writers," as one authoritative study explains, "were perfectly clear that [the market] could only operate within a framework of restrictions. Such restrictions were partly legal and partly religious, moral and conventional, and they were designed to ensure the coincidence of self and community interest… Their attitude towards *laissez-faire* was of a very relativist and conditional kind."[4] In fact, John Elliot Cairnes, the leader of the Classical School after John Stuart Mill, even went so far to declare that "the maxim of *laissez-faire* has no scientific basis whatever, but is at best a handy rule of practice, useful perhaps, as a reminder to statesmen on which side the presumption lies… but [it is] totally destitute of all scientific authority."[5]

The Classical economists saw various circumstances where statist intervention was necessary or even desirable. This understanding is important, as the American Protectionists should not be viewed crudely as champions of statism and interventionism battling it out against the *laissez-faire* of the Classical economists. The debate was not one of free markets versus statism, but rather a debate on the scope and form of government intervention, that is, when and where the government should intervene in a system where the production and allocation of resources is predominantly carried out by private individuals. In this sense, the American Protectionists and the Classical School were operating on the same basic framework with respect to the market system, despite constructing quite different theoretical systems and arriving at different conclusions concerning policy. Explaining how such interventions and restrictions differ between the American Protectionists and the Classical economists, as well as other schools of economic thought for that matter, is a far more meaningful way of understanding their respective systems than comparing them to a hypothetical and non-existent system of perfect *laissez-faire*, which neither the Classicals envisioned nor endorsed.

The American System

Unlike many other schools of thought situated outside the mainstream, American Protectionist thought was not an assortment of complaints and criticisms of the alleged injustices of capitalism. These thinkers were unequivocally in favor of capitalism and private enterprise. They were concerned ultimately with creating conditions conducive to capitalist development and industrial growth. The American Protectionists saw a significant role for government in facilitating the expansion of entrepreneurial and industrial activities, yet they equally recognized that the scope of government's role should be clearly defined, so as not to over-regulate and overburden the productive sectors of the economy.

By way of contrast with both the Classical economists, who generally stipulated the removal of both government restraints and incentives to the private sector, and the earlier mercantilist writers, who affirmed the use of State-based incentives but also onerous and heavy-handed governmental restraints; the American Protectionists stressed the removal of restraints (even more so than the British Classical School in certain areas) but maintained support for State-based incentives and inducements for private sector growth. This view is supported by George B. Curtiss, who notes that:

> The Mercantilists had held extreme and radical views of the means by which industries could best be developed and promoted, as well as upon the system of taxation by which the public treasury should be supplied… On the other hand, it should be noted that those advocating free trade carried their views to an opposite extreme. The Mercantilists and free traders represent the two extreme radical wings of economic parties, while the Protectionists occupy the middle ground between the two, discarding those practices of the Mercantilists which were found to be unnecessary and injurious, and preserving and perpetuating those principles which the experience of the past had demonstrated to be wise, just and beneficent.[6]

This was no late development. Nearly a century earlier, Alexander Hamilton himself expressed the same principle, remarking that "in matters of industry, human enterprize ought, doubtless, to be left free in the main, not fettered by too much regulation; but practical politicians know that it may be beneficially stimulated by prudent aids and encouragements on the part of the Government."[7] The American Protectionists were thus firmly within the capitalist tradition, sharing with Classical economists a commitment to market institutions and private enterprise. Yet, they also retained the elements of mercantilism that aided economic development, including protective tariffs and infrastructure investment, whilst discarding those which hindered it, such as excessive regulations and monopoly privileges.

In agreement with the Classical economists, the American Protectionists took for granted the rule of law, the preservation of private property rights, and the enforcement of contracts. Indeed, as William Elder notes, the "insecurity of property is naturally accompanied by aversion to productive industry which necessarily results in a degraded, ignorant, and dwarfed existence."[8] Willard Phillips follows up in declaring that "giving validity to contracts is of precisely the same importance, as the protection of property. The operations of industry and production must evidently be very feeble in a community which does not supply laws and authority to enforce the obligation of agreements."[9] These protections for property and contracts were seen by the American Protectionists as a necessary precondition for the proper functioning of the market system. Indeed, the American Protectionists were by no means anti-market. Not only were internal free markets, what they dubbed "industrial freedom," compatible with their economic program; it represented a major pillar of it.

On the subject of internal markets, David Rice explains, for instance, how "it is expedient and perfectly necessary, within national boundaries, to abolish tariffs and custom houses."[10] This view is also affirmed by Roswell G. Horr, who declares that "legislation should be so shaped as to protect our people in all laudable enterprises and then carefully to guard the people against the encroachments" from external trade. Yet, "with[in] these restrictions I would give individual capacity, energy and enterprise full scope."[11] The embrace of internal free markets by the American governments of the time was met with approval by Van Buren Denslow. According to Denslow, "the United States… were first in establishing perfect free trade within the borders of one extended nationality, and in surrounding that nationality with a cordon of customs duties which should be equal to all within its boundaries."[12] Indeed, even as early as 1782, Alexander Hamilton noted the distinction between the regulation of internal markets and the regulation of international trade. According to Hamilton:

> The contrary opinion, which has grown into a degree of vogue among us, has originated in the injudicious attempts made at different times to effect a REGULATION of PRICES. It became a cant phrase among the opposers of these attempts, that TRADE MUST REGULATE ITSELF; by which at first was only meant that it had its fundamental laws, agreeable to which its general operations must be directed; and that any violent attempts in opposition to these would commonly miscarry. In this sense the maxim [is] reasonable.[13]

Here, Hamilton is cautioning against price-fixing and other dubious forms of anti-market regulation, while, at the same time, censuring the advocates of free trade who conflate such policies with the regulation of international trade. George M. Steele echoes Hamilton's sentiments against price controls, noting that "government cannot fix the rate of wages, or the price of commodities, or do anything implying either of these."[14]

Along the lines promoted above, internal markets and external trade came to be understood by the American Protectionists as two distinct concepts. The term "commerce" was used to connote transactions with the internal market, while "trade" was used to connote international trade. As Robert Ellis Thompson explains:

> It is charged against our protective system that it has resulted in the destruction of American *commerce*. Objectors… use the word "commerce" in the narrow and conventional sense… affixed to it by English writers… They mean by it the export and import of commodities. The true sense of the word is "the exchange of services or commodities between persons of different industrial functions." In this sense Protection is a great promoter of commerce. It creates variety of industrial function within the nation and fosters… continual interchange of services between persons thus differentiated. It promotes association between members of the same nation by producing variety in their employments.[15]

Whilst international trade was to be subject to regulation, internal free markets were favored by the American Protectionists, and as early as the writings of Hamilton, there was a clear understanding of the market mechanism and natural laws of economics. Indeed, this understanding was cemented further with the introduction of Henry Charles Carey's *harmony of interests* doctrine, which reinforced the view that markets, whilst imperfect, were still generally harmoniously and dynamically coordinated.[16]

Of course, it is important to not overstate their belief in the free market, but what is clear is that there was a general acceptance of the market mechanism over paternalistic and socialistic forms of government interference. This acceptance is perhaps best captured by the Robert Ellis Thompson, who explains that:

> Individualism is a half-truth... It is not always true that if a man be left free to 'do as he will with his own,' he will do what is best for society... But it is true four times out of five, and even oftener. Wherever a social need exists, it generally is to somebody's advantage to meet the want... In this way society is served with a promptness and an economy otherwise impossible... [We should] find reason to be satisfied with the superiority of a policy which throws men on their own resources over one which teaches them to lean on a government. Paternalism... do[es] not make manly men.[17]

Whilst American Protectionists trusted internal markets to coordinate economic activity efficiently, they viewed international trade as operating under entirely different fundamentals.

The heart of the American System was, of course, the protective tariff. While tariffs originated with Hamilton as infant-industry protection, they evolved into something more permanent. In fact, Hamilton himself can even be considered a proponent of a permanent tariff for revenue, declaring that they "must always constitute the chief part of the revenue raised in this country," whilst applauding the incidental protection it would afford.[18] Indeed, it should be noted that it was only after Hamilton became Secretary of the Treasury that revenue considerations came more to the forefront. Prior to this, Hamilton explicitly argued that "vesting Congress with the power of regulating trade ought to have been a principal object of the confederation for a variety of reasons," noting that "it is as necessary for the purposes of commerce as of revenue," while decrying free trade as "one of those wild speculative paradoxes."[19]

It was with Alexander Dallas' *Report on the General Tariff*, however, that a permanent protective tariff was more explicitly endorsed. Van Buren Denslow perhaps best captures this attitude by declaring that "a Protective duty once properly and wisely laid never needs repeal any more than a fort once wisely built needs tearing down."[20] It must be stressed, however, that the Protectionists were under no illusion that protective tariffs, like any other policy, were liable to abuse. Henry Carey thus explains that "protection must not be blind, unchangeable, or excessive; but the principle of it must be firmly maintained."[21]

Tariffs served a dual function. First and foremost, tariffs were used to insulate domestic producers and entrepreneurs from foreign competition, thereby giving them sufficient breathing room to develop their productive capabilities and technical proficiencies. Friedrich List thus explains that "this is our main argument in support of a protective tariff and in opposition to the doctrine of free trade... Import duties should be levied to protect and gradually increase the nation's productive power."[22]

The American Protectionists therefore advocated "tariffs" primarily on the grounds that it "safeguard the industrial enterprises of entrepreneurs who take risks and have no means of knowing if they are going to be a success or not."[23] Indeed, George B. Curtiss echoes List, noting how protection allows "artisans… [to] make experiments and develop a genius and faculty which never could have been brought out under the blighting influence of vigorous [foreign] competition."[24]

The raising of revenue represents the second function of the tariff, and this revenue would be responsible for defraying the costs of internal improvements and infrastructure. This infrastructure would, in turn, improve the competitiveness and productivity of domestic enterprises by reducing transportation costs and lowering barriers to the market. Additionally, the provision of infrastructure would facilitate smooth and efficient transactions between the different sections of the national economy, binding them together into a balanced national economy.

Finally, the revenue collected from import duties eliminated the need for domestic taxation, particularly of the direct form (i.e., taxes on income and property), thereby shifting the burden away from domestic producers. The restructuring from internal to external taxation demonstrates the American Protectionists' emphasis on minimizing restraints but maximizing incentives to private sector growth. Indeed, tariffs were seen as one of the few taxes that possess the unique characteristic of stimulating domestic production. As John Rae observes:

> It is said that capital can only augment by accumulation, and, as the interference of the legislator takes something from individual revenue [taxation], it must also take from the power to accumulate, and consequently, instead of augmenting, must tend to diminish the sum of the capitals of all the individuals in the society, that is the national capital or stock… [Yet] the [import] duty so levied, by directly or indirectly effecting an improvement in the arts, [will] increase the absolute capital of the society.[25]

The unique mix of protectionism, infrastructure development, free internal markets, and low domestic taxation meant that private sector development could proceed unabated by the restraining hand of government, whilst also being insulated from the potentially "destructive" competition of foreign producers.

Industrial Freedom versus Freedom of Trade

Both the American Protectionists and the Classical School saw a significant role for government, but they were still fundamentally market-oriented schools, recognizing that markets tend to function best when high degrees of economic freedom exist. Indeed, as early as *The Report on Manufactures,* Hamilton identifies America's limited taxation and regulatory barriers as an important source for encouraging manufacturers to relocate from Europe to the United States. According to Hamilton, "exemption from the chief part of taxes, burthens and restraints, which they endure in the old world" would operate as a "powerful invitation" for manufacturers to "flock from Europe to the United States… if they were once made sensible of the advantages they would enjoy."[26]

In like manner, the American Protectionists considered socialism and communism o be disastrous, and were thus in lockstep with the British Classical School on the benefits of market capitalism. Henry Carey explains, for instance, that "Communism s everywhere the same… It is a project for reducing [mankind] to a state of barbarism. Hence… its introduction among civilized men have always failed so signally."[27] This aversion is perhaps best expressed by Robert Ellis Thompson:

> Protection cordially accepts the existing [capitalist] order of society, the present distribution of wealth and the lawful freedom of individual action, as right and proper. Its chief advocates have been zealous opponents of Communistic socialism, and the ablest defenders of the rights of property. While it asserts that the industrial growth and welfare of the people must be among the first cares of the statesman, it does not teach—what all experience refutes, that this can be attained through the direct action of the state as the employer and organizer of labor.[28]

Yet on the question of the structure of capitalism, the American Protectionists and the Classical School (and particularly, the more ideologically free trade strands of Classical economics, such as the Manchester and French Liberal School) diverged on their conception of the free market. Both schools were clear that some form of state interference was necessary, but differed over where interference should be tolerated.

Whereas the Classicals were ardent in their support of free trade, they were often more tolerant of state intervention in the domestic market, particularly with respect to taxation and social reform.[29] For the American Protectionists, the opposite was the case. Economic freedom was best achieved through free domestic markets, but the regulation of international trade was well within the legitimate scope of government authority. The combination of protection and the free domestic market was seen as maximizing economic freedom by broadening the opportunities for employment and enterprise. Hezekiah Niles captured this logic precisely:

> The purpose of the protective system being thus directed to the utmost expansion of the industry of the nation into every channel of domestic competition, it would seem to be manifestly erroneous to call such a system restrictive, inasmuch as the avenues of labour in the internal organization of any community are much more numerous and extensive.[30]

According to the American Protectionists, tariff protection does not violate the principles of liberty, because it does not compel or force individuals into any particular pursuit, but instead grants them the freedom to choose between different pursuits. Indeed, as Orrin Skinner explains, "protection… is not an infringement of liberty… It is simply freedom from compulsion. Protection compels neither interests nor individuals. It merely offers inducements, and leaves their acceptance to discretion."[31] This point is echoed by George B. Curtiss, who notes that:

> Under protection the individual exercises the utmost freedom of action in all the pursuits of life. The government does not attempt to direct the individual nor compel him to engage in any pursuit which he does not desire to undertake; neither does it… restrict him in the

> occupation which he may pursue. It simply, by shielding its own citizens from the injurious effect of the unfair and unequal competition of aliens, enables them to... enlarge their opportunities... It is not protection to individuals, but protection to opportunities for individuals.[32]

The American Protectionists termed their system of free domestic markets as "industrial freedom," which they contrasted with the freedom of trade expounded by the Classical, French and Manchester Schools.

It was argued that free trade, which often involves replacing tariffs with domestic taxes and costly policies of colonial expansion, simply meant substituting one form of state interference for another less desirable form. Indeed, "against the fallacy of free trade stands the fact of freedom of industry" argues Ellis H. Roberts. "If you tolerate state interference with industry at any point, it renders its best service in fostering production at home." Thus, "if you magnify industrial freedom, that freedom is nowhere so important, nowhere bears such ripe and nutritious fruit as in removing every restraint, every burden from the production of a nation."[33] Industrial freedom meant freedom from foreign competition, internal taxes, and other restrictive and burdensome domestic regulations. Most importantly, however, by creating the conditions for industrial diversification, protectionism and low domestic taxation create the widest freedom of choice when it comes to pursuing different modes of employment and enterprise. "Hence the scene of greatest diversity of industries," explains Denslow "is at once that in which industrial freedom rises highest."[34]

Industrial freedom allows entrepreneurs to conduct themselves without restraint in the home market whilst allowing them to engage in free competition with one-another. In addition, domestic competition was seen as superior to foreign competition. As the protectionist statesman Thomas Brackett Reed declares:

> What we want is the results of competition? low prices, so that we can buy all we want... [but] the doctrine of competition, most invaluable in its way, has its limitations. Being human, it is not an unmixed good. Destructive competition is an evil. The world cannot afford to have a trade which does not pay a fair profit.[35]

Competition among domestic producers was deemed by the American Protectionists as sufficient and even superior to foreign competition for the purpose of driving down domestic prices. Alexander Dallas, for instance, explains that "the competition among the domestic manufacturers alone would sufficiently protect the consumer from exorbitant prices."[36] More than this, however, by securing sound profits for domestic firms, it allows for competition of a more important kind. That is, competition for new products and inventions.[37] Unrestrained foreign competition may indeed produce more efficient gains in the short term, as even industry-destroying free trade might be efficient in the short term, but the American Protectionists understood that short-term efficiency does not necessarily equate to long-term growth and development. Long-term growth can only be achieved by allowing entrepreneurs scope to experiment and discover new avenues of production. The American Protectionists thus viewed internal free markets within an otherwise protected system as allowing a healthy dose of competition whilst avoiding its potentially destructive excesses.

The American Protectionists thus affirmed a negative view of economic freedom—that is, freedom from restraint and interference—but it differed from the Classical School in that it emphasized freedom of production over freedom of trade. In the words of Calvin Colton:

> Protectionists demand... the free and unrestrained use of American capital and labor... It is a misnomer, therefore, to call it a *restrictive system*, when there is no such thing in it. The design and tendency of an American protective system is not to embarrass, but to disembarrass, American capital and labor; to rescue and shield them from foreign oppression; to encourage them; to bring them out; to open the way for their most profitable employment; and to make them ENTIRELY FREE.[38]

The emphasis which the American Protectionists place on economic freedom is further demonstrated in the next section by their rejection of paternalism and monopoly privileges.

Protectionism versus Paternalism

Protectionism encompasses a broad set of governmental interventions, and what constitutes protectionism is often subject to interpretation. It is therefore important to differentiate between the protectionist measures supported by the American Protectionists and those measures that were not. The American Protectionists were careful in exercising restraint when formulating their system, and they were cognizant that excessive governmental interference, or more importantly, the wrong types of governmental interference, could lead to a system of paternalism or even state socialism. In making this distinction between protectionism and paternalism, the American Protectionists looked to policies that enabled industrial development, as opposed to ones that directed it. This distinction is clearly identified by George Gunton, who explains that:

> Orthodox economists reason that because paternalism is injurious, protection should be abandoned; while on the other hand, socialists conclude that because protection has been advantageous individualism should be abandoned and paternalism adopted. By overlooking the distinction between protection and paternalism, we are logically driven to one of two unscientific theories—*laissez-faire* and socialism.[39]

It should be noted that Alexander Hamilton did, however, support bounties and subsidies. Yet this was only as an initial encouragement for industry and not for the purposes of protection *per se*. After Hamilton, virtually every American Protectionist favored tariffs exclusively. Indeed, even Hamilton cautioned that bounties should only be used as a temporary expedient, noting "the continuance of bounties on manufacturers long established must always be of questionable policy.... But in new undertakings, they are as justifiable, as they are oftentimes necessary."[40] In contrast, Hamilton did back a perpetual, yet moderate, revenue tariff, which he explicitly praised for the incidental protection it would afford.[41]

Indeed, the exclusive preference for protective tariffs was one of design, not convenience or coincidence. The American Protectionists understood that tariffs stimulated domestic enterprise without fostering monopolies. Mathew Carey explains, for instance, that "it is an egregious error to suppose that high duties or prohibitions afford a '*monopoly*' to those in whose favor they are imposed."[42] Unlike tariff protection, which more or less favors all producers within the same industry equally, the use of subsidies and other monopoly privileges—what would now be considered industrial policy—was seen as prejudicial to smaller producers and to potential entrants to the market. This position is well expressed by Daniel Webster, who explains that by "calling for a wise system of custom-house duties… we embrace that policy which we think essential to the good of the whole. We desire no favouritism, no partial system."[43] Indeed, the discriminatory effects of subsidies are even more pernicious since it is almost always the most influential and politically connected firms that stand to benefit. This rejection of subsidies is perhaps best illustrated by William Elder:

> Encouragement sometimes embraces bonuses, extended by the government or exclusive privileges… such as subsidies… [This] is not that protection of the common interests of the community which is strictly defensive in its essence… It is not Protection, in our sense of the term… It is broadly distinguished by the circumstance that it means money paid out of the treasury to the benefit of specific enterprises, and is not general, uniform, and equitable, in its operation.[44]

In short, the American Protectionists supported policies that afforded a domestic preference, but they opposed favoritism or "picking winners" among domestic producers. Protectionism was designed to be applied equally to all producers within the market, as opposed to simply benefiting a few privileged ones. This position is also further demonstrated by the American Protective Tariff League, with their statement of principles explicitly opposing "monopolies and exclusive privileges" including the use of subsidies.[45]

This rejection of heavy-handed industrial policies stood in sharp contrast to the "socialism of the chair" of the German Historical School, and the technocratic planning of their American counterparts, the Progressives. Whereas the Germans and Progressives championed activist industrial policies aimed at directing the internal affairs of industry, the American System was predicated on creating opportunities for individuals to succeed through their own efforts. In the words of Jacob Harris Patton:

> [The American System stands] remarkably in contrast with the so-called paternal governments of Continental Europe. There … [they] are inclined to look to the government for direction in their industrial affairs, while, in the United States, the native-born intelligently and self-reliantly engage in industrial pursuits that are congenial, and look to themselves for success.[46]

The American Protectionists were thus very much aware that the use of subsidies could lead to protectionism morphing into paternalism, and even potentially into socialism

Indeed, in responding to the charge that "protection introduces into government, a principle of *paternalism*, which tends to Socialism," Robert Ellis Thompson counters that:

> [Tariff protection] does not do anything for individuals, or confer personal advantages of any kind on them. It merely creates a new industrial condition, which everyone is equally free to take advantage of. By enlarging the number of employments it also enlarges the range of individual liberty, as it gives greater choice of fields of labor. It thus helps to develop that individuality in the working classes which Socialism seeks to destroy. [Protectionism] leads away from Socialism, not toward it.[47]

At any rate, subsidies and other monopolistic forms of protection were seen as inferior to tariffs due to the fact that an inefficient producer could simply live off the subsidy, and thus live at the expense of the taxpayer. Henry Clay, for instance, objected to bounties, noting that "you tax the *whole* for the benefit of a part *only*, of the community."[48] Under a tariff, on the other hand, domestic producers are simply given breathing space to experiment and engage in entrepreneurial activities, but they are still subject to competitive pressures from domestic rivals. This free competition among domestic producers would in turn guard against market concentration and the development of monopolies. In the words of the Protectionist statesman James G. Blaine:

> Protection, in the perfection of its design as described by Mr. Hamilton, does not invite competition from abroad, but is based on the controlling principle that competition at home will always prevent monopoly on the part of the capitalist, assure good wages to the laborer, and defend the consumer against the evils of extortion.[49]

The passages above highlight what the protectionists considered to be the limits of state aid. As Jacob Harris Patton puts it, "the State cannot and ought not aid the citizens in ordinary circumstances, wherein they can help themselves. Its proper sphere is to protect the individual in his rights and thus afford him an opportunity to develop what may be good… in his own personal capacity."[50] Protectionism was thus conceived by the American Protectionists as a means of affording opportunities to the nation's citizens to pursue industrious activities through which they better their condition. The State was never viewed as an instrument to prop up failing businesses nor was it there to provide direct support to producers. Rather, "what the people need" remarked Roswell G. Horr, "is not that Government should control more patronage or manage more enterprises, but rather that the efforts of each individual should be properly encouraged."[51]

From a more practical standpoint, subsidies were deemed less efficient than tariff protection. This is particularly true since other taxes are required to finance subsidies, and because they require expensive bureaucracies for their administration. Willard Phillips thus explains, "in one respect the granting of bounties [or subsidies] is the most objectionable mode" of protection "as the bounty costs the government more than the amount granted." Indeed, bounties must be "paid out of the revenue, the collection and administration of which is expensive, so that to grant one hundred dollars, a tax of a hundred and two, five, or ten must be levied."[52] This objection to subsidies is perceptive, not only because it points out the paternalistic features of a subsidy, but it also provides a preemptive defense against the dead-weight loss argument, which is often employed by modern economists against tariffs and in defense of subsidies. It was apparent to the American Protectionists that all forms of taxation incur a dead-weight loss. It is not something unique to tariffs. Yet, for the same level of protection, a subsidy will incur an even greater dead-weight loss than a tariff since subsidies require complex and costly bureaucracies for their administration. Furthermore, in contrast to a subsidy, which depletes revenue which could otherwise be spent on the development of infrastructure, a tariff can raise revenue in an efficient manner whilst still serving a protective function. Moreover, this protective function is something unique to tariffs and does not extend to other forms of taxation that also incur a dead-weight loss.

The objection to paternalistic forms of government intervention and its concomitant bureaucratization is perhaps best illustrated by the backlash to FDR's New Deal by the Republican Party, who at the time were still championing the American System. As per the 1936 Republican Platform:

> The New Deal Administration has dishonored American traditions… Regulated monopoly has displaced free enterprise… It has created a vast multitude of new offices, filled them with its favorites, [and] set up a centralized bureaucracy… [which has] bred fear and hesitation in commerce and industry, thus discouraging new enterprises, preventing employment and prolonging the depression.

In response, Republicans were not advocating *laissez-faire*, as often depicted in secondary literature, but rather the standard prescription of tariff protection combined with free internal competition. As the Republican platform continues to explain:

> [Democrats have] secretly made tariff agreements with our foreign competitors, flooding our markets with foreign commodities… We pledge ourselves… to preserve the American System of free enterprise, private competition, and equality of opportunity… Sufficient protection should be maintained at all times to defend the American farmer and the American wage earner from the destructive competition emanating from the subsidies of foreign governments and the imports from low-wage and depreciated-currency countries.[53]

The above captures the scope and form of protection advocated by the American Protectionists. As opposed to affording monopoly privileges and propping up national champions, the aim was to allow "equality of opportunity" among domestic producers with the recognition that subsidies and heavy-handed industrial policies are prone to discouraging smaller producers and potential new entrants to the market. In short, "the distinction between paternalism and protection," as George Gunton explains, "is that a paternal policy implies doing the maximum for the individual, while a protective policy implies providing the individual with the maximum opportunity to do for himself."[54]

Internal Improvements

Aside from tariffs, the other major policy pillar of the American System is infrastructure, referred to at the time as internal improvements. Indeed, as early as *The Report on Manufactures,* Hamilton explains how "good roads, canals and navigable rivers, by diminishing the expence of carriage… are upon that account the greatest of all improvements."[55] The facilitation of exchange and the diminution of transportation costs for industry, whether these costs be monetary or non-monetary (such as congestion costs, cost of time, and so forth), represents the central argument expounded by the American Protectionists in favor of a policy of internal improvements. This position is well illustrated by Lyman Beecher:

> The improvement of roads shortens often the distance to market, increases the amount transported, diminishes the muscular toil, and other wear and tear, of transportation, while it increases the value of the surplus produce… [Similarly,] canals, connecting rivers and lakes with the ocean, break down the distance of three or four hundred miles land transportation, bring the market to the farmer's door, and save millions annually, as the increased reward of industry, and as capital for more extended enterprise.[56]

Beyond these direct economic benefits, the American Protectionists recognized that infrastructure served multiple functions in developing a national economy. Erastus B. Bigelow notes, for instance, how "apart from their greater efficiency and the saving in the cost of transportation which they effect, railroads have many economic advantages." Indeed, among these advantages are that "perishable commodities are safely transported, less capital is in transit, less capital is kept idle in superfluous stock, less time is spent in travel, new markets are opened, and in old markets prices are equalized."[57] In a similar vein, infrastructure investment was also seen as aiding production by connecting resources to industries, industries to other industries, and products to the end consumer. Ezra Seaman captures this perfectly, noting how "roads, canals, railroads, steamboats, and other means of communication and transportation, serve as instruments and agents to aid production, and to promote both industry and commerce." Indeed, using the example of "mining for iron," Seaman explains that this "cannot be prosecuted without facilities for transporting the ore, and fuel to smelt it," and the means to transport it "to the furnace" as well as the means "to transport their manufactured products to market."[58]

The American Protectionists thus advocated infrastructure development for purely structural reasons.[59] They did not justify such expenditures on counter-cyclical grounds. Oliver Putnam expresses this view quite succinctly, noting how, rather than boosting employment, internal improvements are ultimately labor-saving in their effect. Indeed, "internal improvement," explains Putnam, "removes obstructions to the interchange of commodities, and causes labor and capital to be turned from transportation to be employed in production."[60] This view is also well illustrated by Willard Phillips who explains that:

> The expenditure for roads, canals, and bridges are intended to promote production by facilitating the exchange of products. Other public works again are undertaken for motives of piety, national glory, or vanity… We should, for instance, think the Egyptian pyramids scarcely worth their cost, and the building of Babel a sheer folly.[61]

This structural argument contrasts with the counter-cyclical approach to public works that was emerging among American Progressives and later adopted by New

Dealers. These proto-Keynesian thinkers argued that public works spending could boost employment during downturns, regardless of the merit on structural grounds. This view would eventually be formalized by John Maynard Keynes, who argued that "public works even of doubtful utility may pay for themselves over and over again at a time of severe unemployment… pyramid-building, earthquakes, even wars may serve to increase wealth."[62] The American Protectionists rejected this logic, expounding the view that infrastructure expenditure must be justified as a long-term investment in productivity, rather than a short-term stimulus.

The above analysis establishes what the American Protectionists saw as the benefits of internal improvements, but it says little about what they saw as the government's role. According to the American Protectionists, the need for government involvement in the provision of infrastructure essentially comes down to market failure, particularly with respect to the under-provision of infrastructure and issues associated with coordination or what is known today as coordination failure. With respect to the under-provision of infrastructure, the American Protectionists observed that private individuals often lack sufficient capital to finance the construction of large roads and other public works. Moreover, even when sufficient capital exists, these projects often face competition from other investment opportunities. In the words of Henry Clay:

> Some principles drawn from political economists have been alluded to, and we are advised to leave things to themselves, upon ground that, when the condition of society is ripe for internal improvements—that is, when capital can be so invested with a fair prospect of adequate remuneration, they will be executed… unaided by government… [Yet] in regard to internal improvements, it does not follow, that they will always be constructed whenever they will afford a competent dividend… the condition of society may be ripe… before there is… the necessary accumulation of capital to effect them; and besides, there is… not only a scarcity of capital, but such a multiplicity of profitable objects presenting themselves as to distract the judgement.[63]

Coordination issues, on the other hand, arise because the benefits of infrastructure projects are often diffused across a multitude of different individuals within the community, and, as such, there are immense difficulties involved coordinating their efforts to carry out such projects despite the totality of the diffused benefits warranting it. As Henry Clay continues:

> The aggregate benefit resulting to the whole society, from a public improvement, may be such as to amply justify the investment of capital in its execution, and yet that benefit may be so distributed among different and distant persons, that they can never be got to act in concert.[64]

This connects closely with another coordination issue. That is, when the project's expected profitability renders it unviable for individual capitalists, despite the totality of dispersed benefits justifying its development. In these cases, it is only right and proper for the government to enter the market. In the words of John Melish, "it follows, that all public works, which are deemed essential, and which yet do not hold out a prospect of remuneration to individuals, should be executed exclusively by the public, and for public account."[65]

That said, whilst the American Protectionists clearly saw the need for government in the provision of infrastructure, they were far from dogmatic on the question of public versus private provision. Robert Ellis Thompson captures this view, noting that:

> Transportation by sea and land is carried on by individuals and private or semi-private corporations, under the laws which control the common carrier, while the State takes charge of making common roads only, and in some cases leaves even that to turnpike companies.[66]

The ultimate objective was to provide efficient infrastructure for industry, regardless of whether this is facilitated by the private or public sector, or some combination of the two.[67] In fact, the ideal system, it seems, was one where the private sector was free to compete with the public sector in the provision of infrastructure, so as to compel government to maintain sufficient quality and low costs, and vice versa.

Indeed, Henry Carey went as far as to argue that, in addition to public roads, landowners should have the right to construct their own private toll roads and railway lines on their private land. These private roads could thus enter into competition with the public sector as well as with one another. Individuals would thus be free to choose between a range of private and public infrastructure. Writing with respect to the State-sanctioned railroad monopoly of New Jersey, Henry Carey declares that:

> [The state must] exterminate the monster monopoly by passing a general law that would enable all men to associate for the making of turnpikes and railroads, and to select for themselves the road to market, and to go north or south, east or west, as might seem most advantageous to them.[68]

The underlying logic of this mixed (i.e. private and public) and diversified system of infrastructure is that with sufficient competition, whether between the same mode of transportation—one rail line competing against an alternate line—or between different modes of transportation—a rail line competing against a canal or a toll road—the competition, whilst imperfect, still has the effect of guarding against monopoly pricing and provides an incentive for maintenance and improvement.

Indeed, it is far from clear, according to the American Protectionists, that a government monopoly on the provision of infrastructure would necessarily provide quality infrastructure at the lowest costs. Without being kept in check by private competition, the State could well charge transit fees far above what would occur otherwise, or the State could neglect the infrastructure or misuse taxpayer money by building it to an inadequate standard. The American Protectionists thus acknowledged the existence of both market and government failure. By having both the private and public sectors operating within the market, this would act as a check and balance to correct such failures as they present themselves, at least more than what would occur if only one, be it private or public, were present.

It should be recalled that the American Protectionists considered protective tariffs and infrastructure as operating in synergy. Together, both would advance the productivity and competitiveness of American industry more than one would in isolation. Henry Clay declares that "the tariff and internal improvements are intimately connected… if not indissolubly united… their nature, by the tendency of each to advance the objects of the other, and of both to augment the sum of national prosperity."[69] By this, Clay meant that the development of industry makes internal improvement more economically viable by increasing the demand for such services. Nathanial A. Ware captures this view, explaining that "our internal improvements… would be benefited by the establishment of manufactures, for the transportation on them would be more voluminous and varied."[70]

In addition to this protective function, tariffs were also the revenue source for defraying the costs of internal improvements. It is for such reasons that Clay, in another speech, urges the government to "preserve the protective system in full vigor; [and to] give us the proceeds of the public domain for internal improvements."[71] This also connects to broader issue of balanced national economy. Because tariffs are generally more applicable to manufacturing, there was an implicit understanding that agricultural communities should receive more infrastructure funding to offset the costs of the tariff levied on imported industrial goods. Robert Ellis Thompson thus explains that "the Protectionists… have always carried out the policy of subsidizing new roads and railroads, so as to give the farmer free access to his market." The combination of internal improvements and protective tariffs represents the quintessential features of the American System. In the words of Robert Ellis Thompson, the "tariff and internal improvements have always gone together in our political war-cries."[72]

Thus, the American System of Capitalism cannot simply be dismissed as a rudimentary form of industrial policy. It instead constituted its own distinct and complete policy framework. Whilst the American Protectionists recognized a role for the State in creating conditions for the cultivation of private enterprise, they were far from ignorant of industrial policy, and explicitly cautioned against it. With this in mind, it is perhaps fitting to bring this chapter to close with the words of Henry Clay, the father of the American System, who once said that "the American system of protection should be regarded, as it is, an *entire and comprehensive system*, made up of various items, and aiming at the prosperity of the whole Union, by protecting the interests of each part."[73]

Notes

1. Lincoln, "Humble Lincoln," 1; full passage also mentions a national bank.
2. Rice, *Philosophy*, 8.
3. Steele, *Rudimentary Economics*, 45–46.
4. O'Brien, *Classical Economists,* 328; see also Kates, *Classical Theory*, 198–200; Samuels, *Classical Theory,* 104.
5. Cairnes, "Political Economy," 86.
6. Curtiss, *Protection*, 778–779.
7. Hamilton, "Examination," 467.
8. Elder, *Questions,* 17.
9. Phillips, *Manual*, 233.
10. Rice, *Philosophy,* 9.

11. Horr, 'Taxes a Blessing?', 1891, 5.
12. Denslow, *Freedom*, 2–3.
13. Hamilton, "Continentalist 5," 76.
14. Steele, *Rudimentary Economics*, 167.
15. Thompson, *Elements*, 362.
16. See Chapter 7 for harmony of interest doctrine.
17. Thompson, 'Social Reform', 732–733.
18. Hamilton, "Federalist No. 21," 401; see Chapter 11 for an elaboration of Hamilton's views on incidental protection.
19. Hamilton, "Continentalist 5," 75–76.
20. Denslow, *Logic*, 12.
21. Carey, *Financial Crises*, 32; Hamilton ("Federalist 35," 477) similarly warned "all extremes are pernicious" regarding tariffs.
22. List, *Natural System*, 36.
23. List, *Natural System*, 105.
24. Curtiss, *Protection*, 563.
25. Rae, *Statement*, 381–384.
26. Hamilton, *Report on Manufactures*, 11.
27. Carey, *Social Science*, 2:163–164.
28. Thompson, *Elements*, 254.
29. O'Brien, *Classical Economists*, 2004, 228, 328;
30. Niles, *Journal*, 19.
31. Skinner, *American Politics*, 417.
32. Curtiss, *Industrial Development*, 2:425.
33. Roberts, *Government Revenue*, 365–366.
34. Denslow, *Principles*, 122.
35. Reed, 'What Shall We Do?', 748.
36. Dallas, *Report*, 23.
37. Elaborated upon in Chapter 6.
38. Colton, *Public Economy*, 188.
39. Gunton, *Social Economics*, 319.
40. Hamilton, *Report on Manufactures*, 36.
41. Expanded upon in Chapter 11.
42. Carey, *Essays*, 434.
43. Webster, "Convention of Philadelphia," 269.
44. Elder, *Questions*, 205–206.
45. Protective Tariff League, "Principles," 34.
46. Patton, *Political Economy*, 240.
47. Thompson, *High Schools*, 94, 101–102.
48. Clay, "Domestic Manufactures," 10.
49. Blaine, *Twenty Years*, 1:212.
50. Patton, *Political Economy*, 242–243.
51. Horr, "Taxes Ever a Blessing?," 5.
52. Phillips, *Manual*, 207.
53. Republican National Convention, "Platform, 1936," 29–33.
54. Gunton, *Social Economics*, 319.
55. Hamilton, *Report on Manufactures*, 40.
56. Beecher, 'National Prosperity', 265.
57. Bigelow, "Labor and Capital," 478.
58. Seaman, *Progress*, 510.
59. The exception is Daniel Raymond (*Thoughts*, 288–292), who, while emphasizing structural benefits, notes positive employment effects.

60. Putnam, *Tracts*, 32.
61. Phillips, *Manual*, 268.
62. Keynes, *General Theory,* 127–129.
63. Clay, "Internal Improvement," 133.
64. Clay, "Internal Improvement,"133–134.
65. Melish, *Travels*, 573.
66. Thompson, *High Schools*, 103.
67. This often took the form of land grants to the private sector, or private-public partnerships for key infrastructure. Regarding railroads, Jacob Harris Patton (*Political Economy,* 246) notes "the combination of private enterprise with the protecting care of government, accomplishes the end more perfectly than if each acted separately."
68. Carey, *Railroad Companies,* 71.
69. Clay, "Nullification," 408.
70. Ware, *Political Economy*, 143.
71. Clay, "American System," 483.
72. Thompson, *Elements*, 240.
73. Clay, "Nullification," 407.

Chapter Three

THE SOCIAL AND MORAL PHILOSOPHY OF THE AMERICAN PROTECTIONISTS

The American Protectionists insisted that human imperfection was not a problem to be solved, but a foundation to build upon. They rejected socialism because humans were too flawed to plan an economy, and they rejected *laissez-faire* because humans were too flawed to be left entirely alone. Yet this rejection of both extremes was accompanied not by pessimism but by a remarkable optimism about mankind's economic destiny. This optimistic realism formed the basis of their vision of the world. It is a worldview that accepts human imperfection as permanent yet compatible with human progress.

Visions are important for any group of economic thinkers. The great economist Joseph Schumpeter once posited that all economic theory is built upon a vision of the world. Visions can be seen as a "pre-analytic cognitive act," or a view of how things work before any systematic reasoning begins.[1] For the American Protectionists, their foundational vision was grounded in realism and a skepticism toward utopian thinking. This skepticism of utopian thinking stemmed from their belief that human institutions are imperfectible. This view is best articulated by Alexander Hamilton. "It is the lot of all human institutions, even those of the most perfect kind," according to Hamilton, "to have defects as well as excellencies—ill as well as good propensities. This results from the imperfection of the Institutor, Man."[2] By recognizing the defects of human nature, the American Protectionists accepted that imperfections are therefore inherent to the social order.

This aversion to utopianism did not rule out government intervention of course. Instead, it means that interventions must be devised in accordance with human nature and its defects. Alexander Hamilton again exemplifies this view, observing that:

> The true politican on the contrary takes human nature (and human society its aggregate) as he finds it, a compound of good and ill qualities—endued with powers and actuated by passions and propensities which blend enjoyment with suffering and make the causes of welfare the causes of misfortune.
>
> With this view of human nature he will not attempt to warp or distort it from its natural direction—he will not attempt to promote its happiness by means to which it is not suited... but he will seek to promote his action according to the byass of his nature, to lead him to the developpement of his energies according to the scope of his passions, and erecting the social organisation on this basis, he will favour all those institutions and plans which tend to make men happy according to their natural bent.[3]

The hostility which the American Protectionists held toward socialism was no doubt shaped by this understanding. Jacob Harris Patton observed, for instance, that "in theory, socialism professes to aim at elevating man, and the object is a worthy one; but unfortunately, the means employed are antagonistic to human nature and the order of society."[4] Or as Roswell G. Horr explains, "the idea of modern socialism, that the Government should own everything and manage everything, that the people should all work for everybody, and no one for himself, has no foundation in the human organism."[5] Indeed, what the American Protectionists rejected was not intervention, but systematic and heavy-handed economic planning by a central authority. The American System was thus crafted to achieve economic outcomes indirectly, working with the natural tendencies of mankind, instead of against it.

This view that social systems are imperfectible also connects with the assumption that trade-offs are ever-present, and it is for this reason that American Protectionists often disregarded so-called matters of social justice. The American System was not designed to ameliorate every market imperfection or alleviate every social ill. Its purpose was to facilitate the expansion and diversification of national industry and enterprise, which would raise economic well-being over time. Yet, since trade-offs are always present, attempts at complete and sweeping reforms advanced by the more utopian schools of economic thought would invariably clash with the objectives of the American System. Van Buren Denslow perfectly illustrates this worldview in passage of treatise entitled "Can Poverty Be Abolished?":

> So far as the socialist bases his complaint on the assertion that the wealth accumulated in the hands of the few wealthy is so much abstracted or withdrawn from the stock of goods that would be consumable by the poor, he is evidently in error… the surplus wealth of the rich must be invested in such modes as to give society the use of it.… In the existing world the pressure of economic want, present or prospective—in short, poverty—is as potent a force in wealth production as hunger is in causing the body to be fed or cold in causing it to be clothed…
>
> If by the "abolition of poverty" is meant the ensuring a reasonable certainty of comfortable support to all who are ready to do what they can to be useful to their fellow-men, it may be doubted whether any humanly invented system can effect much improvement on than one now in force [that system, being the American System]… [But] the notion that poverty [in the literal sense] can be abolished is a flattering gospel, far more attractive to our human impulses than to [our senses].[6]

Even though Denslow considered the American System as perhaps the best of all possible systems, he nevertheless conceded that it was still an imperfect system. Indeed, the perfect system was an impossibility, it is actually the imperfections of capitalism that allow it to work so effectively. In this case, the fear of impoverishment will always exist, yet is one of the mechanisms that allows for economic progress over time.

Underpinning the American Protectionists' rejection of utopian schemes is also the view that social and economic processes are inherently complex. Because of this, no one individual or central authority is capable of marshalling the requisite knowledge to master the complex array of interconnected social processes. The American

Protectionists even saw this logic inherent in the division of labor. Indeed, "it is well known," explains Denslow, "that the men in each branch of industry become ignorant of the other branches in the ratio that they became skilled in their own, yet that the aggregate result is a vast increase in skill and in rapidity of production."[7] By implication, "it would be as great a waste of time and diversion of effort, on the part… of a legislator to attempt to become an expert fisherman."[8]

Government serves an important purpose, of course, but mastering every facet of society is clearly beyond its capability. It is for this reason that the American Protectionists preferred decentralized institutions and systematic processes, such as markets, to coordinate society. The fear of impoverishment that Denslow described earlier represents one such process, as it motivates productive behavior throughout the social system without requiring direction from a central authority. In the nineteenth century, these systematic processes were viewed as the manifestation of natural law, and as will be shown in the next section, the American Protectionists built their system upon a natural law philosophy. It was this belief in natural law that underpinned their decentralized approach to public policy.

In line with this view of natural law, the American Protectionists envisioned an economic system with a relatively high degree of freedom and flexibility for the individual agents operating within it. Whilst they ultimately desired the development of productive industry and enterprise, the direct and deliberate action of government alone was seen as incapable of bringing about this outcome. Instead, a flexible system of incentives and restraints would allow entrepreneurs to bring about such an outcome within more or less natural or pre-existing social arrangements. Henry M. Hoyt captures this point, declaring that "by *restriction* [protection], industries here will diversify themselves under the operation of natural forces [, and that] the development of society will be as regular and natural as that of [the growth of] a plant."[9] Indeed, even if the individual entrepreneurs within the system are themselves flawed and imperfect, the likelihood that one or more of them will be successful is higher than the likelihood of success from one centralized authority. One can certainly appreciate the divergence between the decentralized entrepreneur-driven industrialization of the American System with that of Soviet-style attempts at industrialization through a centralized system of government planning and state-ownership. Whilst both systems had the goal of industrialization in mind, the divergence in their two visions meant that they both pursued fundamentally different means in attempting to arrive at a similar goal.

Of course, one might object that the American Protectionists, given their fervent support for protective tariffs, were indeed utopian thinkers, likening tariffs to a perfect institution of sorts. Whilst they were no doubt enthusiastic champions of protective tariffs, they did not view tariffs as a cure-all. Giles B. Stebbins remarked, for instance, that "protection is not a panacea, good against crop failures, bad business management or extravagance, but a powerful element in the conservation and development of national resources and of personal skill and power."[10] This point was also humorously illustrated by Robert Ellis Thompson using the example of the 1901 heatwave. In response to free traders who argued that high food prices were due to tariffs, Thompson declared that he "was unaware that there was any clause in the Dingley tariff for the regulation of weather, or that protection was even put forward as a remedy for bad seasons."[11]

The reality is that no matter how well-crafted a tariff schedule is, business failures are inevitable and even to be expected. Tench Coxe explains, for instance, "enterprise and adventure cannot always be expected to be successful. Misfortunes will attend the best concerted schemes."[12] Indeed, it is precisely because certain businesses are bound to fail that the American Protectionists preferred a decentralized network of producers. Moreover, the American Protectionists also recognized that tariffs, like any other government policy, do indeed come with associated costs and trade-offs. Admittedly, these costs tended to be viewed as short-lived and more in terms of opportunity cost, as opposed to direct costs. This is to say, for instance, that a higher price of imports in the short-term was seen as a worthy trade-off for the development of domestic industry over time, and that the cost of an import tariff would eliminate the cost of domestic taxation. But, nevertheless, there was still a clear recognition that certain costs and trade-offs accompanied the use of protective tariffs.

Whilst the above has tended to focus on the utopianism of socialism, the American Protectionists were just as scathing in their rebukes of the perceived utopianism of the *laissez-faire* theorists. This is well-illustrated by the Republican statesman and advocate of the American System, Henry Cabot Lodge:

> The doctrine that the least government is the best, and the economic theory known as *laissez faire* and *laissez aller*... The pendulum under the influence of this great movement [against government] ... swung with corresponding violence to the opposite extreme. Men swiftly concluded that, because the interference of the state under the monarchies of the eighteenth century was evil, the true secret of freedom, happiness, and success was to be found in going as far as possible in the opposite direction, in reducing government to its lowest terms, and in getting as near as possible to no government at all. In other words, the world in its political and economic theories rushed from the system of tyrannous interference... to extreme individualism and unrestrained competition... All this was very natural, but, like all extremes, very dangerous, and, like all Utopias, was in practice very uncertain and disappointing.[13]

The essential character of this criticism of *laissez-faire* goes to the idea of prudence in the crafting of government policy. Since industrial development and economic diversification were high on the hierarchy of values of the American Protectionists, risking the destruction of productive industry for what was perceived as rather minute benefits of unrestricted trade was considered reckless and imprudent. Although their approach differs in some respects from Edmund Burke (such as in their affirmation of natural law), the prudent approach which the American Protectionists had toward public policy places them broadly within the Burkean conservative tradition. Whilst they acknowledged inherent truths of the market system, they were cognizant of not carrying those truths too far. In conservative fashion, historical experience was also used by the American Protectionists as a guide for judging the validity of ideas and policy, and when reforms were sought, they were careful to preserve the beneficial aspects of the existing order that had been tried and tested by past generations. This can be seen most plainly with the preservation of certain elements of mercantilism, as in the case of protective tariffs, whilst rejecting the other heavy-handed and injurious state interventions practiced by the mercantilists. Yet, despite their aversion to utopian thinking, the American Protectionists remained remarkably optimistic about Man's economic destiny.

The Natural Law of the American Protectionists

The scathing critiques of Classical economics by the American Protectionists might suggest that they rejected natural law. Yet, nothing could be further from the truth. The American Protectionists did not reject natural law. They simply rejected the system of natural law as laid down by the Classical economists. Robert Ellis Thompson affirms this commitment to natural law, declaring that "there is a constitution and course of nature in things economical. The statesman has to discover its laws and accommodate his own measures to them." Rather, the issue was "that [Adam] Smith and his followers made mistakes as to what those laws were," but this "involves no deduction from the truth of his main proposition" that natural laws exist.[14] This commitment to natural law connects with their broader Christian worldview, and in the case of Alexander Hamilton even predates the founding of the School. Indeed, "the deity," Hamilton explains, "has constituted an eternal and immutable law, which is, indispensibly, obligatory upon all mankind, prior to any human institution whatever. This is what is called the law of [human] nature."[15]

For the American Protectionists, natural law represents the laws of human nature and human conduct, but it went further. Human nature can, of course, be depraved and corrupt, but natural law are the laws which, if followed, allows for the development of human potentiality and fulfillment. Again, Robert Ellis Thompson explains that "natural rights are such as are necessary to the complete development of our human nature."[16] The discovery of such fundamental principles were also seen as important for guiding proper State action and even moral actions of individuals within society, and it is through the discovery of natural laws that natural rights could be established. It should not be concluded, however, that natural laws are a product of deliberate design. Government is necessary, but its actions must conform and operate harmoniously with human nature. In the words of Robert Ellis Thompson, the statesman "knows that he does not and cannot supply the motive power of the process; that he is gubernator or steersmen merely."[17] This position also echoes earlier pronouncements of Alexander Hamilton, who declared that there exist "fundamental laws, agreeable to which its general operations must be directed; and that any violent attempts in opposition to these would commonly miscarry."[18]

Whereas the natural or iron laws of Ricardo and Malthus can be seen as an equilibrating force which operates to bring living standards back to their natural subsistence level, the American Protectionists saw natural law as a dynamic force which allows for human progress and economic development over time. In both cases, natural law can be likened to systematic processes operating throughout the social system. The

American Protectionists charged, however, that the systematic processes contained in Ricardian and Malthusian economics appealed to the brutish tendencies and impulses of Man. The American Protectionists, on the other hand, saw human deprivation and subsistence not as the result of natural laws inherent in social phenomena, but were the result of human misconduct and human error. The difference in this conception of natural law can be seen in the following passage from Carey:

> Such is the difference between [the American Protectionists], and the doctrines of the Ricardo-Malthusian school… The one inculcates, that the great treasury of nature is practically unlimited in its extent; that there exist great natural laws, in virtue of which, food and other raw materials tend to increase more rapidly than population; that it is the *duty* of the powerful to study and understand those laws; and that if, by reason of failure in the performance of that great duty, vice and misery prevail throughout the world…
>
> The other [Ricardian-Malthusian School] teaches that, by reason of the scarcity of fertile soils, the powers of the earth are perpetually diminishing in the ratio borne by them to the mouths requiring to be fed; that there exist great natural laws, in virtue of which, population tends to increase more rapidly than food… [resulting in] poverty, wretchedness, and death.[19]

Indeed, the American Protectionists did not conceive natural law as a system of mechanical relationships which operated like mathematics—a charge which they levelled against the English Classicals. And it is for this reason that Robert Ellis Thompson declared that through the writings of the American Protectionists that "the science of national economy passes out of the mechanical into the dynamical stage."[20]

For the American Protectionists, mankind as a species is too highly varied to operate in such a mechanical manner. In "Man," explains Carey, "we find individual differences almost as numerous as are those of the human countenance; there being scarcely any two members of the human family precisely alike," but in this "variety there is unity."[21] And in this "unity and universality of law… of which we speak, as in all other instances in which the idea is used… is not identity or sameness, but the harmony of correspondence."[22] In other words, the American Protectionist conception of natural law rests on the notion that orderly patterns emerge from the conduct of highly varied individuals. Even though Man possesses immense individuality and variation, human conduct exhibits regularity and predictability at the societal level, and this regularity and orderliness constitute natural law.

In the modern era, natural law is more often identified with libertarianism, which, especially in its extreme forms, disdains State interference. However, there has always been a tradition which ran through the writers, such as John Locke, which saw the main purpose of government as securing natural rights. The American Protectionists are firmly in this Lockean tradition. The State was not viewed by the American Protectionists as incompatible with natural law. It is natural law which prescribes natural rights, and it is often seen as the role of the State to secure such rights and to remove obstacles to the operation of natural law. Indeed, Denslow even goes so far as to declare that there is a "principle in human nature, which compels the creation of the monopoly known as The State."[23] This monopoly of the State, in Lockean fashion, was likened to an executor of natural rights, or as Robert Ellis Thompson explains:

> The universal element in the vocation of a state is expressed in the statement that it is the institution of rights. This differentiates it from the family, which is the institution of the affections; also from mankind at large, as rights are realized and made positive through the existence of the state.[24]

Thompson continues by declaring that "men have not fewer rights because they have given up some for the sake of making a body politic. Practically they would have none unless the state existed." Indeed, "if a man were to put himself outside the pale of political society… he still would be entitled to so much consideration as humanity suggested, but he would not possess any of the rights which are ideally his as a human being."[25] Affirming Thompson, Denslow thus explains how the "monopoly" of government "by giving to individuals a private title, is essential to each individual having a title to his own labor." "Whilst" it may be argued that "the monopoly seems to build up the individual at the expense of the public, it really is the first step in freeing the individual to serve himself and inciting him to serve the public" through the operation of natural law.[26] In this respect, the State represents a bulwark against violations of natural law, with Thompson declaring that the removal of "obstacles [to the operation of natural law] is the sole function of the state, as regards the active direction of industry."[27]

The American Protectionists conceived a hierarchy of sorts when it comes to natural rights. Paramount among these were private property rights. This was seen as the fountain from which various other rights flow from. Thompson again remarks that "private property is essential to personal liberty… There is no freedom of speech or of action possible to members of communities in which it does not exist." Indeed, "it is only where every man can and most men do possess the means of self-support independently of the will of society, that any man can cherish and assert an opinion which is not shared by the community of which he is a member."[28] This position is similarly noted by Denslow, who explains that "private property in land is essential" to the right of "exchange, because [without] that [right]… no one can sell, and land owned by all does not admit of those permanent crops, orchards, improvements, etc., which extend over years."[29] It is also for this reason that the American Protectionists disdained direct taxation because it represents a direct tax on private property, and is therefore a violation of natural rights. In contrast, indirect taxes levied on consumption are therefore less antagonistic to natural law since the right of exchange is of a lower order than property rights.

In likeness, the right to production was considered natural and of a higher order than the right of exchange since production necessarily precedes exchange. Moreover, even within the domain of exchange, domestic commerce was seen as superseding international trade in the natural order of things. In his piece, *The Rights of American Producers*, Henry Carey Baird declares that "production, furnishing all National power, is to the country, its commerce, and trade… what the water-wheel and the steam engine are to mills and machinery." It is "the prime mover" and "in the absence of this great National prime mover, as it may be called, all motion… must cease."[30] This view is likewise echoed by William Elder who declares that "in natural sequence production precedes exchange, and the answering principle in logic requires that productive power should have precedence of trade interests in the direction of national policy."[31] Or as Stephen Colwell puts it, "industry is the parent of commerce; the latter but distributes what the former produces… Industry is the principle; trade the incident."[32]

It thus follows that if one were to permit taxation anywhere, which is ultimately necessary for the securement of natural rights, taxes on foreign trade are far more congenial to natural law than taxes on domestic production. Indeed, Baird even goes as far as to say that "the American producer has a right to demand that his Government shall levy duties on foreign imports."[33] This is no small matter. Whereas most advocates of tariff protection typically advance their arguments based on expediency, they are frequently on the defensive when it comes to ethical claims. The American Protectionists thus believed that the doctrine of protection was a matter of ethics, and if, as the American Protectionists believed, protectionism can be established as being in harmony with natural law, it passes from a matter of mere expediency to a philosophical imperative.

This view of production preceding exchange in the sequence of nature necessarily lends itself to the view that internal economic freedom, or what the American Protectionist called "industrial freedom" is of a higher order than free trade. Since the ability to support external trade necessarily rests on the power of internal production and exchange, this means that the protection of internal industry is in full accordance with natural law. David H. Mason thus explains that:

> *Freedom within, but restraint against what is without, is the universal rule and the natural law of protection…* There must be a large development of internal power before there can be a large development of external power. No more than an individual can a nation exert great strength outwardly unless such strength exists inwardly… Assertion of selfhood is inseparable from human nature, and is as necessary to the nation as to the citizen. It is the gift of God, [and it] therefore must be beneficial in its exercise. Within the purview of the same doctrine, home industry outranks foreign industry.[34]

Whilst not all American Protectionists would go so far as to characterize protectionism as a natural right, almost all conceived it as operating in harmony with natural law and thus a wise policy to pursue in any event. It was thus argued, in the words of Henry Carey Baird, that "the great cause of Protection can and should be placed upon the high moral ground of right and justice, and its advocates should then, wrest from their enemies the rights and liberties so long and so persistently withheld from them."[35] Having established a commitment to natural law, the American Protectionists then faced the methodological question of how to discover and identify these laws.

The Inductive-Natural Law Method

The American Protectionists not only extended their criticisms to the Classical conception of natural law, they were also critical of the method by which the Classicals arrived at it. The Classical economists, particularly Ricardo, Malthus, and Mill, utilized an *a priori* deductive approach to arrive at natural laws. This approach commences by laying down a set of assumptions and then deducing a system of natural law from these assumptions. It is for this reason that the American Protectionists commonly criticized Classical economics as a "science based upon assumptions," anticipating what later economists would term as the "Ricardian Vice."[36] The issue with this approach is that the underlying assumptions often prescribe the laws and principles that are arrived at without reference to actual experience. These idealized models are then confidently applied to policy recommendations while neglecting the complexities of the real world. Indeed, this view is captured by Peshine Smith in a letter to Henry Carey, writing that "if social science could have been thought by a man with his eyes shut Ricardo would have done wonders."[37] Or as George B. Curtiss elaborates:

> The charge has often been made by protectionists that the theory of free trade had its origin in unreal and imaginary conditions, while the doctrine of protection was drawn from the experience of nations and from the actual practice of man. Free trade has been conceded by eminent economists advocating its principles to be a theory based on assumptions.[38]

The American Protectionist approach differed radically. Instead of imposing assumptions on economic phenomena from the top down, the American Protectionists started by analyzing inductively a vast assortment of economic facts to determine the laws underlying human conduct. Their approach can thus be described as discovering a system of natural laws from the ground up. Robert Ellis Thompson provides perhaps the best rendering of the difference between the two approaches:

> The English [Classical] school adopt the deductive method of the mathematical sciences, and reason down from assumed first principles to the specific facts. They claim that the necessary data for this are already at hand, in the known characteristics and tendencies of human nature, the avarice and the desire of progress, which control and direct the economic conduct of great masses of men. They leave all other elements out of account as inconstant, while they regard these as constant. Theirs is therefore "a science based upon assumptions"; it "necessarily reasons from assumptions, and not from facts."
>
> [The Protectionist] begin[s] with a wide study of the actual working of economical forces, and endeavor to reason upward from the mass of complicated facts to the general laws that underlie and govern all. They begin by recognizing the existence of an actual constitution and course of nature, instead of seeking to devise an artificial one on assumed principles.[39]

It was observed in the previous section that the American Protectionists essentially conceived natural law as an emergent property arising from a social system made up of complex and unique individuals. The purpose of induction, as Thompson points out, is to distil these natural laws from the complex array of facts and tendencies in human conduct. Indeed, particularly after the writings of Henry Carey, the American Protectionists stylized their natural law approach along the lines of Comtean positivism, which places a similar emphasis on the use of historical methods to discover general laws of social phenomena.[40]

Yet it should also be noted that the American Protectionists cautioned against pure empiricism, arguing that induction requires certain metaphysical foundations that cannot themselves be empirically verified. William Elder articulated this view, explaining that "the science of observation, experiment, and induction... builds its certainties as much upon the harmonies of the system of creation, and as confidently as upon the evidence of the senses." Indeed, "we have ideas and ideals, that come not from observation or experience. Our intellectual and moral faculties are equipped with innate activities that have no patterns in the perceptions of outside things." Elder thus warned that "the inductive system [can be] abused [and] pushed beyond the boundary assigned to it... and forced into a province of knowledge of which it is wholly incapable... [such as the] metaphysical or supra-physical" claims.[41] This position connects with their broader Christian worldview, which posits a divine lawgiver behind natural law and who imbued Man with certain innate intellectual faculties which can be used to understand the world.

This approach also helps to explain the fundamental difference between them and the German Historical School. Whilst their inductive approach might seem similar to that posited by the German Historical School, Progressives, and Institutionalists, these similarities are superficial. Whereas the American Protectionists used induction as a means of uncovering a system of natural laws, the German-derived schools outright rejected the existence of universal natural laws.[42] This German tradition instead assumes that economic phenomena are contingent on their particular social, institutional, and historical context. Economic laws, according to them, were relative, and since laws are relative, so too are rights. There is thus nothing fundamental or natural about private property rights and the market system. They are merely institutions like any other and thus have no claim to preeminence. Progressives therefore tended to view themselves as scientific technocrats, who with the right tools and knowledge, obtained through induction, could successfully fine-tune and engineer the economy. This is, of course, antithetical to the approach of the American Protectionists. The purpose of induction, for the American Protectionists, was to discover natural laws so that statesmen could craft policies in such a way that they are compatible and in harmony with human nature.

Since Progressives viewed all economic relations as contingent on institutional context, this also meant that human nature itself is malleable. And because human nature is a product of the institutional setting, it thus follows that through the right policies, the State can modify human conduct. Robert Ellis Thompson mockingly compared such attempts at social engineering to that of "the statesman [who] embodying the will of the nation could do anything he pleased [and] could make water run up hill if he were so disposed."[43] The disdain for heavy-handed governmental planning is further echoed by Ellis H. Roberts. Indeed, "do not exaggerate the interference of government," explains Roberts, for "nature has its own law... regardless of human statutes." Because there is a certain nature in human conduct, "trade has its laws also, and the wise ruler will give them free scope. Prices are not made by statute, and markets pay little heed to law makers."[44]

It is important, however, not to exaggerate the American Protectionists' rejection of institutionalism. The American Protectionists were at odds with the institutionalism of the German Historical and Progressive Schools, with their latent socialist tendencies and their extreme relativistic methodology, but the American protectionists did not deny the importance of institutions *per se*. The approach of the American Protectionists can be likened to that of "New Institutional Economics," whereby society and the economy still fundamentally operate within a framework of general or natural economic laws, whilst also being shaped by institutional factors. Denslow captures this New Institutionalist approach by declaring that "society is made up in part of principles of human nature which are lasting, and of manifestations, which change every hour. It combines much that is transitory with somewhat that is permanent."[45] Similarly, William Elder notes how "natural laws are ever operative, but subject to modification, so far as… conventions can effectively work under them."[46] These conventions or institutions, to borrow a phrase from Thompson, take on a "gubernator or steersmen" like function. Indeed, even Friedrich List, who is sometimes depicted as an old-style Institutionalist, was more nuanced with his approach also resembling that of New Institutionalism, as illustrated in the following passage from List:

> [Without nations] there would be no national interest, no national law contrary to the freedom of the whole race, no restriction, no war. All would flow in its natural current… I am yet by no means of [the] opinion… that Adam Smith's system, in a scientific view, is without its merits.
>
> I believe, on the contrary, that the fundamental principles of the science could only be discovered by his researches in the economy of individuals and of mankind. His error consists in not adding to those general principles the modifications caused by the fraction of the human race into national bodies… To complete the science, we must add the principles of national economy.[47]

In spite of its name, this New Institutionalist approach of the American Protectionists differs substantially to that of the German-derived Institutionalism. Since the American Protectionists adhered to a general system of principles, their social philosophy was far closer to that of the English Classical School. It is quite ironic, in fact, that by the end of the nineteenth century, the American Protectionists were defending their former archrivals, the English Classicals, from the Germans. Writing with respect to the German "criticisms [of] the English school," Thompson declares that "we are thoroughly at war with [them], and we are astonished at being obliged to say so much in…defence" of the English. "But we do maintain with [the English], in opposition to their continental critics, that there is a science of economy, that it is a science whose function is to master laws common to both nature and human nature, and that all true economic progress, like all true political progress, is toward freedom."[48] Of course, by freedom, the American Protectionists meant industrial freedom, as opposed to the free trade of the English Classicals.

Critique of Economic Man

Of all the aspects of economic thought where the American Protectionists diverged from the Classical School, none was greater than their conception of Man. The American Protectionists detested what has come to be known as "economic man," or *homo economicus*. Although economic man is commonly ascribed to the writings of John

Stuart Mill, the American Protectionists traced its origins to the writings of Malthus and Ricardo (and in some cases Adam Smith). The economic man concept was an anathema to the American Protectionists because it deprived "Man" of his humanity. In the case of Mill, Man is depicted as a narrowly self-interested and rational agent only concerned with maximizing utility and minimizing disutility, whereas the economic man of Ricardo and Malthus was marked by Man's brutish and impulsive lower order qualities which destined him for a life of depravity through iron laws of subsistence. In either case, Man was viewed solely as an economic being bereft of his distinct human qualities. The American Protectionist critique of economic man, however, was not only polemic, but also constructive.

As we have seen, the American Protectionists considered Man as an inherently flawed creature, but, at the same time, they were incredibly optimistic about his capacity for improvement. This is grounded in their Christian worldview, whereby Man is a fallen creature for disobeying God, but through divine grace and being created in God's likeness, Man is also endowed with knowledge and discernment which gives him capacity for progress. The Bible thus provided the foundations of their view of Man, which was then confirmed and elaborated upon through empirical observations of human conduct.

In any event, the result is a far more realistic depiction of Man than the economic man of the English Classical School. In short, the Protectionist conception of Man considered the full spectrum of Man's benevolent and wicked qualities. Alexander Hamilton, as noted earlier, saw human nature as "a compound of good and ill qualities," and Henry Clay was also acutely aware of "all the violent prejudices, embittered passions, and implacable animosities which ever degraded or deformed human nature."[49]

In spite of these flaws, however, the American Protectionists saw that Man was also endowed with reason, moral duty, and intellect. William Elder explains, for instance, that "his ignorance and nakedness he is the slave of nature; but as he acquires knowledge, he gains its power and grows into the mastery of his proper dominion" of nature.[50] It was these higher order qualities which differentiated him from the rest of the animal kingdom and gives him the capacity for betterment. This point is well observed by John Rae:

> The Chief distinction between man and the inferior animals consists in this. They [the animals] are moved only by the immediate impressions of sense, and, as its impulses prompt, seek to gratify them… scarce regarding the future or endeavoring from the experience of the past to provide against what is to become. Man… is endowed with reason, by which he is able to connect effects with their causes… The same intellectual powers… which nature has bestowed on him, give scope to his affections, and join him to his fellows by the ties that spring from language and the connexions of social life.[51]

Because man's nature is complex, consisting of both lower and higher order qualities, the American Protectionists rejected the mechanistic "iron-law" approach of the English Classicals, with William D. Kelley noting how the American Protectionists "have recognized the fact that national and individual life are not governed by a ystem of equations, but influenced by cupidity, ambition and all human emotions and passions."[52] Or as George Gunton puts it, "human desire and human will, neither of which admits of exact quantitative statement. Although economic phenomena are not susceptible of being reduced to exact mathematical statement, they are susceptible of positive explanation."[53]

Most American Protectionists considered economic man to have originated in he writings of Malthus and Ricardo, as typified by their theories of population and listribution, albeit through somewhat different mechanisms. Paradoxically, in each case, the American Protectionists saw the economic man of Ricardo and Malthus as behaving in an animalistic, but also in a mechanistic, manner. According to Malthus's ron law of population, Man would be unable to control his sexual urges and would eproduce in a geometric manner (e.g., 1, 2, 4, 8, etc.), which would outpace the growth in he means of subsistence, which only grows arithmetically (e.g., 1, 2, 3, 4). This destined Man to a future of economic depravity. Ricardo likewise borrowed from Malthus the assumption that wages must always and everywhere press on the food supply or level of subsistence. In the long run, however, Ricardo considered that through diminishing eturns on agricultural land, the price of food would continue to increase over time, but ince real wages were fixed by subsistence, this meant that laborers would continually lemand higher money wages due to rising food prices. By demanding higher wages, this vould increasingly deplete the capitalists' profits, causing investment to grind to a halt, and would similarly result in economic subsistence and stagnation.

However flawed, Man was not viewed by the American Protectionists as a mere brute animal or automaton directed thoughtlessly by iron laws of subsistence. Indeed, "it is no matter of surprise," remarked Carey, "that modern English political economy sees in man only an animal that will procreate, that must be fed, and that can be made to work… It repudiates all the distinctive qualities of man and limits itself to the consideration of those he holds in common with the beast of burden or of prey."[54] Malthus and Ricardo, according to Carey, thus "excludes from consideration [Man's] feelings and affections, and the intellect which he has been endowed." Indeed, "such s the error of modern political economy… it presents for our consideration a mere brute animal… which desecrates the word man."[55] A similar assessment of Classical conomics is also made by John Rae, who explains that "Malthus… assimilates Man to the lower animals which is not correct… [there is] a radical difference in that the one [the animal] is guided by mere instinct, the other [Man] by reason, fancy, [and] that heerful thing we call moral feeling."[56]

It was inconceivable to the American Protectionists that such an all-wise and benevolent God, having created Man in his image, could create such a wretched destiny or mankind. According to Henry Carey, the economic man of Malthus and Ricardo is "retrograde throughout," because "it requires that we should at once, and forever, ignore the existence of an all-wise and all benevolent Deity, and put our trust in a Being by whom had been instituted great natural laws in virtue of which men should necessarily, nd regularly, die of want."[57] Along similar lines to Carey, Calvin Colton also castigates he English economists, explaining that "it is shocking to ascribe such a want of wisdom nd goodness to the Creator!… the European economists of the Free-Trade school" assumes this "as a postulate, putting it in the place of one of the foundation-stones of their edifice!" This is the economic man "resulting from Malthus's theory, which dooms the masses to work for bare subsistence."[58] Since Man is in the image and likeness of God, Man, in God's likeness, possesses the power and the unique ability to harness and direct the forces of nature. Henry Carey thus explains how the "all-wise, all powerful, and all benevolent Creator" created "the being [Man]… in his own likeness and gifted [him] with power to control and direct all the forces of nature to his use."[59] Man does this through his higher order faculties, such as intellect, moral restraint, and thrift, which allows him to construct various tools and inventions.

Man is thus uniquely considered to be a tool maker of sorts, a position well put by Peshine Smith, who declares that "Man has been defined a tool-making animal," and "we nowhere see him working without artificial aid." Indeed, "even the rudest savages possess some simple implements, which they employ in fishing and hunting… and building their huts." Thus, according to Smith, "it is difficult, indeed, to conceive man as destitute of every kind of implements."[60] This view of Man as toolmaker who perfects his workmanship through invention is well illustrated by Abraham Lincoln by way of comparison to the animal kingdom. In the words of Lincoln:

> Beavers build houses; but they build them in nowise differently, or better now, than they did, five thousand years ago… Man is not the only animal who labours; but he is the only one who improves his workmanship. This improvement, he effects by *Discoveries,* and *Inventions.*[61]

Whilst optimistic about Man's ability to better himself by securing the bounties of nature by the use of artificial aid, the American Protectionists were under no illusion that great misery persists in the world, with such "vice and misery" being viewed by Carey as "consequences of human error."[62] Man was thus considered in his totality encompassing both the benevolent and flawed aspects of his nature and being.

In positing their view of mankind, the American Protectionists also stressed how Man exists as a social creature. Although there is a clear individualist streak in American Protectionist thought, these thinkers were opposed to treating Man in an isolated or atomistic manner. Instead, "Man," according to Rae, "hardly exists but in the social state," and David H. Mason likewise explains that "God has constituted man a social being."[63] This rejection of the atomistic view of Man, a view that pervades mainstream economic thinking, is best summarized by Thomas Brackett Reed, who explains that "whoever considers the human being as a creature alone, by himself, isolated and separated, and tries to comprehend mankind by mathematically adding these atoms together, has utterly failed to comprehend the human race and its tremendous mission."[64]

Indeed, the American Protectionists understood that even though Man possesses certain natural tendencies, they were also clearly aware that such tendencies are shaped by the community and societal institutions. In the words of John Rae:

> [Man's] mental and bodily capacities and energies seem… to be moulded by the condition of the society of which he is a member… it is very certain that they exist, and that the moral and intellectual condition, as well as the bodily organization of men, vary, as they

> belong to this, or that society. Besides this, institutions, forms of government, and laws, influence somewhat the genius, and… the conduct, of every people, and these also are very various.[65]

Thus, if society's institutions are organized in such a way as to encourage private enterprise and personal industry, this would appeal to the better angels of human nature and channel human conduct away from Man's lower-order instincts. As Ezra Seaman explains, "industry supplies man's wants and removes him from many temptations and hence it is the parent of many virtues; on the contrary, idleness leads to poverty, suffering, temptation, vice and crime."[66] Or, as the Home Market Club puts it, "through industrial activity chiefly, harmonies pervade society, men increasingly serve each other, and the depravities and discords, calamities and misfortunes, crimes and cruelties of society" dissipate.[67]

In the second half of the nineteenth century, as Mill's influence within the economics discipline grew and the theories of Ricardo and Malthus became increasingly discredited, the American Protectionists shifted their attention away from the economic man of Malthus and Ricardo, and toward the economic man associated with John Stuart Mill. The destiny of Mill's economic man was far less pessimistic than that depicted by Ricardo and Malthus, but it was no less problematic. Whilst more of an analytical tool rather than a description of how people actually behave, Mill asserted that economics ought:

> Not treat the whole of man's nature as modified by the social state, nor of the whole conduct of man in society. It is concerned with him solely as a being who desires to possess wealth, and who is capable of judging the comparative efficacy of means for obtaining that end.[68]

This rational and narrowly self-interested economic Man conducts his economic affairs through the calculus of pleasure and pain in order to maximize his own personal utility. Indeed, with the Millian takeover of the economics discipline, and in contrast with the American Protectionists, the British Classical School was quickly dispensing with their natural law approach and now predicating their ideas on utilitarian grounds. The British Classical School was also not the only school of thought which adopted this concept of economic man. The French Liberal School also affirmed this depiction of man, with Fredric Bastiat declaring that "the subject of political economy is man. But it does not embrace the whole range of human affairs…. To political economy is left only the cold domain of personal interest" with "utility… [being] the perpetual object of his search."[69]

The American Protectionists took issue with this narrow depiction of Man for many of the same reasons which they had with Ricardo and Malthus, but also for very different reasons as well. Two issues were prime among these. First, is what is known as Mill's utilitarian calculus, which in the economic context, suggest that all economic decision making is the result of a perfectly rational and self-interested calculation of what maximizes utility. The second issue takes this even further, and relates to French Liberal Schools' refinement of economic man, typified by them redefining political economy, by the likes of Arthur Latham Perry, as the "science of sales or exchanges."[70] This science of sales considers Man only in relation to the exchange of goods and services, and nothing else. This was not only problematic because it downgraded the importance of production, it was also problematic because it conceived of man only in relation to the exchange of material things. Thus, in his sweeping critique, George B. Curtiss declares that:

> Economic man [is] an imaginary being… The protectionists dealt with man as they found him in society and business, considering all of his hopes, aspirations, and all of the elements which necessarily contribute to his elevation and improvement. Instead of a science in which commodities and money transactions were alone to be dealt with, the protectionist school held to that time-honored policy which made man the chief factor, and the best means of improving and advancing his social, intellectual and material welfare the prime object… [These] visionary theorists… [have] formulated an economic policy for an imaginary man in an unreal world.[71]

For one thing, in the utilitarian calculus of pleasure and pain, industry and employment were simply viewed as a necessary pain to be endured in order to finance future consumption or pleasure. To this, Cyrus Elder replied that "the proposition that Man has a natural aversion to labor, and, therefore, gives the least possible services for the largest possible reward" represents one of "the principles of human nature" set forth by the English Classical School. This principle is, however, often inconsistent with reality. "Man" explains Elder, "has not a natural aversion to labor" especially if "his activities are instinctive and naturally pleasurable." For the American Protectionists, enterprise and industry were not simply a means of financing future consumption, but were often a worthy and meaningful activity in itself. Moreover, Elder also explains that "pleasure in serving others is a motive in the worker often as powerful as the desire to better his own condition."[72] Enlightened individuals would frequently put the needs of their family and community above that of their own.

Indeed, enlightened self-interest was viewed by the American Protectionists as quite different to selfishness. Robert Ellis Thompson explains, for instance, that "individual selfishness is always shortsighted."[73] Similar to Smith's invisible hand, the American Protectionists considered the pursuit of self-interest as a benefit to society when properly tempered and channeled through the right pursuits. Indeed, even Ezra Seaman explains that:

> Even avarice, when it exists in a moderate degree, is consistent with the nature and end of man, and becomes a vice, only when it is in excess, and leads to covetousness and oppression. The same may be said of ambition; it is laudable as long as its ends and objects are good; and vicious when its ends and objects are evil.[74]

The American Protectionists thus saw that "among the distinguishing qualities of man is *responsibility* for his actions," and it was this which differentiated civilization from barbarism.[75] When applied to the matter of self-interest, the creation of wealth through personal initiative and private enterprise was seen as a virtuous act, but acquiring wealth through theft or business malpractice was a vice to society. This view is well expressed by Horace Greeley, who penned "let no man… think to relieve himself from the common troubles by means detrimental to the welfare of his neighbors—by encrusting himself in the armor of narrow selfishness… Let him rather prosper by feeding than starving his neighbors."[76]

Thus, in a not so subtle critique of economic man, Carey explains how "the real MAN capable of self-direction, and responsible for his actions holds his existence in virtue of laws of universal force and effect, and that the teacher who fails to familiarize himself with them, and with their bearing on societary and Christian life, fails in the performance of his duty to his Creator and to his fellow-men."[77] The existence of such virtues was often seen as an important restraint tempering conduct in the marketplace. Of course, the American Protectionists never entertained legislating morality, but they did see that virtues could be encouraged indirectly through proper institutions and conformity to natural law. Property rights and protectionist policies would, for example, encourage the creation of wealth through industry, whereas a court system and police force would discourage the acquisition of wealth through theft and malpractice. It was also thought that the development of industry would help foster community spirit with its members coming together in what Henry Carey termed "association," which will be the subject of a later chapter.

The American Protectionists thus conceived human nature in a broader manner than his connection to material processes, as in the Ricardian and Malthusian (and even Marxist) thought, or his connection to pleasure and pain as with Mill and Bastiat (and continuing through Neoclassical economics). Because Man possesses both higher and lower order qualities, this naturally produces a flawed creature, but one that is immensely capable of progress and improvement. The optimism which the American Protectionists had for Man's economic destiny stemmed from those higher-order faculties that gifted Man with ingenuity, through which he could obtain mastery over nature.

Individual versus National Wealth

The subject of individual versus national wealth represents a common thread running through the writings of the American Protectionists. The wealth of the nation, according to the American Protectionists, cannot simply be viewed as commensurate with the wealth of the individuals that compose it. In particular, they recognized the limitations of using exchange value as a measure of wealth. In some contexts, the American Protectionists accepted the use of exchange value when calculating individual wealth, but they had serious doubts that national wealth could simply be determined by aggregating the accumulation of exchange values which made up individual wealth. The equating of individual with national wealth is captured in the writings of the Southern free trader Thomas Cooper, who explains that "the aggregate [exchange value] of individual wealth is national wealth. In fact, I wish it to be well understood and therefore I repeat it, that there is no such thing as a nation distinct from the individuals who compose it."[78]

The view that individual and national wealth often diverge dates to the very founding of the School. Tench Coxe had already identified the tension between private and national interests, observing that "the private interest of individuals, is very often directly opposed to the general interest of the nation" and that "that which is the best calculated to promote the common interest of the nation, is undoubtedly to be regarded in preference to the… private interest of any individual."[79] Whilst it would be left to the second generation of American Protectionists to develop this insight into a systematic critique of exchange value as a measure of national wealth, it is clear that the groundwork was laid from the School's inception. Building upon this insight, the later generations of American Protectionists maintained that whilst it is sometimes true that individual wealth can be expressed in terms of exchange value, this represents a poor measure of the wealth of nations.[80] John Rae, for instance, saw that "as individuals seem generally to grow rich by grasping a larger and larger portion of the wealth already in existence, nations do so by the production of wealth that did not previously exist. The two processes differ in this, that the one is an acquisition, the other a creation."[81] This view was widely held among American Protectionists, with Henry M. Hoyt stating that "an individual and a nation became opulent by means of entirely different orders of procedure," or as even more forcibly declared by George B. Dixwell, "the identity of individual and national interests has been abundantly disproved."[82]

This conception of use value differed in some respects from that of the Classical economists. Whereas the Classicals typically emphasized the utility or pleasure gained through the use of a commodity, the American Protectionists tended to place more emphasis on productivity. That is, its usefulness in augmenting the nation's capacity and capability to produce. This led earlier protectionists, such as Daniel Raymond, to declare that "the true definition of national wealth is the *capacity* for acquiring the necessaries and comforts of life." With an emphasis on capacity, Raymond observed that "more than anything else, this capacity depends on the industrious habits of the people."[83] This is what Friedrich List would term "productive powers."[84] This definition of national wealth became a staple of American Protectionist thought, with William Elder declaring that "political economy is not a theory of market values, but it is, or ought to be, a system or theory of the productive power of a people."[85]

Critics of the American Protectionists naturally held this definition of national wealth in low regard because it lacked a quantitative measure, especially since the American Protectionists emphasized qualitative changes in the nation's productive powers. Yet, the idea that economic phenomena must be quantifiable to be meaningful was viewed as a complete fallacy by the American Protectionists. "Indeed," William Elder writes that, "estimates and computation fail to grasp the effective value of the adjuvants that human ingenuity employs to enhance its mastery of matter. And as a source of wealth to the civilized world."[86]

In spite of its inability to be easily quantified, the American Protectionists maintain that the development of productive powers represents a far superior determinant of national prosperity than the level of aggregated exchange value. Hence, "the prosperity of a nation," explains Friedrich List "does not depend, as [Jean-Baptiste] Say thinks, on the quantity of riches and of exchangeable values it possesses, but upon the degree in which the productive power is developed."[87] This point is well illustrated by Daniel Raymond, who alludes to the fact that "there are a great many things indispensable to [a nation's] existence which are nevertheless said to have no value… and the reason is, because they cannot be exchanged."[88] Indeed, it is along such lines that Andrew Stewart, using the example of public roads, declares how immense benefits can be bestowed upon the nation from things which lack exchange value entirely. In the words of Stewart:

> As to the [exchange] value of public works… What would the Cumberland Road bring? Nothing! Yet, does it follow that they are worth nothing to the nation? The value of public works is not estimated in dollars and cents, but by the benefits and blessings they confer to the country.[89]

In a similar vein to the above, the distinction between use and exchange value was also extended to the American Protectionists' analysis of profit or income generation. As a general rule, the American Protectionists viewed private profitability as operating in harmony with the national interest, but like all general principles, there exist exceptions. There are cases where private profitability is sometimes at odds with national productivity and the expansion of productive powers. Peshine Smith, for example, explains that whilst "the capital of a society is the same as that of all the individuals who compose it" you cannot simply "jump to the conclusion that progress of a community is measured by the prevailing rate of profit."[90] Or as Van Denslow explains "many things are wealth and profit to individuals which are not wealth or profit to the nation of which they are citizens, and vice versa."[91]

The profit motive of merchants was sometimes cited as an example, since an increase in imports may indeed be profitable to individual merchants, but it may also come at the expense of the nation's agricultural and industrial sectors. William Jarvis explains, for instance, that "whenever commerce is profitable to the merchants, say some, it must be necessarily profitable to the nation to which the merchants belong." Yet, "this mode of reasoning is far from being conclusive… it may happen, that the individual success of the merchants, is not the sure and invariable sign of national prosperity."[92] This could, in turn, suppress the general prosperity of the economy and reduce national wealth by diminishing the nation's productive power. Willard Phillips perhaps illustrates best, however, how national prosperity may be at odds with individual profitability:

> This distinction [between individual and national wealth] may be illustrated more clearly, perhaps, by the instances of a canal and navigable river, for if navigation can be done on a river, without tolls, as cheap as it could be done on a canal of the same length paying tolls, the river gives all the facility and advantage to industry, that could be derived from the canal; yet the canal is of great value to the proprietors as a navigable channel, and the river of no value at all [because it is unprofitable].[93]

That said, private profitability generally failed to fully reflect national prosperity, not because private enterprise has a tendency to exploit the community for its own gain, but because the benefits that accrue to the community are often over and above that received by the entrepreneur who sacrificed his own time, effort, and resources in the process of invention. This is to say, that an individual private enterprise is often of far greater benefit to the nation itself than it is to the individual undertaking it. George M. Steele captures this view, explaining that:

> Sometimes the man [or entrepreneur] has spent a large fortune and given many years to the devising of plans and instruments, by which humanity will be benefited for ages to come. To such a man, no compensation likely to be bestowed will be more than a small fraction of the good conferred [to society].[94]

Indeed, the view that society as a whole benefits more than the individual entrepreneur bringing it into existence is also well attested to by Daniel Webster, who explains that "the application of science to art [i.e., invention] is the main cause of the sudden augmentation of wealth." Indeed, "this augmentation of wealth is general and diffusive, reaching all classes, embracing all interests, and benefitting, not a part of society, but the whole. There is no monopoly" derived from invention. Both "the poorest, as well as the richest man in society, has a direct interest… in the successful operation of these arts."[95]

At first glance, it may appear that the American Protectionists from Henry Carey's generation onwards broke with the earlier protectionists and dismissed the debate around individual versus national wealth. To some extent, they did, but not for the reasons one might expect. The American Protectionists of the Carey era, rather than viewing individual wealth in terms of exchange value, tended to treat individual wealth solely in terms of productive power. Productive powers came to represent both individual and national wealth. Indeed, "the wealth of a man, or of a nation," as William Elder declares, "consists of, and is measured by, their power to command the services of nature for their uses; their productive power."[96] Of course, exchange value or price was seen as important for economic coordination, but it was rarely spoken of as wealth. In fact, as we shall see in the chapter on value, wealth and exchange value were often seen as the inverse of one another.

In any event, instead of viewing wealth and value as commensurate, from the writings of Henry Carey onwards, wealth in both individual and national terms was considered as the power to command the always gratuitous services of nature. Yet, William Elder rightly showed that "the power to command the always gratuitous services of nature" was for all purposes synonymous with "the productive power of the people," yet simply expressed in a more philosophical manner.[97] Productive power, according to Elder represents the "power" necessary to command nature. However, perhaps without even realizing it, this equating of individual and national wealth, albeit on a very different basis to that of the Classicals, undoes much of the analysis of the second generation of American Protectionists.

It was Van Buren Denslow who sought to correct this issue by reintroducing the distinction between individual and national wealth, whilst maintaining what he considered as Henry Carey's "excellent" contribution.[98] In the spirit of Carey, Denslow notes how Man is both a part of nature, but also conducts himself in the nature exterior to himself. Indeed, "whatever there be in man, which obtains command of the forces of exterior nature," Denslow explains, "must of course be part of man's nature. It is not, therefore, a contest between man and nature, but between nature in man and nature exterior to man."[99] Denslow viewed national wealth as concerning the contest between Man and the nature exterior to him, which effectively corresponds with Carey's definition. If Man, in the general sense, increases his productive power and thus his ability to command the forces of nature, then national wealth will increase. Yet, it does not simply follow that the individual will automatically benefit from this increase in national wealth. Instead, Denslow explains that "we [the individual] get what we enjoy gratis, from nature, by paying our fellow men to bring it to us."[100] Denslow thus defined individual wealth as:

> That power in me, however and whenever obtained, which gives me command through the services of my fellow men, which it enables me to pay for, of all those gifts or services, which nature brings gratuitously to some member of society, at some time or place, but which only through his toil or that of others, is brought to me.[101]

This definition of individual wealth is far superior to simply viewing individual wealth as an individual's accumulated exchange value. Ultimately, an individual benefits more from his capacity to acquire, as opposed to living off accumulated exchange values. In fact, there are many aspects of a person's character which allow him to command the services of his fellow man which cannot be considered to have an exchange value. In the words of Denslow:

> The highest elements of [individual] wealth do not always exist in a form in which they may thus be seen to have an economic value without being in the least exchangeable. Yet a judge's reputation for integrity on the bench, a clergyman's reputation for purity, a manager's reputation for successful enterprise, an author's repute as entertaining... Indeed, all modes of intellectual and social power give their possessor a command over the services, destinies, and material commodities of others, and are therefore not only wealth but capital, and yet are not exchangeable. Character, religious faith, moral influence, courage, sagacity, rank, titles, political office, a chair in a university as an instructor, all are wealth, but not exchangeable.[102]

Denslow's definition thus avoids the mistake of conflating individual with national wealth, which Henry Carey's generation of protectionists were in danger of running into. Like the pre-Carey protectionists, Denslow saw plainly that nations only gain through creation, yet the individuals gain through both creation and acquisition, with the wealth of the individual being contingent on his ability obtain this new creation or presently existing goods through commanding the services of his fellow man.

In bringing this chapter to a close, it is worth highlighting how the American Protectionists' conception of national wealth represents a fundamental departure from traditional mercantilist thinking. Whereas the mercantilists primarily sought to expand national wealth by grasping a larger portion of wealth already in existence and acquiring a larger sum of precious metals through favorable trade balances, the American Protectionists looked to human ingenuity, invention, and industry as the means of creating the wealth of nations. This represented the true foundation of national prosperity.

Notes

1. Schumpeter, *Economic Analysis*, 39.
2. Hamilton, "Defence 1," 393–394.
3. Hamilton, "Funding System," 59–60.
4. Patton, *Political Economy*, 241.
5. Horr, "Taxes a Blessing?," 2.
6. Denslow, *Principles*, 76–78.
7. Denslow, *Modern Thinkers*, 126.
8. Denslow, *Principles*, 136.
9. Hoyt, *Protection*, 206–207.
10. Stebbins, *Manual*, 10.
11. Thompson, "National Policy," 146.
12. Coxe, *Essay*, 31.
13. Lodge, "Tariff," 95–96.
14. Thompson, "Kathedersocialism," 382.
15. Hamilton, "Farmer Refuted," 87.
16. Thompson, *Divine Order*, 89.
17. Thompson, "Kathedersocialism," 384.
18. Hamilton, "Continentalist 5," 76.
19. Carey, *Social Science*, 1:365–366.
20. Thompson, *Elements*, 29.
21. Carey, *Unity*, xiii.
22. Carey, *Unity*, 122–124.
23. Denslow, *Principles*, 135.
24. Thompson, *Elements*, 36.
25. Thompson, *Divine Order*, 89.
26. Denslow, *Principles*, 137.
27. Thompson, *Elements*, 30.
28. Thompson, *Divine Order*, 90–91.
29. Denslow, *Principles*, 137.
30. Baird, *Rights of Producers*, 10.
31. Elder, *Questions*, 224.
32. Colwell, *Relative Position*, iii.
33. Baird, *Rights of Producers*, 11.
34. Mason, "Natural Law," 120–125.
35. Baird, *Rights of Producers*, 11.
36. e.g., Curtiss, *Industrial Development*, 2:451; Kelley, "Science," 285. "Ricardian Vice," was coined by Schumpeter, *Economic Analysis*, 473.
37. Smith to Carey, July 17, 1858, box 18, folder 2, *HCCP*.
38. Curtiss, *Industrial Development*, 2:451.
39. Thompson, *Elements*, 31.
40. This should not be confused with the logical positivism associated with the Vienna circle, focuses on the logical structure and verification of scientific statements.
41. Elder, *Conversations*, 83–84.

42. Self-reported by Seligman, *Essays*, 15–16; and Ely, *Outline*, 669–670. Note that whilst the younger generation of the German Historical School associated with Gustav von Schmoller rejected general laws of economics, the older generation associated with Wilhelm Roscher were at least open to possibility of an economic science, yet one of more empirical (as opposed to theoretical) nature.
43. Thompson, "Kathedersocialism," 383.
44. Roberts, *Revenue and Labor*, 4.
45. Denslow, *Principles*, 5.
46. Elder, *Conversations*, 35.
47. List, *Outlines*, 7–9.
48. Thompson, "Kathedersocialism," 392.
49. Hamilton, "Defence 1," 393; Henry Clay, "Abolition," 157.
50. Elder. *Conversations*, 18–19.
51. Rae, *Statements*, 80–88.
52. Kelley, "Science," 287.
53. Gunton: *Social Economics*, 117.
54. Carey, *Social Science*, 1:470.
55. Carey, *Social Science*, 1:30–31.
56. Rae to Mill, [c. 1854], 430.
57. Carey, *Social Science*, 1:468.
58. Colton, *Public Economy*, 159.
59. Carey, *Social Science*, 1:93.
60. Smith, *Manual*, 63.
61. Lincoln, "First Lecture," 438.
62. Carey, *Social Science*, 3:486.
63. Rae, *Statements*, 95; Mason, *Impending Crisis*, 3.
64. Reed, *The Tariff*, 7.
65. Rae, *Statement*, 95.
66. Seaman, "Human Progress," 412.
67. Home Market Club, "Champions: Denslow," 464.
68. Mill, *Questions*, 137.
69. Bastiat, *Harmonies*, 38–40.
70. Perry, *Political Economy*, 96. Whilst American, Perry was an adherent of the French Liberal School.
71. Curtiss, *Industrial Development*, 2:452.
72. Elder, *Man*, 8–12.
73. Thompson, *Elements*, 48.
74. Seaman, *Progress*, 43.
75. Hayes, "Carey's Law," 307.
76. Greeley, "Return of Prosperity," 3.
77. Carey, *Unity*, 127.
78. Cooper, *Lecture*, 77.
79. Coxe, *Observations*, 9.
80. Raymond, *Thoughts*, 28–29.
81. Rae, *Statement*, 12.
82. Hoyt, *Protection*, 168; Dixwell, "Perry," 35.
83. Raymond, *Thoughts*, 112.
84. List, *National System*, 222.
85. Elder, *Memoir*, 10.
86. Elder, *Questions*, 55–56.

87. List, *National System,* 222.
88. Raymond, *Thoughts*, 47.
89. Stewart, *American System*, 336.
90. Smith, *Manual*, 140.
91. Denslow, *Principles*, 43, 67.
92. Jarvis, *Republican*, 209–211.
93. Phillips, *Manual*, 13.
94. Steele, *Rudimentary Economics*, 180.
95. Webster, "Diffusion," 136.
96. Elder, *Doctrine*, 5.
97. Elder, *Doctrine*, 17.
98. Denslow, *Principles,* 43.
99. Denslow, *Principles,* 43–44.
100. Denslow, *Principles,* 44.
101. Denslow, *Principles*, 45.
102. Denslow, *Principles*, 46.

Chapter Four

THEORETICAL FOUNDATIONS OF AMERICAN PROTECTIONIST THOUGHT

Not only did President Lincoln declare his support for the American System, he would also affirm the principles underpinning this system. Against the dismal science of the Classical School, Lincoln reportedly termed the theory of the American Protectionists the "beautiful science."[1] Yet for more than a century, this beautiful science of the American Protectionists has been dismissed by scholars as unoriginal. Their ideas are said to be mere adaptations of the dismal science to divergent policy conclusions.[2] The words of the American Protectionists reveal something else entirely. Far from deriving their ideas from Classical economics, the American Protectionists saw themselves as pioneering a distinct intellectual tradition. This rejection of Classical economics is well articulated by Hezekiah Niles, who declared that "a different system of political economy is maintained by a certain school of theoretical writers… which has been lately called enlightened," or Classical. "We," continues Niles, "believe it to be founded on mistaken views; and that a practical application of it would paralyze the industry of the country."[3]

Indeed, the American Protectionists not only differed from the Classicals on trade policy, their differences cut to the very core of economic theory. As Robert Ellis Thompson explains, "the differences that exist between the two schools are not merely in regard to the details. It is a difference about foundations and first principles," and "neither can concede to the… other the name and rank of a science, without giving up its own claim to that name and rank."[4] It is precisely because the American Protectionists started from different foundations that they arrived at divergent policies concerning trade. By identifying these foundational principles, this chapter will demonstrate how the American Protectionists did indeed construct a distinct and beautiful science of political economy, with these foundations going on to shape every aspect of their economic system.

The Individuality of Man

The first and most fundamental of these principles concerns the very nature of mankind itself. Nowhere does American Protectionist thought diverge more fundamentally from the British Classical School than in their conception of the nature of mankind. Since economic science concerns Man's conduct in the production, distribution, and exchange of goods and services, the conception of Man is the bedrock upon which all economic theory is built.

In positing their alternate conception of Man, the American Protectionists observed how Man is distinguished from the animal kingdom by a high degree of individuality. Henry Carey explains, for instance, that the "distinctive quality of man is individuality." Whereas "each rat or robin, fox or wolf, is the type of his species wherever found, possessing habits and instincts in common," such is not "the case with man, in whom we find differences of tastes, feelings, and capacities almost as numerous as those observed in the human countenance."[5] Such a view is likewise affirmed by Erastus B. Bigelow who explains that:

> There is nothing more manifest in the constitution and course of nature than the law of diversification… Of the millions of human beings, the features of each one are so unlike the features of all the others as to be distinguishable; and observation and experience prove a similar diversity to exist in their mental organization and aptitudes.[6]

This represents a sharp break with the Classical economists. Whereas this conception of Man emphasizes the existence of natural differences and distinctions among individuals, Classical economic thought depicts human beings as more or less uniform and homogeneous.[7]

The rejection of innate individual differences by the Classical School can be traced to its founder, Adam Smith, who asserts in the *Wealth of Nations* that "the difference of natural talents in different men, is, in reality, much less than we are aware of." According to Smith, "the very different genius which appears to distinguish men of different professions is not upon many occasions so much the cause, as the effect of the division of labour." And hence, "the difference between the most dissimilar characters between a philosopher and a common street porter, for example, seems to arise not so much from nature."[8] This conception of the individual is likewise affirmed in Smith's lesser-known *Lectures on Jurisprudence*, which asserts that the "disposition to barter is by no means founded upon different genius and talents. It is doubtful that there be any such difference at all." Indeed, according to Smith, individuals in their natural state possess the "greatest uniformity of character" and "there is hardly any diversity of temper or genius."[9]

The importance which American Protectionist thought attaches to individual differences and distinctions is perhaps most clearly demonstrated by Henry Carey going so far as to define social science as "the science of the laws which govern man in his efforts to secure for himself the highest individuality, and the greatest power of association with his fellow-men."[10] The view that individual differences are ever present across the different members of the human species was shared unanimously across the school of American Protectionists, and was a defining feature of their thought since the movement's very inception.

Even before the drafting of the *Report of Manufactures*, Tench Coxe had already voiced how "the creator and benefactor of men… in great wisdom and goodness, so diversified the natural abilities, genius and disposition of mankind."[11] Indeed, going further North the Bostonian protectionists likewise affirmed this view, which comes despite some sources incorrectly placing them outside the broader School of American Protectionists. Alexander Everett, the intellectual leader of Bostonians, explains that:

> The labor of individuals is by no means a fixed quantity, but varies with their natural dispositions, and with the motives that determine their conduct. We observe a remarkable difference in the activity and industry of different communities, and of different persons in the same community, resulting from varieties of situation and character.[12]

Indeed, it is this law of individuality which underpins the American Protectionists' commitment to economic diversification. Since individual differences are ever present, much of which is determined by nature, it means that different individuals are predisposed and suited to different modes of employment and enterprise. Alexander Hamilton explains, for instance, that "furnishing greater scope for the diversity of talents and dispositions which discriminate men from each other… is a… powerful mean[s] of augmenting the fund of national industry." This is because the "minds of the strongest and most active powers for their proper objects fall below mediocrity… if confined to uncongenial pursuits… It is hence to be inferred, that the results of human exertion may be immensely increased by diversifying" national industry. Hamilton therefore concludes that "when all the different kinds of industry obtain in a community each individual can find his proper element, and can call into activity the whole vigor of his nature."[13]

Hamilton thus clearly observes that mankind as a species is uniquely characterized by its high degree of diversity, differentiation, and individuality. Furthermore, without a diversity of employments, there will necessarily be unique qualities which will remain dormant and unutilized. This view is affirmed by Rufus Choate who explains that "in a country of few occupations, employments go down by an arbitrary, hereditary," and even "coercive designation without regard to the peculiarities of individual character," noting that "the son of a priest is a priest; the son of a barber is a barber" and so forth.[14] Having a diversified economy would break this cycle and rouse the unique talents and qualities of each individual. In the words of Choate:

> A diversified, advanced, and refined mechanical and manufacturing industry, co-operating with these other numerous employments of civilization which always surround it, offers the widest choice; detects the slightest shade of individuality; quickens into existence and trains in perfection the largest conceivable amount and the utmost possible variety of national mind… Every fragment of mind is gathered up. Nothing is lost… Every taste, every faculty, every peculiarity of mental power finds its task, does it, and is made the better for it.[15]

Because the American Protectionists accepted that individuality represents an innate and distinctive feature of Man, it follows that they did not believe in the notion of a blank slate or a *tabula rasa*. American Protectionists believed that everyone was equal before God and that everyone deserved equal treatment before the law, but they did not believe that different individuals had equal abilities and aptitudes. This rejection of the blank slate view of mankind can even be seen in the writings of Stephen Colwell who happens to represent one of the more egalitarian thinkers within the School:

> Men are not born equal; they do not grow to equality in physical or mental qualifications. No human training could produce an equality evidently not contemplated in the human constitution.[16]

Envisioning everyone as equal in all respects ultimately reduces Man into a uniform and generic creature. The American Protectionists thus saw individual differences and distinctions as making each person special and unique. Even though there was an acceptance that no two individuals are created equal, everyone has a disposition or aptitude for a particular pursuit, and thus possesses the capacity for excellence in their particular field. In spite of this, however, the fact still remains that since Man is not created equal, true genius tends to be the product of nature, which contrasts sharply with the Smithian view highlighted in the passages above. In the words of John Rae:

> Genius is, by many, considered synonymous with learning… A refined and cultivated mind does not properly constitute genius; but it consists in a gift of nature… Education may embellish the mind… but there is something noble and majestic in a great natural genius… There is something divine in a true genius that raises the soul above itself, and enables it to attain objects beyond the sphere of intellect.[17]

As will be demonstrated through subsequent chapters, the emphasis which the American Protectionist School places on Man's individuality would go on to shape virtually all aspects of their thought and would culminate in two fundamentally different sets of ideas. This divergence cannot simply be dismissed as an archaic squabble over details with no bearing on modern economics. Since the three leading contemporary schools of economic thought—Neoclassical economics, Keynesianism, and Marxism—all have their roots in Classical economic thought, the American Protectionist conception of Man is very much distinct from the view which still pervades and dominates mainstream economics and the leading heterodox schools of economic thought till this day.

The Law of the Endless Circulation of Matter and Force

The second principle is the law of the endless circulation of matter and force. This principle recognizes that all economic activity must operate within the first law of thermodynamics. In other words, matter and energy can neither be created nor destroyed, only changed in form or transferred. Since economics cannot escape this law, wealth necessarily involves Man's transformation of earthly substances and forces into instruments and services fit for human use. Connecting this with their Christian worldview, Jacob Harris Patton provides perhaps the best rendering of this, explaining how:

> The benevolent Creator has placed within man's reach in the storehouses of the earth those substances, that when properly prepared can add to his comfort and improvement. Man can neither create a particle of matter nor can he destroy it; he can only change its form by making combinations of its various properties, produce results that become useful and adapted to gratify desires.[18]

To demonstrate the significance of this law for economic thought, it is perhaps useful to observe how the absence of this understanding can lead to exceedingly defective conclusions. It must be remembered that the chief arguments against Hamilton's *Report on Manufactures* were rooted in Physiocracy. It was assumed by the Physiocrats that agriculture, and only agriculture, was productive. All other industries were unproductive since only land was said to produce. This stemmed from the belief that only agriculture involved the creation of new matter. The Physiocrats and their American counterparts, thus asserted that manufacturing did not create anything new and was therefore "sterile." It merely involves the reshuffling of matter, and thus does not add any value to production. Hamilton summarizes the Physiocratic position, writing that "labor of artificers does nothing more than replace the stock which employs them" (as such stock is derived purely from agriculture) and "neither does it add anything to the total value of the whole annual produce of the land and labor of the country [agriculture]."[19]

Yet, in reality, agriculture, like manufacturing, does not lead to the creation of any new matter at all. It merely changes it from one form to another. Peshine Smith explains that "in this world, nothing is created except human souls and the souls of other animals… Every particle of matter was made from some other matter already existing."[20] Or as Henry Carey puts it:

> Man can neither create nor destroy a particle of matter, nor can he affect the quantity of force in the world. His power is limited to altering the mode of its manifestation, its direction and distribution… He may do this by giving the appropriate direction to some independent force existing in the storehouse of Nature… Every development of force, however, involves a consumption of matter—not its destruction, but its change of form.[21]

In a dualistic fashion, economic activity is thus characterized by the human soul and mind interacting with and rearranging earthly substances into useful instruments.

Hamilton lacked this understanding of the law of thermodynamics since he was writing prior to its discovery. Nevertheless, he still rightly points out that the artificer or manufacturer must bestow at least some incremental amount of value when furnishing the products of the soil, since these finished products earn "an amount sufficient, not only to repay the farmer" but to "furnish the artificer himself with a supply of similar commodities" after wages are deducted.[22] In other words, it is self-evidently true that value is added through manufacturing because furnished goods generally command a higher value than raw goods.

Whilst Hamilton's observation is correct, if he understood the law of the endless circulation of matter developed by later American Protectionists, he could have more thoroughly demolished the Physiocratic position. Indeed, the original matter contained within a good can never be the inherent source of a furnished good's final value since, in the words of Horace Greeley, "industry applies itself to the transmutation of certain substances into others presumptively of greater value."[23]

The critique of Physiocracy is perhaps the clearest instance of where grounding economic theory within the law of the endless circulation of matter and force produces far sounder theories, but its importance extends well beyond this example. The American Protectionists would proceed to characterize economic growth more broadly as Man using his ingenuity and intellect to manipulate matter and energy, transforming it for human use.

The Nature and Origins of the Division of Labor

The American Protectionists fundamentally agreed with the Classical School on the power of the division of labor. Even as early as the *Report on Manufactures*, Hamilton explains "that it has justly been observed, that there is scarcely any thing of greater moment [importance] in the oeconomy of a nation than the division of labour."[24] Despite this common ground, however, the American Protectionists differed when it came to discussion of the origin and nature of this division. Indeed, it should come as no surprise that the Classical view, which reduces individual beings to uniform and homogenous factors of production, considers the division of labor not to be the result of individuals seeking out different modes of employment based on their unique characteristics. This is made clear by Adam Smith who attests that "it is not the difference of natural parts or genius (which if there be any is but very small)… that occasions this separation of trades."[25] Smith, instead, sees the division of labor as the "consequence of a certain propensity in human nature… to truck, barter, and exchange."[26]

Although the American Protectionists emphasized the existence of natural differences, they partially agreed with Smith that these differences alone cannot explain the initial emergence of the division of labor—at least not without some intermediate cause. Tench Coxe, for instance, notes that "those who have been peculiarly qualified by nature for the useful arts, should find the encouragement [of manufactures] necessary to *call forth their various talents*."[27] If the division of labor emerges automatically from the mere existence of individual differences, it follows that there would be no need to call forth such talent through the cultivation of manufactures, as this should emerge naturally.

However, the American Protectionists firmly rejected Smith's explanation that the division of labor somehow arises from an apparent "propensity to truck, barter, and exchange." Rather, the true cause of the division of labor was invention and human ingenuity. It is new inventions and innovations that multiply and bring forth the variety of employments and industry that allows the division of labor to take place. Ezra Seaman expresses this point well by explaining that the "division of employments cannot take place until man has made some progress in making tools and instruments," and it is thus "the division of employments, which follows, and cannot precede the mechanic arts."[28]

Classical theory does not provide a satisfactory explanation for the cause of invention and innovation, often treating it as an exogenous force. To the extent that it was discussed, invention was seen to be the result of the division of labor.[29] American Protectionists, on the other hand, argued that the Classicals mistook the line of causality. Whilst some American Protectionists recognized the existence of bi-directional causality between the division of labor and invention, they stressed the role of innovation and invention as the first mover and driving force which begets the division of labor. John Rae, for instance, directly challenges Smith's causality, explaining that:

> In the *Wealth of Nations*, the division of labor is considered the great generator of invention and improvement… [But] the division of labor, is to be held as an effect…

> It will appear…to be… a result, not a cause; and ranks properly, not as a prime mover… but as a consequence of the actions of the prime movers.[30]

Indeed, in an earlier article, Rae more explicitly identifies this prime mover to be discovery and invention:

> In the early stages of human society, some persons, more ingenious than the rest, make discoveries and improve the natural products in a variety of modes, whence gradually arise the division of labour, [and] the difference of professions… From making clothes and utensils for his family, the man of an inventive mechanical turn will be led by degrees to a profitable employment of his time and talent in working for others… [and] the utility of this division of labour in process of time will establish the distinction.[31]

Thus, rather than the division of labor giving rise to inventions and innovations, it is the exact opposite. Inventions give rise to the division of labor, as it multiplies the number of industrial pursuits within society and creates more opportunities for laborers to be subdivided into separate tasks. Of course, natural talent and inventive genius shape the propensity to invent, but invention itself remains the direct cause of the division of labor.

The American Protectionists also took issue with the Classical conception of the division of labor because of the undue emphasis placed on the internal division of labor within an individual firm. This is highlighted by Smith's emphasis on workers in a pin factory.[32] On this point, Ezra Seaman, whilst acknowledging that the "division of employments beyond a doubt contributes greatly to increase the productive industry of a nation," observes that "quite too much importance has been generally attached to a minute subdivision of employments" within the individual firm.[33] In fact, the American Protectionists argued that the Classicals remained virtually silent on the far more important division of labor which takes place between different economic pursuits. This broader conception of the division of labor is well captured by Friedrich List:

> The [Classical] School has erred in confining [the division of labor] to a manufacture… it should have perceived that the same law extends over the whole of manufacturing and agricultural industry, and… the whole economy of a nation.
>
> As the manufacture of pins can prosper only by the combination… of individuals, every manufacture, of whatever kind, can flourish only by the combination of its productive power with those of all other manufactures.[34]

The emphasis which the Classicals attached to the internal division of labor within a firm seemingly stems from their rejection of innate differences between individuals. Since, in the view of Adam Smith, individual differences are the result, rather than the cause of the division of labor, there is no need to emphasize the diversity of employments across industries, as each individual can become accustomed to the narrow range of tasks within any particular firm, no matter what those tasks may be. Because the American Protectionists started off with the opposite view, that individuals will seek out different employments based on their unique individual characteristics, they thus downgraded the importance of the internal division of labor, and elevated the importance of the diversity of employments which exists across industries.

Nature as a Factor of Production

In the traditional model of political economy, there are typically three or four factors of production depending on how they are identified. The standard model includes land, capital, labor, and sometimes, the entrepreneur. In the case of the American Protectionists, however, there exists an additional factor of production not commonly recognized by the other schools. This factor of production is nature. The American Protectionists considered nature and Man as the two original factors of production. In the words of George M. Steele, "there are two great agencies which must co-operate in production—*nature* and *man*... Nature furnishes all the material upon which labor is to be exerted."[35] Since Man and nature are the two original factors, it follows that capital goods have their origin in Man's transformation of nature's bounties into instruments, with successive capital goods coming about through the conjoined operation of labor and capital in the exploitation of nature. In the words of Ezra Seaman:

> Man by his inventive powers and his own efforts and industry during a series of years, can alter the face of nature... and mineral substances... of the earth... into instruments and mechanical powers, to augment the productiveness of his own industry... the more labor saving machinery he can invent and bring into use, the more easily he can subdue the earth; convert its resources and products to his use.[36]

The American Protectionists saw nature as possessing unique properties which differentiates it from the other factors of production. For one thing, nature is essentially a free factor. Henry Charles Carey refers to this as "the always gratuitous services of nature."[37] And, as described in the example above, all that is required to access this free gift is for Man to combine his labor and capital with it.

Nature, as a factor, can be further subdivided into two categories. The first is raw materials of nature, such as timber, minerals, and so forth. The second is natural services and energy, which include sunlight, wind, and waterpower.[38] The natural energy of nature was also perceived as existing in its active and potential forms. William Elder notes, for instance, how there "exists latent capabilities of service" within the earth including the likes of coal and oil deposits.[39] In the case of natural energy, this free service can be harnessed through the use of special inventions and machinery. Tench Coxe, as one of the originators of this concept, provides a perceptive treatment of how machines can tap into the natural energy and access the free service of nature. As Coxe explains, "machines ingeniously constructed will give us immense assistance." The "combinations of machines with fire and water have already accomplished much more than was formerly expected from them by the most visionary enthusiast on the subject."[40] This view was echoed by Alexander Hamilton, who, likely inspired by Coxe, highlight the productivity improvements attainable from the naturally-powered machine, noting that "the vast extension given by late improvements to the employment of machines which substituting the agency of fire and water, has prodigiously lessened the necessity for manual labor."[41] Thus, natural energy when harnessed through machinery thu allows nature to act as a substitute for labor power.

The other aspect of nature which requires comment is its immense diversity, which complements the diversity in individual talents, aptitudes, and dispositions mentioned earlier. Giles B. Stebbins notes, for instance, how "we have a broad land of varied [natural] wealth, cotton and wool and food. With these gifts of a beneficent Creator, we must build up a diversity of occupations, giving complete scope to all powers of body and brain."[42] Indeed, Alexander Everett likewise comments on how the great diversity of natural substances lends itself to the cultivation of an immense variety of industrial pursuits. As Everett writes:

> When we reflect upon the variety and excellence of the natural products, animal, vegetable, and mineral, that enrich the different parts of our magnificent and almost boundless territory… with inexhaustible and incalculable treasures their hitherto almost unexplored recesses… we cannot hesitate to affirm that our situation is eminently auspicious for the establishment of almost every branch of industry.[43]

This immense diversity within nature was also seen to aid invention, with John Rae explaining that the "diversity of materials, must have increased very much the chance of discovery in the arts"—an argument expressed earlier by Hamilton.[44]

The above passages focus on nature with respect to its role in production, but the inclusion of nature as a distinct factor of production has profound implications for distribution. What is unique about nature is that, unlike labor and capital, it does not require a return for its use. Nature is always a "gratuitous service." Whereas Marxists emphasize the apparent exploitative nature of relations between capital and labor, the inclusion of nature fundamentally changes this dynamic. According to the American Protectionists, the exploited factor in capitalist production is not labor, but nature. Through labor and capital working in combination, they both benefit through nature's exploitation. Peshine Smith explains, for instance, that "the wages of labor and the hire of capital, both come out of the product of their co-operation in directing the natural forces to the service of man. This joint work of labor, capital, and the natural forces, we call production."[45] In light of this, the American Protectionists did not view exploitation with a negative connotation, as is now commonly the case within modern literature. Indeed, Van Buren Denslow even explains how:

> The choice of the word "exploitation" by the socialists is particularly happy, since it is in fact truthful when accurately understood. Exploitation does not mean "spoliation," but simply creating or causing exploits or achievements … It implies that capital energizes labor, but this implication is ignored. Its perversion into a term signifying robbery is part of the general system of "exploitation" of economic terms carried on by socialist writers.[46]

Workers and capitalists working together to exact the bounties of nature underpins what the American Protectionists considered a harmony of interests between capital and labor. The notion of a class struggle was thus rejected by the American Protectionists. Capitalism was not marked by class struggle, but by Man's struggle for mastery over nature.

Theory of Heterogenous Capital

Similar to their views on labor, and Man more generally, the American Protectionists saw a high degree of heterogeneity between capital goods. By failing to clearly distinguish between different types of capital goods, they argued that the Classical economists were falling into the trap of equating capital goods with capital funds. This treatment meant that capital, even when it takes the form of highly specialized or immobile pieces of machinery, tends to be expressed in highly liquid terms, with the presumption that it can flow effortlessly in and out of different industries as they expand and contract. This tendency in Classical thought is again well demonstrated by Adam Smith, who notes that:

> [Al]though a number of people should, by restoring the freedom of trade, be thrown all at once out of their ordinary employment, and common method of subsistence, it would by no means follow, that they would thereby be deprived either of employment or subsistence… To the greater part of manufactures, there are other collateral manufactures of so familiar a nature, that a workman can easily transfer his industry from one to the other… [Thus,] the capital of the country remaining the same, the demand for labor will still be the same, though it may be exerted in different places, and for different occupations![47]

Against this view, the American Protectionists saw that capital goods, or any other factor of production for that matter, are almost always heterogeneous and, at times, fixed and immobile. Such resources are therefore unable to shift between industries with anywhere near the ease assumed by the Classicals.

Of course, Mathew Carey did concede that there is some affinity between related industries, such as "the weaving of cotton and woollen," but this could in no way be treated as a general rule. Challenging the great Scotsman, Carey posed the question of "where will [Adam Smith], or any of his disciples, find collateral manufactures to employ… the great variety of other artists and manufacturers?" Noting that "there is no such affinity as… presumed" by Smith, it may therefore "be asserted, without scruple, that" if through the introduction of free trade "ten thousand hatters, shoemakers, printers, or chandlers, are thrown out of their ordinary employment, there is no collateral manufacture of so familiar a nature that they can easily transfer their industry from one to the other."[48] Indeed, Smith's assumption becomes even more problematic when one considers that investment decisions are largely irreversible. Whilst a capitalist can observe and predict changes in the economy and channel his capital funds into new capital goods accordingly, this "direction," as Ezra Seaman notes, "may [only] be given to it before it is invested, but when once invested in agriculture, real estate of any kind, mills, factories, tools or machinery, it is invested forever, and can never be recalled."[49]

Because capital is heterogeneous and cannot be seamlessly transferred from one industry to another, the process of deindustrialization often results in the destruction of capital, as opposed to it being freed up for use elsewhere in the economy. The Protectionists thus accused the Classicals of likening capital movements to a reticulation system diverting idle water to its ideal equilibrium point. In the words of Ezra Seaman

> The theory of Free Trade… involves the farther assumption that… capital be changed from one employment to another with as much facility as water runs down hill; that by a sort of instinct, natural or gravitating tendency, the moment the price of an article falls below its cost, both laborers and capital leave the employment by which it is produced, and it ceases to be produced until the price rises; and that these shifting laborers, and this floating capital, are moved on by some irresistible natural impulse, and rush into that species of employment whose products are above the assumed standard of cost.[50]

Friedrich List was more generous, conceding that the Classical School did in fact distinguish between "capital fixed and capital circulating."[51] That is, capital goods, such as machinery and equipment, and liquid capital funds. He even notes that they acknowledged the difference between material, intellectual, and social capital. Yet, List explains that, whilst the Classical School acknowledged this fact, they remained silent in every instance where this distinction was relevant:

> The [Classical] School ought, of course, when it speaks of capital, to indicate whether it intends material capital or material instruments of production, or intellectual capital, or capital arising from moral or physical power… The omission of this distinction in cases where it ought to be made, cannot fail to lead to false conclusions, or to conceal the truth.[52]

This failure to distinguish between different types of capital and capital goods when it mattered leads to a tendency in Classical thought to treat different capital goods as if they were identical.

The French Liberal Jean-Baptiste Say did attempt to qualify the Classical view of capital homogeneity and liquidity by pointing out that, whilst capital goods themselves are not homogeneous, they still function as if they are homogeneous because the capitalist can always sell existing capital goods from one branch of industry and exchange them for capital goods in another branch of industry with relative ease.[53] Still, the American Protectionists considered this qualification to be far from satisfactory. List notes, for instance, that a nation cannot sell the entire stock of capital goods in a declining branch of industry, as simply as an individual leaving that branch of industry can:

> [Jean-Baptiste Say] has blended individual with national capital. A manufacturer or a merchant may withdraw his capital from manufacturing industry or commerce by selling his manufactories or his ships to another, and by purchasing with the proceeds real estate; but a whole nation cannot perform such an operation without sacrificing a large portion of its material and intellectual capital.[54]

Say's qualification thus represents a complete fallacy of composition. What is true for the individual, in this case, cannot be true for the nation as a whole. Indeed, the American Protectionists recognized, as noted by Seaman, that "the owner of [capital] may exchange it for other property, yet… it is the owner only that is changed, and not the capital" itself.[55] It is not true, therefore, that specialization under free trade necessarily increases the stock of national capital and capital goods. On the contrary, national capital can be laid to waste if an entire industry declines as a result of enacting free trade policies, since capital goods often lack the ability to be easily transferred between industries.

The American Protectionists understood, of course, that innovation and technological change may render capital obsolete, but this represents a very different situation from trade-induced obsolescence. Technology-induced obsolescence is inevitable, and they saw how the benefits derived from technological change more than compensates for the loss of existing capital. George B. Curtiss summarizes this view, noting that:

> The general benefits and advantages of the new inventions, to the whole people, so outweighed the temporary and individual losses [of capital and employment] which [has] occurred, that nothing could stop or check the full play of inventive genius, and the progressive development of man's powers over the forces of nature went steadily on.[56]

Indeed, productivity enhancing inventions tend to reduce the cost of capital goods, creating a more than compensatory increase in the total stock of capital over time.

Finally, whereas the above mainly focuses on the destruction of capital through free trade and deindustrialization, the theory of heterogeneous capital also provides a positive argument in favor of protection. The American Protectionists observed that there is often capital within the economy which remains dormant because it lacks the industry to stimulate it into effect. Alexander Everett explains, for instance, that:

> Persons of great discretion believe that there is… what has been contemptuously called an *imaginary dormant capital*… a certain portion of the capital and labor of almost every community, is at all times either unemployed, or not employed… A circumstance which renders practicable the introduction of a new branch of industry that did not exist before, by stimulating enterprise, has a tendency to bring this dormant capital into activity…. [Yet] the *dormant capital* of the country is not so entirely *imaginary*, nor… completely insignificant, as some [free traders] have supposed… [When] this dormant capital… [is] brought into action, [it] may be regarded as a real addition to the previously existing capital of the country, resulting… from the protecting policy… The capital which is put in motion… is therefore not withdrawn from other employments… That this increase, if not taken up by manufactures, might be employed in some other way, is a mere baseless assumption.[57]

This represents an argument against the position put forth by free traders, and in this case, Albert Gallatin, who argued that the encouragement of manufacturing through protective tariffs would only serve to divert capital away from existing and more profitable pursuits, which, according to Gallatin, was agriculture. Since the American Protectionists conceived capital as being heterogeneous, it stands to reason that the establishment of manufactures would more often tend to stimulate dormant capital that is unsuited for existing industries, as opposed to diverting existing capital goods away from more profitable pursuits. Indeed, protective tariffs, it must be remembered, do not coerce capital into alternate channels of production, but merely widen the scope of activities and opportunities in which capital and labor can be employed.

Mental and Intellectual Capital

The American Protectionists stressed the importance of what is known today as human capital—the mental and intellectual capabilities of the individual. Friedrich List captured this emphasis when he declared that the "greater part of the productive power consists in the intellectual and social conditions of the individuals, which I call capital of mind."[58] This focus on intellectual capital represents another fundamental departure from Classical economics, one that would profoundly shape their approach to economic development.

The American Protectionists recognized that the productivity of labor depends not merely on physical effort but on skill, training, and intelligence. Erastus B. Bigelow, for instance, observed that "the efficiency of labor, on whatever objects it is exercised, depends not only upon the natural power of the laborer, but also upon his training and general intelligence."[59] This contrasted sharply with the English Classical economists, and particularly David Ricardo, who dismissed such considerations. Ricardo himself declared that "the consideration of the comparative skill and intensity of labour required for [a] particular commodity needs scarcely to be attended to… [as it] continues nearly the same from one generation to another; or at least, that the variation is very inconsiderable from year to year."[60]

When combined with Adam Smith's tendency to downplay differences in natural talents and aptitudes, Ricardo's dismissal of human capital development means that labor is essentially an abstract and uniform factor of production. This flaw in Classical economics was well observed by Francis Bowen:

> The great mistake of Ricardo and his followers, who have done so much to reduce Political Economy to a mere deductive science, all the conclusions in which are obtained by abstract reasoning from a few arbitrarily assumed premises, is, that they generally treat of labor *in the abstract,* and make no allowance for these differences in the *quality* of the labor.[61]

The American Protectionists were thus highly critical of this tendency in Classical thought of ignoring the role of intellect and skill in production. Henry Carey argued, for instance, that "the English school of political economy treats Man as a *mere* machine" and "takes no account of him as being capable of intellectual and moral improvement."[62] This view is echoed by Stephen Colwell who similarly chastises the Classicals for ignoring Man's "agency [as] a moral and intellectual being" and thus "not distinguishing the labor of man from that of beasts, or that of machinery."[63]

For the American Protectionists, intellectual capital assumed even greater importance than material capital. Peshine Smith, for instance, declared that "Man's office in the world is that of engineer; all his real power is mental."[64] The importance placed on intellectual capital over material capital is perhaps best captured by Ezra Seaman who explains that:

> Immaterial [or intellectual] capital is even more necessary than material capital, to the progress of individuals and communities in productive industry… If he live[s] in a country of great natural resources, and [has] an abundance of immaterial capital, no matter

> how destitute he may be at first of material capital, in a few years, by means of properly directed industry and frugality, he can accumulate sufficient… capital to make his industry effective.[65]

Indeed, whilst the productivity of manual labor has definite limits and is thus subject to diminishing returns, the productivity of intellectual capital was viewed as virtually limitless with a tendency toward increasing returns. In the words of Calvin Colton:

> A man's power of labor is limited; but his skill is unlimited. Skill is often a thousand times more productive than what is commonly called labor. But it is to be remembered, that, skill itself is the fruit of the labor of mind, or is the employment of mind, as muscular effort is labor of the body. But skill is capital.[66]

Referring to skill as capital was deliberate, as it signifies an underlying importance. Whereas modern socialist literature views the term "human capital" as condescending and dehumanizing to workers, the American Protectionists employed the term in a positive manner.

Indeed, the American Protectionists considered skilled and educated workers to be micro-capitalists of sorts. Since the decision to invest in one's education and training is the result of deliberate decision making—often requiring the worker to sacrifice a portion of his income and to forego other enjoyments—the process of intellectual capital accumulation is similar to how industrialists accumulate capital through investing in new equipment. Moreover, this intellectual capital is owned by the laborer and is merely leased out to the capitalist for the contracted period. Skilled labor can thus be viewed in a similar vein to independent contractors. As Calvin Colton explains:

> The relative position of the capital of labor and moneyed capital, is, not that the latter commands the former, but that the former commands the latter. Moneyed capital employs labor, because its owner has need of the service… Labor is the master here; it is the great capitalist… within his own skin, and deep down in his own soul, lies the capital, the productive power, with which he is to trade.[67]

As with their analysis of heterogeneous capital, their theory of intellectual capital has important implications for trade policy. Although the same rules largely apply, the implications for trade are greatly magnified when considering intellectual capital. Unlike material capital, intellectual capital often takes far longer to develop. This provides an even greater justification for infant industry protection, as workers need time to develop the requisite skills to compete internationally. In the words of Ezra Seaman:

> As a general rule, it requires several years of training and discipline of both body and mind, to fit persons for any… manufacturing employment, and make them skillful workmen. Great difficulty has, therefore, been experienced in every country, in introducing the mechanic arts… and obtaining skillful workmen to carry them on successfully… [thus] the mechanic arts and manufactures have never flourished in any country, without the fostering care of the government.[68]

By implication, the loss of industry through free trade means a far greater loss of investment than simply the destruction of machinery and tools, since the outlay involved in accumulating intellectual capital often represents a far greater cost.

Land as Capital

The traditional model of political economy holds that there are three basic factors of production—land, labor, and capital. Not only did the American Protectionists differ from this by including nature as a distinct factor, they rejected the view that land constitutes its own separate factor of production. Land instead represents a form of capital. This concept has its origins in Hamilton's *Report on Manufactures*, and it is a view that remained remarkably consistent throughout the entire history of the School.

Hamilton's treatment of land as capital emerged through his critique of Physiocracy. Reflecting their bias toward agriculture and their disdain for manufacturing, the Physiocrats asserted that manufacturing was inferior to agriculture because it failed to produce a "net product" (or rent) that accrues to the proprietor of land.[69] Hamilton countered, however, that while manufacturing does not produce a source of income denoted as rent, this issue is purely nominal. The ordinary profit of the manufacturer captures what would otherwise be called agricultural "rent." Indeed, Hamilton explains that "the rent of the landlord and the profit of the farmer are therefore nothing more than the ordinary profits of two capitals belonging to two different persons." The problem is thus merely "verbal rather than substantial."[70] In other words, land represents a form of capital which yields an income like any other form of capital. Hamilton's observation, while simple, is perceptive, and this insight formed the foundation for the American Protectionist analysis of land.

This treatment of rent as profit and land as capital would continue throughout the later generations of American Protectionists. Indeed, commenting on how the Classical economists "have taken great pains to establish a distinction… between rent paid for the use of land and the price paid for the use of commodities," Daniel Raymond echoes Hamilton, declaring that "in fact no such distinction exists, except in name."[71] The Carey generation of American Protectionists would extend this analysis of land even further, grounding it in their broader system of theory. Recall that American Protectionist theory considers nature as a distinct factor of production. Man and nature represent the two original factors, with capital goods arising from Man's transformation of nature into instruments. Land, insofar as it is a productive factor, adheres to the same principle. It thus represents a form of capital. This led William Elder to declare that among the "fundamental propositions… credited to the [American Protectionist] system" is the "doctrine [that] land is a machine in functions and uses."[72]

The American Protectionists emphasized that land becomes productive capital only through human transformation of nature. This point is well articulated by Robert Ellis Thompson, who explains that "a farm is like a ship. Nature gives us the materials out of which to make it, but it is labor which gives these their value in adapting them to human use."[73] In other words, it is through the application of labor and capital that land, in the form of nature, is transformed into new capital. William D. Wilson captured this dual nature, describing land as both a natural force and "a tool, an implement, or a machine by which man is able to unite these elements into the forms in which they serve him."[74] William Elder further reinforced this view:

> The primary fact is that Land in the state of Nature… must be subdued in order to be brought into service [that is, transformed into capital]. Its forests must be felled, its swamps drained; its mould must be broken up, and the seeds of the required harvest must be sown; and the implements of clearing and culture must be provided.[75]

This conception of land as capital diverges significantly from the Classical treatment of land and land rents. The Classical economists, in particular David Ricardo, and later, Henry George, likened landlords to parasites on society who receive an unearned rental income based solely on what Ricardo labels "the original and indestructible powers of the soil."[76] Against this view, the American Protectionists argued that landlords were indeed a productive class. Like any other capitalist, landlords were responsible for transforming land into productive capital and were responsible for maintaining its productivity.

Thus, in response to Ricardo, Henry Carey poses the question: "what are indestructible powers? The most fertile soil, if not renewed, will have its powers destroyed."[77] The implication is clear. According to the law of the endless circulation of matter and energy, cropping and cultivation must necessarily deplete the elements and nutrients of the soil. This lowers the productive power and the fertility of land. The process can thus be likened to the wear and tear of capital goods. Just as capital goods require repair and maintenance, so too does land through the application of fertilizer and organic waste (reintroducing lost nutrients), rotational cropping, clearing of regrowth, and so forth. In relation to the loss of fertility, Peshine Smith illustrates how land functions as a form of capital:

> [Land] is a great machine, differing from others in the circumstance that it is immovable. But, like other machines, whatsoever of its force is due to the past operation of natural agents [in this case, nutrients] having been gratuitously produced, must be gratuitously parted with [as it is expended through production] … Such is that accumulation of organic and inorganic matter, which constitutes its fertility, and gives it what Ricardo calls its original and indestructible powers.[78]

In this case, landlords, operating not unlike other capitalists, must replenish the soil of elements and nutrients as they are exhausted in order for it to remain productive. The landlord thus adheres to the same principles as any other capitalist maintaining a piece of machinery. This principle, of course, encompasses all improvements and maintenance to land. American Protectionists thus avoided the Ricardian trap of equating the productivity of land with fertility. The productivity of land more generally was the result of investment. Indeed, Van Buren Denslow even went so far as to declare that "rent… has almost nothing to do with fertility, even in the case of agricultural land."[79]

This treatment of land as capital has important philosophical implications and underscores the American Protectionists' commitment to the Lockean theory of property rights. Since land, as a productive resource, comes into existence through the application of labor and capital, it necessarily follows that the person responsible for bringing about such improvements should have an exclusive natural right to the land. It is for this reason that the American Protectionists rejected the Ricardian–Georgist–Millian proposal of taxing away land rent. This rejection can be seen in the following passage by William Elder:

> Is [the] English theory of political economy, like that of the French [communist] Proudhon, based upon the axiom, "Property is robbery?"... [Ricardo, George, Mill, etc.] put land upon a different economic basis from all other machinery of industrial production... If that property [land], though it be in fact like any other property, wholly due to labor and capital applied to its creation, is based upon a different right, or no right at all, the theory is answerable for the result [that] it is no man's land.
>
> Every occupant is an usurper; but curiously enough, not of the rights of other people, for nobody has any right to any portion of it... [Their view] is invented to support... the principle of depriving landlords of the power of raising rent; the principle, therefore, of imposing on the State the obligation of saying what a *fair rent is*... I [say] these people reason in a circle.[80]

A similar view is expressed by George B. Dixwell in his critique of Henry George. "It is *assumed*," writes Dixwell, "that the value of land of these United States is the product of nature; but nearly all of it is the product of capital slowly acquired by self-denial." If it were not "for this antecedent labor and thrift," continues Dixwell, "no piece of ground would command any rent. The whole value then would seem to belong to those who are here"—that is, those who own it.[81] In other words, since all forms of property, including productive land, are the product of Man's transformation of nature, the only internally consistent position is that property rights must either extend to land ownership, or it does not extend to anything at all. It is for this reason, among others, that Van Buren Denslow declared that "Karl Marx begins with Ricardo, and ends with thuggism."[82]

Linkages

Whilst the concept of economic linkages is typically traced to the development economics subfield that emerged after World War II, American Protectionist thinkers had already articulated this principle more than a century earlier. Linkages, in this context, represent the connection between different firms or industries involving purchases, particularly with respect to inputs. As early as 1810, Tench Coxe clearly acknowledges the significance of industrial and agricultural linkages, explaining that:

> The manufacturing [firm] uses... the productions of the earth, [and] occasion a regular and extensive sale and consumption of them, in places, where there would otherwise be no market. Agriculture and the landed interest are materially benefitted [through manufactures], and the country prospers by [the] convenient internal exchanges and operations.[83]

Indeed, Coxe further emphasizes this interconnection, noting that "the manufacturing arts all depend upon, and are connected with each other."[84] The implication of these linkages is that the expansion of a particular industry will have the tendency to expand connected industries. As one industry expands, this will necessitate the expansion of industries down and upstream of it. A. B. Stone explains, for instance, how "the industries of a nation are interconnected… one is an aid to the other." It thus follows that the expansion of one industry "fosters the growth of all related industries."[85]

As this concept relates to protective tariffs, it follows that even non-protected sectors will have a tendency to benefit from protective legislation. Indeed, this logic extends even to service sector industries, which are commonly overlooked when discussing the benefits of protection. Yet this observation is clearly captured by Ellis H. Roberts:

> [Free traders] assume that all industries not included directly, and by name, in the imposts, do not secure protection through the tariff… [But] the effect of a given duty is to stimulate production in all its [connected] branches, to protect industry in every one of its phases. When you seek to raise a chain of which the links are all connected, and to raise it for a considerable height, you need not fasten your hook to every link. If you grip closely a single link, you lift the whole chain as far as that link is raised.[86]

Roberts' description illustrates what modern development economists call "cumulative causation." This is the tendency for industrial development to act in a mutually reinforcing manner, whereby growth in one industry tends to produce growth in connected industries. In this case, the development of a particular industry, or a "link in the chain," to use Roberts' analogy, will progressively increase demand for products along the chain of production.

This concept of linkages underscores the "harmony of interests" doctrine of the American Protectionists. With linkages in mind, Daniel Webster explains that all "great interests of the country are united and inseparable… [and] will prosper together, or languish together."[87] Indeed, it is precisely because different "employments are," as Rufus Choate writes, "so interwoven with all the nerves of business," that what affects one tends to affect all.[88] Henry Carey, however, provides one of the most detailed expositions in his work entitled *The Harmony of Interests*:

> It is not so much that coal needs protection for itself—or that iron or cotton need it for themselves—but that each needs it for the other. The producer of coal suffers because the furnace is closed, and the producer of iron suffers because the factories are no longer built, and the maker of cloth suffers because labour is everywhere being wasted, and the power to buy cloth is diminished. The harmony of interests—agricultural and manufacturing—is as perfect as is that of the movements of a watch, and no one can suffer without producing injury among all around. The grower of cotton suffers when the operatives in cotton factories and the workers in mines and furnaces are unemployed, and the latter suffer when adverse circumstances diminish the return to the labour of the farmer and planter.[89]

By implication, the presence of linkages means that the stagnation or decline of a particular industry will drag down all those connected with it. In any event, this emphasis placed on the interconnectedness of different industries led the American Protectionists to stress the importance of having a balanced and diversified economy, with Daniel Raymond explaining that it is "manifest, that in a national point of view, [agriculture, manufactures, and commerce], are but parts of one great system, each of them essential to the other."[90]

Now that the principles that underpin the beautiful science of the American Protectionists have been established, this book can proceed with a more direct discussion of their system of economic laws. The first of these discussions will concern their theory of value, which will be the focus of the next chapter.

Notes

1. William Herndon quoted in Boritt, *Lincoln*, 125.
2. For example, Dunbar, "Economic Science," 131–140; Schumpeter, *Economic Analysis*, 514–520; Galbraith, *Affluent Society*, 121; Conkin, *Prophets*, 142–147; Barber, *Economic Thought*, 117.
3. Niles, *Journal*, 19.
4. Thompson, *Elements*, 31.
5. Carey, *Social Science*, 1:52.
6. Bigelow, "Labor and Capital," 481.
7. Cannan, *Production and Distribution*, 44; Schumpeter, *Economic Analysis*, 180; Rothbard, *Austrian Perspective*, 1:454.
8. Smith, *Wealth of Nations*, 19–20.
9. Smith, *Jurisprudence*, 341.
10. Carey, *Manual*, 47.
11. Coxe, *Observations*, 25; For Coxe's influence, see Frith, "Hamilton, Coxe, and Talents."
12. Everett, *New Ideas*, 24.
13. Hamilton, *Report on Manufactures*, 11.
14. Choate, "Mechanical Industry," 127.
15. Choate, "Mechanical Industry," 127.
16. Colwell, *Claims*, 23.
17. Rae, "Genius," 320–321.
18. Patton, *Political Economy*, 17.
19. Hamilton, *Report on Manufactures*, 3.
20. Smith, "Notes: Chapter 1," 80.
21. Carey, *Social Science*, 1:65.
22. Hamilton, *Report on Manufactures*, 7.
23. Greeley, *Essays*, 44.
24. Hamilton, *Report on Manufactures*, 9; 'moment' was expressed as 'importance' in Hamilton, "Fourth Draft," 249.
25. Smith, *Jurisprudence*, 238.
26. Smith, *Wealth of Nations*, 16.
27. Coxe, *Memorial*, xi.
28. Seaman, *Progress*, 58; Seaman (p. 62) also emphasizes the science and ingenuity embodied in the mechanical arts: "it may therefore be truly said that a division of employments… all depend upon the mechanic arts and cannot exist without them; and that… no nation or people can advance… any faster than they make progress in the mechanical arts, and the science [on] which they are based."
29. Smith (*Wealth of Nations*, 6, 9) speaks of "the invention [of machinery] of which the same division of labour has probably given occasion," and explains that "the invention of a great number of machines" is a "consequence of the division of labour,"; see also Smith, *Jurisprudence*, 340.

30. Rae, *Statement,* 352, 357.
31. Rae, *Sketches*, 195–196.
32. Smith, *Wealth of Nations*, 6–7.
33. Seaman, *Progress,* 136.
34. List, *National System,* 232–233.
35. Steele, *Outline*, 11.
36. Seaman, *Progress,* 23.
37. Carey, *Social Science,* 1:149, 18.
38. Steele (*Outline*, 12) also explains that "nature furnishes not only materials, but also forces, to aid man in his productive efforts."
39. Elder, *Conversations*, 18.
40. Coxe, *View*, 40.
41. Hamilton, *Report on Manufactures,* 18;
42. Stebbins, *Manual*, 16.
43. Everett, *Opinions*, 42.
44. Rae, *Statements*, 251; see also Hamilton, *Report on Manufactures*, 13.
45. Smith, "Notes: Chapter 3," 89.
46. Denslow, *Principles*, 184f.
47. Smith quoted in Carey, *Essays*, 27.
48. Carey, *Essays*, 27–28, emphasis and internal quotations have been omitted to improve readability.
49. Seaman, *Progress*, 318.
50. Seaman, *Progress,* 317.
51. List, *National System*, 314.
52. List, *National System*, 307.
53. Say, *Treatise*, 350–351.
54. List, *National System*, 315.
55. Seaman, *Progress*, 318.
56. Curtiss, *Protection*, 123.
57. Everett, "Memorial," 138–140.
58. List, *Outlines*, 20.
59. Bigelow, "Labor and Capital," 479.
60. Ricardo, *Principles*, 14.
61. Bowen, *American Economy*, 77.
62. Carey, *Harmony*, 210–211.
63. Colwell, *Claims*, 32.
64. Smith, *Manual*, 74.
65. Seaman, *Progress*, 134.
66. Colton, "Labor and Capital," 2.
67. Colton, "Labor and Capital," 2.
68. Seaman, *Progress*, 135.
69. Groenewegen, *Eighteenth-Century Economics*, 241.
70. Hamilton, *Report on Manufactures*, 5.
71. Raymond, *Elements*, 1:184.
72. Elder, *Conversations*, 51.
73. Thompson, *High Schools*, 19.
74. Wilson, *Principles*, 90–91.
75. Elder, *Conversations*, 28.
76. Ricardo, *Principles*, 53.
77. Carey, *Political Economy*, 1:189.
78. Smith, *Manual*, 102.

79. Denslow, *Principles*, 239.
80. Elder, *Conversations*, 50–51.
81. Dixwell, *Progress*, 41.
82. Denslow, *Principles*, 91.
83. Coxe, *Statement*, iix.
84. Coxe, *Essay*, 24.
85. Stone, "Protection," 26.
86. Roberts, *Government Revenue*, 260–261.
87. Webster, "Tariff," 96.
88. Choate, *Speech*, 43.
89. Carey, *Harmony*, 49.
90. Raymond, *Elements*, 1:205.

Chapter Five

THEORY OF VALUE

If Classical economics earned its reputation as the dismal science due to its emphasis on iron laws of diminishing returns, it should come as no surprise that the "beautiful science" of the American Protectionists was predicated on the exact opposite: laws of increasing returns. This is best illustrated by looking at their theory of value. The American Protectionists referred to their theory as the reproduction cost theory of value, and whilst it has sometimes been dismissed as clumsy modification of the Ricardian labor theory of value, this represents a fundamental misunderstanding of their approach. For one thing, the American Protectionists rejected Ricardo's pursuit of a so-called "invariable standard of value." They instead embraced a dynamic world where values perpetually decline as mankind obtains mastery over nature. In this beautiful science, the diminution of value did not signal economic decline, but a triumph of human ingenuity. Yet, to fully grasp the American Protectionists' approach to value, it is important to first understand the Classical framework which they sought to overturn.

The Reproduction Cost Theory of Value in the Classical Context

From the time of Adam Smith (1776) until the Marginal Revolution (circa 1870s), value theory was predicated on cost of production. Chief among these theories was David Ricardo's labor theory of value, a theory which was later adopted by Karl Marx. According to this theory, value is determined by the amount of labor embodied in a commodity, or in Ricardo's own words, "the value of a commodity… depends on the relative quantity of labour which is necessary for its production."[1]

In positing his theory, one of Ricardo's chief concerns was establishing what he called an "invariable standard measure of value," and this invariable standard would be his concept of embodied labor.[2] In order to make this work, however, Ricardo had to assume that productive activity must always adhere to laws of constant returns. Or to express it using a labor theory of value, all production must adhere to a law of constant value. This means that a unit of labor, or a unit of labor time, will always produce an equal amount of output, and adding additional laborers to productive activity will only ever produce a proportional increase in output. Indeed, since value is determined by the amount of embodied labor, the amount of value bestowed upon a commodity must remain constant. This position is well captured in the following passage from Ricardo:

> The scale, when once formed, is liable to little variation… In comparing therefore the value of the same commodity, at different periods of time, the consideration of the comparative skill and intensity of labour, required for that particular commodity, needs scarcely to be attended to, as it operates equally at both periods.[3]

The American Protectionists were under no such illusion. Indeed, despite writing prior to the introduction of the reproduction cost theory of value, Daniel Raymond had already rebuked efforts to derive an invariable standard, declaring that "a permanent standard of value is in the nature of things an impossibility, nay, a palpable absurdity."[4]

Nevertheless, for Ricardo to preserve embodied labor as an invariable standard, he had to assume away concepts that were foundational to the American Protectionists. For one thing, maintaining a constant value of labor meant upholding Smith's assumption that labor is essentially homogeneous and uniform in nature, something which was antithetical to the American Protectionists' emphasis on individuality and the diversity of talents. Moreover, the importance of intellectual capital, technology, and productivity was dismissed in the elusive quest for an invariable standard. The reproduction cost theory of value of the American Protectionists thus emerged as a direct challenge to Ricardo's assumption of constant returns. In supplanting Ricardo's static approach to value, the American Protectionists would establish a dynamic theory of value predicated on rising productivity and increasing returns.

The Reproduction Cost Theory of Value

Prior to the mid-nineteenth century, most American Protectionists tended to avoid the question of what determines exchange value. This would change with the introduction of the reproduction cost theory of value, which would become a mainstay of American Protectionist thought. Although the more conventional and refined version of the theory was first developed by Henry Carey, a rudimentary version based on declining reproduction costs as measured in labor can be traced to John Rae. Writing in the 1830s, Rae observed that:

> It follows that, whenever an article comes to be made with less labor than formerly [i.e., lower labor cost of reproduction], articles of the same sort which may have been previously manufactured, procure for their owners less of other articles in exchange than they did before. They exchange, not for what labor has been actually wrought up in them, but for what is now required to make others similar to them.[5]

Unfortunately, however, the theory's reputation as a modification of the Ricardian labor theory of value obscures the profound differences in their approach and that of the Classicals. First, the reproduction cost theory of value as developed by the Carey generation of protectionists is not, strictly speaking, a labor theory of value, or even a pure cost of production theory of value for that matter. It can be more properly understood as a utility-productivity theory of value, and even a rejection of the Ricardian and later Marxian labor theory of value.[6]

Indeed, unlike Rae's earlier formulation, Carey and the post-Carey protectionists did not equate reproduction costs solely with labor costs. Instead, the reproduction cost theory of value considers all elements under Man's command, whether this consists of manual labor, labor-saving machinery, intellectual capital, harnessed services of nature, and so forth. As Robert Ellis Thompson explains, "the price of a thing being fixed by the cost of its reproduction, *every improvement in the methods of production* lowers the price of what has been already produced."[7]

Perhaps more importantly, however, the American Protectionists denounced the Ricardian notion of an invariable standard and the idea that commodities maintain a constant value. The American Protectionists argued instead that there is a tendency for prices to fall as productivity increases and this reduction in price was seen to be inclusive of pre-existing goods. There is thus no fixed and invariable standard underlying value, as assumed by Ricardo and Marx, as cost or value tends to diminish over time.

The central idea behind the reproduction cost theory of value is relatively simple. As the cost of reproducing a commodity becomes less through improvements in productivity, the value of the commodity will decline. In the words of Henry Carey:

> Value is measured by the resistance to be overcome in obtaining the service of things required for human use. It is the cost of re-production. As the value of commodities declines, the worth of man advances. In advancing communities, the cost of reproduction constantly diminishes, and in the ratio of such advancement.[8]

This decline in reproduction costs also means that the price of pre-existing goods will also tend to fall. Indeed, "if we can reproduce or replace them with less outlay of labor than when they were made," writes Robert Ellis Thompson, "we will not pay more for them than they would now cost." Thus, "the price of anything, therefore, is not the cost of making it, but the cost of replacing it, or making another like it."[9]

Whilst the value theory of the American Protectionists rejects the notion of natural price, or an invariable standard, they did conceive of reproduction costs in terms of both in the abstract and in terms of market value. In the abstract sense, the value of production diminishes as the resistance to producing a good or service is overcome through advancements in productivity. That is to say, that the cost of reproduction, in terms of Man's effort, even in the absence of a market with exchangeable values, will tend to diminish as he becomes more proficient at producing the good which he desires. As a frame of reference, value is thus measured, and subsequently diminishes, relative to Man. Market value is an extension of this process, with real market prices approximating the diminution in reproduction costs. Thus, for all practical purposes, a declining reproduction cost leads to lower real prices on the market over the long run. The reproduction cost theory of value thus represents a productivity theory of value.

It is important to note, however, that whilst this theory of value rests primarily on production or the resistance imposed by nature, utility also represents an important element of the theory. In order for a product to have value, it must first have utility, or a use or reason for Man to desire it. Yet, having utility does not automatically bestow a commodity with value, unless there is resistance to be overcome in obtaining the commodity. Robert Ellis Thompson, for instance, explains that:

> Value is the measure of nature's power over man—of the resistance that she offers to his efforts to master her. Some of the natural substances are to be had everywhere, always and in the form needed for man's consumption. These have no value, though the very highest utility. Others, such as the water for the supply of a great city, need to be changed in place, and have a value proportional to the cost of their transfer. Others need to be changed in form by manufacture as well as changed in place before their use, and have a still higher value. In other instances, the resistance takes the form of scarcity.[10]

Value thus represents an intersection between resistance and utility. If a good has utility, but there is no resistance to be overcome, or no cost involved in acquiring the good, then the good is valueless. Conversely, if the good has no utility, but there is resistance to be overcome to obtain the good, it is equally valueless. Thus, "to be valuable," explains Robert Ellis Thompson, "a thing must be wanted for use, or for ornament, or as a curiosity, and also must be something we cannot get without an effort."[11]

However, the absence of value does not mean the utility disappears. Rather, utility now simply exists as a gratuitous gift of nature, and it therefore follows that the excess of utility over resistance represents a form of economic surplus. Peshine Smith elaborates on this intersection between utility and resistance further, explaining that:

> Utility [is] the capacity a thing has to satisfy a man's wants and desires—[it] is something more than Value, which is the sum of the obstacles to its attainment. The difference between them—between the gross amount of service, in the satisfaction of wants, that the possession of a thing will bestow, and the gross amount of labour which must be undertaken to secure it—is the sum of the effects—produced by the gratuitous operation of the forces of Nature.
>
> Men differ in their estimate of the utility of objects… In proportion as this estimate is high, the demand for a commodity is urgent. In proportion as the obstacles to its production are reduced… its value is diminished.[12]

Thus, unlike the Ricardians, the American Protectionists were completely aware of the role of utility in the determination of value. The cost of reproduction simply attracted a greater degree of attention in their theory than utility of value because reproduction costs were seen as exerting a greater influence on the determination of value over the long run, as it is conditioned by improvements in technology and productivity.

In fact, the American Protectionists were perfectly clear that in scenarios where goods cannot be reproduced (i.e., maximal resistance) that value is determined exclusively by utility. As Henry Carey explains:

> It may be asked, why should a very rare copy of an ancient work sell for many times its original price? Value is limited to the cost of reproduction; and where an object cannot be reproduced, its value has no limit but the fancy of those who desire to possess it.[13]

Although improvements on the reproduction side are emphasized by the American Protectionists, it is important to note that they did not view utility as unchanging either

Whereas economic development leads to a lessening of resistance, that is, a declining cost of reproduction over time, it generally produces the opposite effect with respect to utility. By stimulating human intellect, economic progress multiplies the uses of instruments and earthly substances, giving utility to things which formerly possessed none. In fact, Alexander Hamilton had already alluded to this tendency, noting how industrial development "creates a demand for such as were either unknown or produced in inconsiderable quantities." And thus through the cultivation of new pursuits, "the bowels as well as the surface of the earth are ransacked for articles which were before neglected. Animals, plants and minerals acquire a utility and value, which were before unexplored."[14]

This tendency for industrial and intellectual development to create new use values by giving Man the ability to harness new instruments and earthly substances was well put by Henry Carey, who notes that "the capability of [something] being useful to man exists… but, in order that it may have utility, man must have the power required for overcoming the resisting force of nature."[15] Economic progress is thus marked by declining resistance or reproduction costs, on the one hand, and an increase in potential use, or utility, on the other.

In relation to prices on the market, this means that existing commodities will tend to experience declining reproduction costs, whilst at the same time, new commodities will tend to emerge that command a high price. Price determination is therefore marked by a process of new uses giving rise to higher prices, yet new processes of production will constantly press down upon price as reproduction costs diminish. William Elder illustrates this tendency, noting that certain "raw material rises in value as it is made more useful by labor; but commodities of every kind decline in cost as they are made more readily to decline in resistance." Indeed, whilst, "the machine costs more as it is the more efficient [i.e., has a higher utility due to its efficiency], its product costs… less as its capability enhances."[16]

The long-run trajectory, however, is that as society progresses, there will typically be diminution of value due to diminishing reproduction costs. In fact, reflecting their emphasis on increasing returns, it was even implied that the emergence of new uses will have a tendency to produce an even greater reduction in reproduction costs over the long-run, as it allows for the scale of production to expand. John L. Hayes thus observed that "manufactured commodities are invariably cheapened… as the home demand for them enlarges…. This demand justifies production on vast scale, diminishing [reproduction costs] to the lowest point."[17]

Markets, Value, and Individuality

Markets were seen as playing an important role in the determination of value for they tended to synchronize final price with the cost of reproduction. This synchronization comes about due to consumers constantly comparing relative sacrifice. That is to say that they will compare the cost which they would otherwise have to incur in reproducing a similar good themselves, relative to them producing a different commodity which could then be traded for the commodity in question. The estimated resistance to be overcome if they were to produce the good themselves is what rounds out final value. As Henry Carey explains:

> [The] idea of comparison [is] inseparably connected with that of value… [Value] is simply our estimate of the resistance to be overcome before we enter upon the possession of the thing desired.[18]

The relative resistance to be overcome in reproducing a commodity is therefore an important element in the determination of exchange and relative value between commodities. Individuals will estimate and compare their own estimated cost of reproducing different commodities to that of other producers on the market. It then follows that individuals will typically seek to specialize in producing the commodity which they are relatively more efficient at producing and will then trade these commodities for commodities which would incur a higher cost if they were to reproduce it themselves. If the general reproduction cost is high in terms of absolute sacrifice or resistance to be overcome, this will confer a high price on the market, since individuals are prepared to pay the high price as compensation for the resistance they would face if they were to make it themselves.[19]

The perception of the relative reproduction cost of different commodities among different individuals is also important for establishing the basis for exchange as well as for coordinating production and exchange within society. It is the interplay in the variation in the costs of reproducing different commodities between different individuals in the market which coordinates relative prices. In the words of Henry Carey:

> Exchanges establish measures of value suited to the places and times at which they are made… The perception of value leads to a comparison of values [with value being the measure of nature's power over man or resistance to be overcome in obtaining a good], and finally to those exchanges which demand an adjustment of the relations of things to be exchanged.[20]

An important element of this concerns the concept of individuality. Unlike in the Ricardian labor theory of value, which assumes that a unit of labor time is always simply a unit of labor time, the American Protectionist thought assumes that factors of production are heterogeneous. Since individuals possess different talents and aptitudes, it follows that no two individuals will be equally productive at producing the same commodity. William Elder captures this point well, noting how "instance of genius and natural endowments… diminish the cost of acquirement by lessening the time and effort required to develop their availableness."[21]

This influence of individual differences on value is well illustrated by Henry Carey's example of Jenny Lind, a famous songstress from the time. On the question as to why "Jenny Lind could get a thousand dollars a single evening; while young women who sing in the chorus receive less than a single dollar" Carey explains that if there "were some enterprising [showman]… determine[d] on raising a new Jenny Lind, he would find it necessary to make the experiment on some hundreds, or even thousands, of individuals." It would only be "after enormous outlay, [that] he [could produce] one prodigy who could earn as much as that famous songstress." So, "why is Jenny Lind so highly valued?" asks Carey, "because of the obstacles to be overcome before an equal voice can be reproduced."[22]

This variance in the productivity and talents of different individuals thus conditions relative reproduction costs, both real and perceived, and it likewise follows that these individual differences constitute the basis for specialization and exchange. It is for this reason that Van Buren Denslow declares that "commerce grows, not out of the unequal powers of various peoples to produce the same things, but out of their equal powers to produce different things. It is not inequality, but diversity of production, that promotes exchange."[23] Because productivity necessarily varies among different individuals, there is thus no concrete mathematical formula for setting relative prices, but there is rather a general tendency for prices to apportion themselves on the basis of relative reproduction costs as conditioned by individual variation.

National Wealth and the Paradox of Value

The reproduction cost theory of value also has important implications for national wealth. Because the theory posits that in order for something to possess exchange value there must be both resistance to be overcome, in addition to it possessing utility, this necessarily leads to the view that wealth and value are not commensurate. Instead, wealth and value tend to be inversely related to one another. As Robert Ellis Thompson explains:

> Closely connected with the term wealth is the term value. The one is the antithesis of the other. If wealth is the measure of man's power over nature, value is the measure of nature's power over man—of the resistance that she offers to his efforts to master her.[24]

In other words, if the resistance to obtaining something useful increases, this tends to diminish wealth. In the case of water, for instance, if there is great abundance and thus no resistance involved in obtaining it, then water is valueless, but the community is all the wealthier for it. Conversely, if water was to become scarce, meaning that there is now resistance to obtaining it, this results in water now commanding a price. This means that the wealth of the community has diminished. In a similar vein, it follows that a diminution of value through falling reproduction costs represents an increase of wealth, as opposed to a reduction of it. National wealth is thus generally advanced by diminishing reproduction costs of commodities, and as such, improvements in productivity and technology were thus seen as key to unlocking the wealth of nations.

This understanding also demonstrates that the American Protectionists solved the so-called "paradox of value," a discovery which predates the marginal revolution. This paradox of value is often illustrated using the example of diamonds and water, and asks why water, given its high use-value, commands a low exchange value compared to the likes of diamonds which commands high exchange value despite its lower use value. According to the reproduction cost theory of value, because water possesses maximum utility yet there is often minimal resistance to obtaining water, water will therefore possess a low exchange value despite its utility. In contrast, diamonds possess a moderate utility due to their use as ornaments, yet there is very often a high degree of resistance to be overcome when obtaining diamonds due to their scarcity and the efforts involved in their extraction. Indeed, William Elder even notes how in the "fancy case of finding a diamond on the seashore at no greater expense than the trouble of picking it up… That stray diamond is, perhaps, not overvalued by the cost of reproduction, if… [someone] were put to work to find another in the same way."[25]

It is for the same reason that the American Protectionists perceived the forces of nature as constituting a free service. Since nature provides services as a free gift, the only resistance to be overcome are efforts involved in harnessing these forces. As William D. Wilson explains, "the fundamental fact is, that these forces are *gratuitous*, they have no exchangeable value, they cost nothing; and the only cost in using them is the labor of making the tools, machinery and other apparatus necessary for their utilization and use."[26] Thus, in the case of water, costs only come into existence due to the resistance involved in tapping into sources of water and transporting the water to consumers.[27] However, as this resistance to accessing water is diminished through improved modes of obtaining water, wealth is increased by lessening the resistance involved in gaining a given amount of utility. In this case, wealth thus increases as exchange value decreases.

Thus, despite predating the marginalist explanation to the diamond–water paradox, the value tradition of the American Protectionists arguably provides a more complete solution to the paradox. Marginal analysis solves the paradox by shifting the focus to the marginal unit, but this side-steps the deeper philosophical issue at the core of the paradox. It does not contend with the fundamental question as to why water which possesses maximal utility commands a low value. Instead of explaining the apparent disconnect between market value and societal wealth, the marginalists transformed the paradox into a technical question about price formation. By demonstrating that falling prices are actually a sign of rising economic prosperity, and that value and wealth exhibit an inverse relationship, the American Protectionists contended with the paradox directly. Low prices combined with high utility are not paradoxical at all. It is instead a sign of increased wealth. It is thus a far more comprehensive solution, and one which connects with their broader views on individual versus national wealth.

Of course, the American Protectionists did not view wealth and exchange value as always at variance with one another. It was instead treated as a general or guiding principle. George Steele clarifies this position noting that:

> Value and utility are often found in the inverse ratio of each other; that is, as value increases, utility [wealth] diminishes, and vice versa. But it is not correct to say that this is always the case. If it were, infinitude of value would imply zero of utility. But, as we have seen, an object destitute of utility can have no value. Mr. Carey's description of the two is, that 'the utility of things is the measure of man's power over nature'; while value is 'the measure of nature's power over man,' or of 'the resistance which nature makes to man.' These statements, while not altogether adequate as definitions, imply profound philosophical truths.[28]

In line with this thinking, it may be added that the discovery of new uses giving utility to an object which formerly possessed none also increases wealth at the same time as increasing value in aggregate terms, which suggests that the two are not always the inverse of one another. This inverse relationship therefore holds specifically for changes in productivity and resistance, not for changes in utility *per se*. Rather, new use-values coming into existence is a mark of economic progress.

The Price of Land

The price of land, and by extension rent, represents a special case in the reproduction cost theory of value. Land was seen as unique because it possesses elements which are reproducible, such as buildings and other improvements, and elements that are not, specifically the space it occupies. Indeed, because the American Protectionists considered land to be a form of capital, and like any other form of capital, land is thus subject to the laws of diminishing reproduction costs. This is the element of land which captures buildings and improvements. In relation to houses, for example, Robert Ellis Thompson notes that:

> As nearly everything we have… keeps falling in value, through our devising better ways of getting it… the price we pay for articles is not always what it costs to produce them. If we can reproduce… them with less outlay… we will not pay more for them than they would now cost. Thus a house that has stood for a century is not worth what it cost to build it. All the materials of which it is made had to be hauled to the site by horses or oxen. The bricks in the walls were made by hand… The boards were planed by hand. The glass was made by a laborious method. All these things are done more cheaply now, mostly by machinery and steam-power. So we are willing to pay for such a house only what it would require to build another house like it, using modern tools, machinery.[29]

This capital element of land in isolation is thus priced according to the principle of what it would cost to improve, or to reconstruct such improvements, on a similar piece of land. The physical space of land, however, does not follow this same law of diminishing reproduction costs, simply because the space cannot be reproduced. The space of land can thus be viewed differently to the capital element of land. Van Buren Denslow notes, for instance, that rent in its strictest sense represents "a payment for space," as opposed to profits for the use of capital, which includes profits on capital improvements applied to land—though they still basically considered the difference between rent and profits as nominal in nature.[30]

Because the space of land cannot be reproduced, land is, as with other non-reproducible goods, priced according to its utility. The American Protectionists saw that there were several factors which influenced the final utility, and consequently, the price of land. In the first instance, for land to have utility, Man must have the means to subdue it. Indeed, similar to how use-values come into existence through economic progress more broadly, it is through the development of Man's intellectual and technological capabilities that land comes to possess utility. It is also for this reason that Henry Carey somewhat controversially reversed the Ricardian order of cultivation. In contrast to Ricardo who argued that cultivation progresses from the most to the least fertile parcel of land, Carey argued the exact opposite. Cultivation tends to proceed from the least to the most fertile. This is due to the fact that the most fertile lands are usually covered by forests and swamps which need to be cleared and drained first in order for them to be rendered useful. Man must therefore develop the requisite technical capabilities or productive powers to perform such a task.[31]

Utility in itself, however, is not sufficient to bestow a good with value. Value only comes into existence when there is resistance to be overcome. In the case of land, this resistance comes in the form of fitting it for human use. "Nature," explains Robert Ellis Thompson, "gives us the materials out of which to make it, but it is labor which gives these their value in adapting them to human use." Indeed, "there is no value in mere soil, however fertile, unless it has acquired value either through cultivation or through its situation."[32] This view is also echoed by George Steele, who notes that "land itself, in its natural relations, has no value. It is that which is done on it, or in some relation to it, which gives it value."[33] There is thus resistance involved in making the space useable, and hence this leads to the emergence of value, even if the space itself cannot be reproduced.

Robert Ellis Thompson helps to illustrate this using the example of Amazon rainforest, noting that "nobody would give a dollar for a square mile of the Amazon valley, which is the most fertile soil in the world. No doubt it will yet become the most valuable through conquest of nature's forces by labor."[34] In this case, the Amazon rainforest does not possess utility, at least with respect to its use in cultivation, even though it is potentially very useful. This potentiality will only be realized, and will thus only command a value, if man has the power to subdue it. Of course, the Amazon rainforest does render a service of great utility to mankind in the form of oxygen, but this service does not command a value, as it is a gratuitous gift of nature, and there thus no resistance involved in utilizing this free gift of nature.

Nevertheless, in addition to the rise in value that results from the resistance that has been overcome, the improvements made in adapting land for use, as well as any subsequent improvements, also adds to the utility of land. This increase in utility has the tendency to further raise the value of land. William Elder saw, for instance, that:

> [Value] is the measure of the resistance which nature opposes to our command of the things… Now land under improvement is in proportion less reluctant, and in capability richer, or worth more. Principal value, thus produced, and rent are equivalents of the labor saved to the purchaser [that is, resistance involved in rendering a similar piece of land productive]… [Higher value is] the reward of industry applied in bringing… its serviceableness to the degree attained. Enhancement of every good and valuable thing increases its utility, and therefore… [it] commands a higher price, and a higher rent.[35]

Prices and rents therefore increase as improvements are made upon land. This is on account of the resistance which would otherwise have to be overcome in improving an alternate parcel of land, but also because of the higher utility which accompanies such improvements.

There is, of course, a countervailing tendency on price, arising from the falling reproduction costs of such improvements, but in the case of land, the growth of utility typically outpaces the fall in reproduction costs, since these declining costs only apply to the capital improvements themselves, whereas the space itself is non-reproducible. This sets land apart from virtually every other kind of commodity. In every other case, diminishing reproduction costs exhibit the tendency to outpace the growth in utility. Therefore, as a "guiding principle," explains Elder, "nothing can increase in value except land and labor."[36]

The growth in utility was also seen as broader than the improvements made to the individual parcels of land. An equally important factor contributing to the price of land is the rise in utility resulting from improvements made upon properties within its vicinity. This can be viewed as a geographically bounded spillover of sorts, whereby utility-enhancing improvements to one property will increase the utility, and thus, the pricing of neighboring properties. These two elements of land price are sometimes described as the earned and unearned increment. Robert Ellis Thompson notes, for instance, that:

> That part of the value of a piece of land which is due to labor expended on itself is called the *earned increment.* It is represented by the clearing away of timber, fencing… drainage… houses… and whatever else would not be on the land except through the labor of man… All these add to the value of the land… The part of the value of a piece of land which is due to labor expended on land in its vicinity, we call the *unearned increment.*[37]

Anything that theoretically enhances utility tends to raise price. Thompson notes, for instance, that "whenever a railroad establishes a station at any point, the land near it rises at once and decidedly in value."[38] It follows from this, however, that prices tends to be "greatest where the population is most dense" on account of the utility derived from being situated within or within close proximity to larger towns and cities.[39] William D. Wilson, for instance, observes that:

> With a population increasing in density, something is done every year on the land or around it, to improve its value… giv[ing] it an increased [utility], as a means of getting a living and supplying human wants… at each successive stage, we should find it increasing in value and in price, as… more labor will have been bestowed upon it… *New [utilities arise] with increasing population…* [and] the proximity to market… The English writers are extremely unwilling to admit this doctrine of rent… We find, therefore, no occasion to regard land as constituting any exception to our rule [of value].[40]

The price of land is thus internally consistent with the broader value tradition of the American Protectionists despite it representing a special case. Land prices and land rent increasingly become a payment for the use or utility of a "productive space," and this utility is conditioned by its nearness to town and city centers. Hence, Van Buren Denslow exclaims that "Carey found rent defined [as by Ricardo] as a payment for [an] area of soil because of its fertility. He left it defined as a payment for space, because of its nearness to the societary movement," that is, because of its proximity to populated centers.[41] In other words, as George B. Dixwell puts it, "high rents in the cities appear to be a *consequence* of the fuller occupation of the population."[42]

It should be noted, however, that even though the American Protectionists sometimes used the terms earned (the result of resistance that has been overcome by the individual owner) and unearned increment (the result of utility arising from improvements external to the individual piece of land) to describe the two elements composing price, they did not believe that the State had any basis to tax the unearned increment. Even though the owner of an individual piece of land gains higher land value and receives higher rent without having earned it *per se*, the American Protectionists saw that there is no possible way, or it is at the very least extremely difficult, to differentiate between the earned and unearned since both are rooted in improvements effected by human exertion, whether by the individual owner or by society at large. In the words of Robert Ellis Thompson:

> One proposal is to tax only land-values… to take the annual value of the unearned increment… It is said that this increment owes its existence to the growth of society, and not to the labor of the land-owner, and that society has the right to take what it has created. To this proposal there are several grave objections… The task… of levying such a tax would be one of extreme difficulty. It is hard enough to assess the lump value of land… It would be vastly harder to determine how much was due to labor expended on that farm, and how much to labor expended on land in its vicinity. The attempt… would lead to social bitterness, and would be open to many abuses.[43]

Furthermore, since land is considered to be a form of capital and taxes on capital are necessarily injurious to production, it follows that the State arbitrarily deciding what is and what is not earned or unearned would constitute an unsound basis on which to base tax policy, when there are other less injurious taxes available. In addition, the price of land also serves as an important function in the coordination of population movements and the geographical distribution of industry in the American Protectionist theory of agglomeration.

Notes

1. Ricardo, *Principles,* 1.
2. Ricardo, *Principles*, 42.
3. Ricardo, *Principles*, 13–14.
4. Raymond, *Elements*, 1:56.
5. Rae, *Statements*, 168; Dorfman, *Economic Mind*, 2:795 suggests Carey adapted the theory from Rae.
6. Granted, Ricardo (*Principles,* 2) explains that "utility… is not the measure of exchangeable value, although it is absolutely essential to it." Yet, for Ricardo, this forms not part of value with him maintaining that "commodities derive their exchangeable value from… the quantity of labour." This is fundamentally different from the American Protectionist approach, since in their theory, utility is an active and dynamic component in price determination, as opposed to a binary condition that must be met for a good to possess value.
7. Thompson, *Elements,* 139.
8. Carey, *Social Science,* 1:148–149.
9. Thompson, *High Schools*, 13.
10. Thompson, *Elements*, 41.
11. Thompson, *High Schools*, 8.
12. Smith, *Manual,* 70.

13. Carey, *Manual*, 88. In contrast, Ricardo (*Principles*, 2) views the value of such goods as "determined by their scarcity alone," and not utility.
14. Hamilton, *Report on Manufactures*, 13.
15. Carey, *Social Science*, 1:178.
16. Elder, *Conversations*, 58.
17. Hayes, 'Customs Duties,' 117.
18. Carey, *Social Science*, 1:148.
19. Carey, *Manual*, 84.
20. Carey, *Manual*, 89.
21. Elder, *Conversations*, 102.
22. Carey, *Manual*, 94–95.
23. Denslow, *Principles*, 513.
24. Thompson, *Elements*, 41.
25. Elder, *Conversations*, 103.
26. Wilson, *Principles*, 80.
27. Thompson, *High Schools*, 8.
28. Steele, *Outline*, 4.
29. Thompson, *High Schools*, 13.
30. Denslow, *Principles*, 240.
31. Carey, *Past, Present, Future*, 10–15.
32. Thompson, *High Schools*, 19.
33. Steele, *Outline*, 180.
34. Thompson, *High Schools*, 19.
35. Elder, *Conversations*, 52–53.
36. Elder, *Conversations*, 58; *Questions*, 89.
37. Thompson, *High Schools*, 20.
38. Thompson, *High Schools*, 20.
39. Thompson, *High Schools*, 20.
40. Wilson, *Principles*, 98–100. 'Intrinsic value' is substituted for 'utility' in the quote for ease of exposition, as Wilson uses the terms synonymously: "utility, or intrinsic value, is the capacity to satisfy human wants" (p. 32).
41. Denslow, "American Economics," 21–22.
42. Dixwell, *Progress*, 34.
43. Thompson, *High Schools*, 68–70.

Chapter Six

THEORY OF GROWTH, DEVELOPMENT, AND ENTREPRENEURSHIP

The American Protectionists developed a theory of economic growth that fundamentally challenged the prevailing emphasis on static capital accumulation. Where Adam Smith and his followers saw savings and parsimony as the engine of progress, the American Protectionists looked to human ingenuity, invention, and entrepreneurship. Indeed, this knack for invention and technology has been likewise recognized by historian of economic thought Stephen Meardon, who observes that "American economic thinkers… believed that a distinctly American system of economics was needed. It would be a *system of ideas* spotlighting the *role of ideas* in economic development."[1]

The emphasis on human ingenuity represents a fundamental difference between the American Protectionists and other nineteenth-century schools of economic thought. Whereas most other schools of economic thought treat the technological base of society as a given, the American Protectionists sought to explain how the technological base comes into existence. The American Protectionists characterized economic activity as Man using his ingenuity to transform nature, and this connects directly with the American Protectionist conception of wealth and production. Indeed, on the question "where does wealth come from?" Thomas Brackett Reed declares that:

> It comes from the power of man to let loose and yet guide those elemental forces, the energy of which is infinite. It comes from the power of man to force the earth to give her [treasures]… To grasp the full powers of nature…. we must utilize the full power of man… both of muscle and brain, of body and of soul, in the great enterprise of setting in motion the ever gratuitous forces of nature.[2]

Wealth and production thus directly concern the interaction between Man and nature. It is through Man using his intellect and ingenuity to manipulate nature that new products and inventions come into existence. This view that economic progress is ultimately the result of Man utilizing his intellect to manipulate nature is well demonstrated in the following passage by Jacob Harris Patton:

> The Creator has constituted him [Man] lord of the earth and endowed him with mental capacity to search out the hidden treasures of nature and utilize them for his own benefit… *He inspired him with intellect*, that he might investigate the mysterious powers that are hidden in nature and by controlling them compel them to do his bidding.[3]

It would therefore be an understatement to say that the American Protectionists exhibited technological bias. Technology, invention, and entrepreneurship represent the focal point of their system of economic thought, and as will be demonstrated, the American Protectionists saw protection and technological change as intimately connected. Indeed, the American System was designed precisely to create conditions conducive to invention and the exercising of Man's ingenuity, or as Robert P. Porter explains "the American System… [has] brought into play the ingenuity and mechanical invention of the country."[4] It is thus for this reason that David Rice declared that "invention and protection march hand in hand, one and inseparable."[5]

Inventive versus Accumulative Growth

The American Protectionists were dynamic thinkers. Virtually all their writings are from the standpoint of an economy in the process of change. This can be seen most explicitly when comparing their theories of growth with that of the English Classical School. Growth, according to the Classicals, was said to be the result of the accumulation of capital, and this was seen as dependent on the level of private savings within the economy.[6] This emphasis on the static accumulation of capital is perhaps best demonstrated by the founder of Classical economics, Adam Smith:

> Whatever a person saves from his revenue, he adds to his capital, and either employs himself in maintaining an additional number of productive hands, or enables some other person to do so, by lending it to him for an interest… the capital of an individual can be increased only by what he saves from his annual revenue… Parsimony and not industry is the immediate cause of the increase in capital.[7]

In contrast, the American Protectionists viewed the level of private savings and investment as playing an important, but ultimately a subordinate and supportive role. The true cause of the wealth of nations was not savings, argued the American Protectionists, but ideas and inventions. This is perhaps best illustrated in the following passage from John Rae:

> Invention is the only power on earth that can be said to create… The ends which individuals and nations pursue, are different. The object of the one is to acquire, of the other to create…. industry and parsimony increase the capitals of individuals… [while] the wealth of all nations cannot be increased, but through the aid also of the inventive faculty.[8]

This emphasis on invention and human ingenuity was shared by virtually every American Protectionist. Even as early as Hamilton, there was a recognition "that there is, in the genius of the people… a peculiar aptitude for mechanic improvements." However, the sharpest separation between statics and dynamics in economic analysis can be found in the writings of Rae. Rae termed the static component of growth as the "accumulative," and the dynamic component as the "inventive." The static increase in capital or stock through the process of accumulation operated through what Ra termed the "accumulative principle." This accumulative principle essentially describes economic growth which operates in Classical growth theory. The more important aspect of growth, however, concerns the introduction of an invention or the augmentation of existing knowledge into new capital or products. This operates through what Rae terms as the "inventive principle."[10] It is this "faculty of invention," explains Henry M. Hoyt, "by which we [have] turned material forces into use."[11]

The conjoined operation of the accumulative and inventive principle was seen as the key to unlocking the nation's productive powers, but primacy was always placed on inventive growth in American Protectionist thought. Indeed, on a theoretical level, Rae implies that accumulation would eventually cease due to an exhaustion of investment opportunities if invention was to stall. This implies that the economy will verge toward an equilibrium or stationary state if deprived of new sources of invention. In reality, however, the American Protectionists observed that there exists a positive feedback loop between invention and accumulation. In other words, accumulation tends to promote invention and improvements via a process of learning by doing. This makes the accumulative and the inventive aspects of growth intimately connected. As Rae explains:

> The means, or instruments, [serve] to unlock the stores which the nation possesses; but it is not so easy to conceive how, or for what purpose, a general increase of these means or instruments [capital accumulation] should take place without some accompanying discovery of an improvement in their construction… We can easily conceive, that the national capital also, might accumulate in this shape, were some discovery, producing an improvement in the manufacture, to occur.[12]

This process of learning by doing is also a feature of the writings of other American Protectionists. Henry Carey, for instance, observes that:

> The great object of man… is to acquire dominion over nature, compelling her to do his work; and with every step in that direction labor becomes less severe, while its reward increases…. each successive triumph is attended by increased facility for further combinations, to be followed by new and greater triumphs.[13]

For all practical purposes, the American Protectionists saw invention and technological progress as an endless frontier that was far from being exhausted. Erastus B. Bigelow explains, for instance, that as "great as mechanical progress has heretofore been, we are still very far from its ultimate limit."[14] Jacob Harris Patton, likewise, explains how "in the storehouse of nature there may be more forces yet to be discovered and utilized in numerous ways, that are now to us incomprehensible."[15] Finally, Ezra Seaman notes that "the amount of knowledge and skill which the entire human race can acquire, accumulate, and perpetuate, may be regarded as almost boundless."[16]

The American Protectionist conception of technology therefore surpassed nineteenth-century understandings, and even those held into the modern era. Whereas Neoclassical theory typically treats technology as an exogenous factor that saves labor, the American Protectionists saw technology as an endless frontier of possibilities serving to transform matter from one state to another by which Man could obtain mastery over nature. This not only captures changes to the production process (process inventions), it also captures the introduction of new and original instruments (product inventions), or what John L. Hayes refers to as "novelties."[17] Indeed, the pioneering role of the American Protectionists on the economics of technology and invention is brought home by the fact that a member of the School even independently coined the term "endogenous growth," some 100 years prior to its usage in mainstream economics, as demonstrated by the following passage by John L. Hayes:

> All American inventions... in hardware so perfect that British manufacturers admit, in their own journals, that they cannot imitate, much less compete with us. The tools and inventions of this industry have helped the mechanics of all industrial nations. They have aided man to subdue the earth. The fruits of protection have overflowed our own borders; nationalism has become cosmopolitanism; for it is through the internal, the endogenous growth of nations that the world's progress is achieved.
>
> Let me refer to but one other illustration of endogenous growth... compelled by the restrictive policy... The existence of the textile manufacture in this country, and especially the industry of manufacturing machinery... Up to the time of [t]his advent in this country... there were substantially no machines in this country, no steam-engines, no engine-lathes, no machine tools... These early textile machine shops became the great schools of American inventions.[18]

The distinction between inventive (or endogenous) and accumulative growth made by the American Protectionists also has important implications for the issue of international trade, as it dispels the underlying assumption in Ricardian trade theory that allocative efficiency, in the static sense, is the cause of sustainable and long-term growth. Even if it is granted for the sake of argument that trade specialization promotes static allocative efficiency, these efficiency gains pale in significance to the gains made possible through invention and technological change. The American Protectionists were thus operating on a completely different framework from the Classical economists, and under this framework, protective tariffs were designed to facilitate inventive growth by giving entrepreneurs scope to engage in new pursuits—or in the words of Tench Coxe, "protecting duties *alone* can give encouragement to men of genius to pursue complex and difficult manufactures."[19]

Technological Diffusion and National Wealth

As noted in an earlier chapter, the American Protectionists acknowledged that there is a difference between private and national wealth. In a similar vein, the American Protectionists also saw that the private profitability of an invention could not be equated with the prosperity which the invention bestows upon the national economy. Since new technology is absorbed into the nation's technological base and because such technology exhibits a tendency to transfer from one industry to another in a process of technological diffusion, this necessarily means that inventions bring about permanent change to the economic structure of society. In other words, because of the diffusive nature of technology, inventions will tend to spill over and seed successive inventions. The rate of technological progress will thus tend to grow exponentially if the economy is conducive to entrepreneurship. Such thinking is well captured by Horace Greeley, who explains:

> That our people are ingenious and energetic is undoubted… [But] no great invention ever yet sprang full-armed from the brain of its author; as a general rule… nearly every machine of great value is the product of a score of successive inventions.[20]

This tendency for invention to give rise to other inventions was also well observed by Calvin Colton:

> Every new art or pursuit… almost necessarily calls into existence other new arts and pursuits, to supply its demands; and these latter, the offspring of the former, themselves become parents of other arts and pursuits, in their turn; and so on, in almost endless progression… diffusing its benefits all around.[21]

The American Protectionist thus clearly observed that inventions will tend to spill over and seed new inventions. Or as put by Peshine Smith, "every machine facilitates the construction of new ones" and "each new truth discovered is the key to a whole magazine, and each new art the parent of a thousand."[22] This observation therefore implies that in order for an economy to be innovative, it must be also be diversified. For if it is true that each new industrial pursuit propagates a thousand more, then the more varied domestic industry is, the greater the capacity for invention and the more exponential the rate of inventive growth will be.

Indeed, not only did the American Protectionists see new industries and inventions as propagating a score of others, the American Protectionists understood that new inventions will also have the tendency to spillover and reinvigorate mature and seemingly stagnant ones. As John L. Hayes explains:

> In all the manufacturing nations, and particularly in our own, a passion for invention has been developed with the new facilities for putting in practice the conceptions of inventive power. The arts succeed each other by a true generation. Idea begets idea, and the invention of to-day gives birth to the invention of to-morrow. In the genial atmosphere of invention, new industries take root in the old [industries], like epiphytes in the humid forests of the tropics.[23]

This is one of the reasons why the American Protectionists supported protected diversification, as opposed to so-called "strategic trade policies." Since it is always unclear how inventions and technological spillovers will affect seemingly stagnant industries, it follows that diversification is a far more prudent approach than targeting a specific industry in isolation.

In any event, since the initial invention and subsequent technological spillovers are a permanent benefit to society due to its diffusive character, it thus follows that these benefits can never be fully captured in the entrepreneur's private returns, as the benefits persist long after the entrepreneur's earthly existence has ceased. John Rae explains, for instance, how in "spite of every obstacle to be overcome, or pain to be endured, to task themselves to the performance of works of permanent and diffusive utility," the entrepreneur "receives now less recompense than even in ages not so able to appreciate the benefits conferred" by his invention.[24] In other words, the entrepreneur only receives a partial return for the benefits which he affords to society. Instead, the social or national wealth derived from an invention will invariably eclipse the private return to the entrepreneur. Van Buren Denslow thus argued that "all inventions and discoveries is necessarily social, and the wealth they give rise to is imperishable—albeit it is often too social in its use to be the subject of any private appropriation whatever."[25] Indeed, it is for this reason that John Rae declared that "the fruits of the labors of genius… are the property of the whole human race."[26] Or as Willard Phillips put it, "the [industrial] arts are the inspiration, no less than the trophies, of inventive genius. They are social and gregarious."[27]

It is on such grounds that the American Protectionists argued that pure *laissez-faire* conditions would generate suboptimal rates of invention. Since inventions generate immense positive externalities for the nation, it is in the national interest to skew incentives in such a way as to encourage and foster entrepreneurship. This led to the conclusion that the State had an indispensable role in encouraging the adoption and discovery of new inventions and technology. As John Rae explains:

> Before capital can increase, there must be something in which it may be embodied [i.e., inventions]… [Without invention, there] can never, by simply urging on their production, be rationally expected to be much augmented. It is invention… that may most fitly be esteemed the cause of the existence of [wealth]… It is certainly, therefore, very far from being a self-evident truth, that the legislator, by employing the resources of the country in rousing this principle to activity, necessarily retards, instead of advancing, the increase of wealth and the prosperity of the state.[28]

Indeed, to the extent that technology has a tendency toward diffusion, it does not necessarily follow that it can be easily transferred from one economy to another. The American Protectionists recognized the immense difficulties associated with establishing new technologies in a different location from their origin due to barriers to entry and geographical constraints. It was on such grounds that the American Protectionists argued that infant-industry protection was necessary for the "successive passage of the same arts from country to country."[29] This encouragement of new industrial arts was more than justifiable. Even though technological diffusion was seen to be of immense benefit in the abstract, the American Protectionists saw that the benefits arising from the diffusive nature of technology would be severely limited if the economy lacked the industrial capacity and capabilities to absorb and embody said knowledge and technology in the form of industrial production. Indeed, regarding "the diffusion of knowledge," Willard Phillips explains, that "such diffusion is of no utility if the knowledge, when diffused, is sterile and does not show itself in the arts."[30]

The American Protectionists recognized, of course, that the transfer of industry nay initially consist of what Rae referred to as "servile imitation," or simple import ubstitution.[31] In the long run, however, these new industries could surpass those of he established industrial centers due to the influence of positive feedback between ccumulation and invention. Moreover, because of the nature of learning by doing, echnological spillovers are often confined to the particular location where production akes place, which further underscores the importance of the State in creating conditions onducive to domestic production. This is well illustrated by Nathanial A. Ware:

> This habit of inquiry and freedom of thought appertains to all, even the operator and common mechanic, who have not only this vigor of intellect thus cherished, but time to think and experiment much, because his wages are good and the means of living so certain and easy that he can afford to hazard something. It is generally the common mechanic or operator who is with and near the machinery that makes or suggests improvements, and most of the valuable patents and inventions issue from such persons.[32]

s Ware notes, this means that the positive feedback between accumulation and nvention is often geographically bounded since it is generally those directly engaged in roduction who bring about improvements or apply the technology in different ways. t is thus clear that the American Protectionists understood that in order for a nation to apture and maximize these beneficial externalities, production must take place within he domestic economy. When this fact is viewed in conjunction with the need to elevate he rate of capital accumulation and invention closer to the national optimum due to the ermanent and diffusive benefits that invention affords, the importance of substituting ncome tax for tariff protection was apparent to the American Protectionists. The emoval of income tax would eliminate the forced reduction in savings that necessarily ccompanies these taxes. In doing so, this would elevate the rate of private capital ccumulation, while the imposition of protective tariffs would promote the establishment f new arts and industrial pursuits.

The Entrepreneur as Adventurer and Discoverer

losely connected with the theory of growth and development is the theory of the ntrepreneur. The entrepreneur plays a central role in American Protectionist thought. Vhereas mainstream economics typically treats the entrepreneur as either a bearer of isk or as an agent who works to bring markets back into equilibrium, the American rotectionists see the entrepreneur as essentially a discoverer and someone who dventures into new economic pursuits. Indeed, as early as 1804, Tench Coxe, sees enterprise" and "adventure" as intimately connected.[33]

Because economic progress in American Protectionist thought is marked by a reater capacity for Man to control and manipulate the forces and substances of nature r his bidding, the entrepreneurial function is characterized as a process of discovery nd experimentation with nature to obtain mastery over it. By discovering new ways of anipulating nature for man's bidding, the American Protectionists did not consider the entrepreneur as an equilibrating force, but rather as an agent who brings about economic change and diversification. Van Buren Denslow, observes, for instance, that "the enterpriser… leads forwards the industrial host into enterprises in which other dare not." It is through this process that the entrepreneur "creates all industry," and thus the entrepreneur's "title of profit-maker rests on his utility as a creator" of new industrial pursuits.[34] Thus, profits, in the true entrepreneurial sense, can be seen as the reward for invention and undertaking new pursuits. This point is again well captured by Denslow who notes that it is "only invention and enterprise, in perceiving avenues to wealth where others failed to see them," that profits come into existence. Indeed, "profits of such inventive energy or enterprise are the wages which society justly awards to the man who can teach it what is both new and valuable."[35]

This emphasis on the entrepreneurial process involving the discovery of new industrial pursuits is present throughout American Protectionist literature. John Rae for example, sees discovery as an element which sets the entrepreneur apart from the rest of the population, explaining that "men are so much given to learning, that they do not readily become discoverers. They have received so much, that they do not easily perceive the need of making additions to it, or readily turn the vigor of their thoughts in that direction."[36] And Jacob Harris Patton likewise explains that "the multiform productions of every kind and grade… are the results of the application of the several powers of nature" combined with the entrepreneur's "genius and will and perseverance in discovering the properties of these materials, and combining them to accomplish the desired purpose."[37] Finally, although referring to them as an inventor class, William Dexter Wilson also emphasizes this discovery function and connects it with the class of producers—what could be considered as a class of entrepreneurial producers:

> There is indeed another class of persons who at first sight may appear to deserve a special recognition among the creators of wealth, the inventors… agriculturists and manufacturers are often inventors and discoverers… By their discoveries and inventions they enable men to accomplish results with less time and expenditure than they could have done without such inventions and discoveries.[38]

It can thus be said that the American Protectionists had a clear conception of entrepreneurship and one which relates specifically to invention and discovery in an economic context. As is shown throughout the course of this study, this conception of the entrepreneur as discoverer has far-reaching implications for their system of economic analysis.

Indeed, one such implication of conceiving entrepreneurship as a process of industrial discovery concerns trade policy. Since the discovery of new industrial pursuits necessarily involves some degree of experimentation and risk-taking, protective tariffs are necessary to provide up-and-coming entrepreneurs with breathing room to engage in exactly this. Friedrich List explains, for instance, that "tariffs safeguard the industrial enterprises of entrepreneurs who take risks and have no means of knowing if they are going to be a success or not."[39] Moreover, since humans tend to be habitual creatures and are reluctant to change modes of enterprise, the protective function of the tariff works to skew incentive structures toward discovery and undertaking new avenues of production. This is well observed by Alexander Hamilton:

> Experience teaches, that men are often so much governed by what they are accustomed to see and practice, that the simplest and most obvious improvements, in the most ordinary occupations, are adopted with hesitation, reluctance and by slow gradations. The spontaneous transition to new pursuits, in a community long habituated to different ones, may be expected to be attended with proportionably greater difficulty.[40]

On face value, the transfer of industry through protection represents a form of imitation, as opposed to an original discovery. In practice, however, the American Protectionists saw that this has the effect of breaking the population out of old habits and awakening the spirit of enterprise. Indeed, this tendency for protection to break the population out of old habits and to arouse the entrepreneurial spirit is also noted by Nathanial A. Ware, who observes that "the labour of the country… will be benefitted by a protecting tariff" due to "the creative genius that it calls into existence, and with which it works the wonders and magic that astonish and enrich."[41] Furthermore, as John Rae notes, because different nations face different circumstances, the imitation of foreign industries is virtually always accompanied by adaptation, invention, and improvement. In the words of John Rae:

> There is no art in existence… which may not be shown to have attained perfection by continual changes from place to place, and material to material, and by encountering consequently alternate difficulties and facilities, the former developing its powers, the latter extending their field of action, and both, by helping to introduce general principles, weakening the restraining power of the tendency to servile imitation, and advancing the progress of science. This successive passage of the same arts from country to country, and from one into another, seems to be the great exciting cause of the progress of them all.[42]

John L. Hayes echoes Rae's position, viewing the process of local adaptation as essentially one of entrepreneurial discovery itself which brings forth new inventions. Indeed, Hayes goes even further than Rae, arguing that the cultivation of domestic industry is a virtual pre-requisite for adapting production to the peculiar circumstances and necessities of the local population, even seeing this process of adaptation as extending across different industries. In the words of John L. Hayes:

> To resume the main argument for the encouragement of the production… It is only by domestic production that commodities are exactly adapted to the necessities of a people… The close contact of consumer and producer in this country has given to our mechanical industry and its products this distinguishing characteristic—adaptation; we commonly call it ingenuity, but ingenuity is only a genius for adapting means to a desired end… Adaptation to American wants made the first cast-iron plough, and the thousands of improved forms which followed it; it made our seeders, reapers, mowers, harvesters, threshers, grain-elevators; in fact, the whole system of agricultural machinery substantially originated in this country [via the adaptation of the mechanical to the agricultural].[43]

Thus, even though entrepreneurship is viewed as a process of discovering new industrial pursuits, the imitation of existing pursuits tends to produce its own discoveries as production is adapted to the different circumstances peculiar to the nation, community, or the individual producer. This is in addition to the rousing of the entrepreneurial spirit which the establishment of industry tends to produce. With the above in mind, it is therefore clear that the American Protectionists conceived an entrepreneurial function which involves discovery and experimentation to harness nature and render it fit for human use. In doing so, the entrepreneur is responsible for bringing about the discovery and creation of new industrial pursuits.

Individuality, Diversification, and Entrepreneurship

Even though it is implied in the writings of the American Protectionists that it takes a particular kind of person to be an entrepreneur, it must be remembered that entrepreneurship was still viewed within the context of human individuality.[44] Recall that the American Protectionist conception of Man is predicated on the principle that no two individuals are the same, with each possessing unique talents, aptitudes, and dispositions. With respect to entrepreneurship, this naturally implies that whilst an individual may possess the characteristics to be a successful entrepreneur in a given field, it does not mean that they will be successful in any given field. This view is well illustrated by Ezra Seaman:

> The faculties of mankind are almost infinitely various, so as to adapt men to a great variety of pursuits… Some constitutions produce intellectual faculties best adapted to particular pursuits, while the different constitutions of other persons tend to adopt their intellectual faculties to very different pursuits and acquirements. The peculiarities which adapt a person to the highest degree of excellence in one field of employment, [can make him] unfit… for many others.[45]

This means that in order to maximize the entrepreneurial potential of the economy, so that more of the nation's population can move into the entrepreneurial class, industry must be varied and diversified. Giles B. Stebbins explains, for instance, that "the individual, if wise, seeks such occupation as will give scope to his genius… The nation should so shape its policy as to give scope to the varied genius of its people."[46] Indeed, this very argument was a feature of American Protectionist thought as early as the *Report on Manufactures*, with Hamilton explaining that:

> To cherish and stimulate the activity of the human mind, by multiplying the objects of enterprise, is not among the least considerable of the expedients, by which the wealth of a nation may be promoted.... Every new scene which is opened to the busy nature of man to rouse and exert itself, is the addition of a new energy to the general stock of effort. The spirit of enterprise, useful and prolific as it is, must necessarily be contracted or expanded in proportion to the simplicity or variety of the occupations and productions, which are to be found in a society.[47]

In other words, if there is a diversity of industry, this means that those with an entrepreneurial flair for a particular pursuit will have the opportunity to exercise it. It is for this reason that Thomas Brackett Reed explains that "the diversification of our industries that has stimulated inventions. Otherwise, all the inventive power of America would have run to waste."[48] Thus, in the absence of such diversity, talents will inevitably remain dormant, and this will, in turn, reduce the inventive and entrepreneurial capacity of the society.

This represents a significant point of departure from the Classical economists. Since the Classicals conceive the individual as abstract and uniform, it leaves no room for any consideration of how an individual's natural differences might impact the nation's entrepreneurial and inventive capacity. It may be perfectly reasonable therefore for Adam Smith to say that "if a foreign country can supply us with a commodity cheaper than we ourselves can make it, better buy it of them." Indeed, if everyone is essentially the same, it is only logical to source products from where they are cheapest since individuals cannot, as a matter of first principles, be locked into uncongenial pursuits and have their inventive talents laid to waste.

Yet, since the American Protectionists were perfectly aware that natural differences are ever present, they saw that buying from where is currently cheapest does not necessarily result in the most efficient outcome since inventive talents will necessarily remain dormant. Francis Bowen thus challenges Smith, arguing that:

> It is as wasteful, to say the least, to allow mechanical skill and inventive genius to remain unemployed, as it would be to permit water-power to run without turning mills… To give full scope to all the varieties of taste, genius, and temperament; to foster inventive talent; to afford adequate encouragement to all the arts, whether mechanical or those which are usually distinguished as the fine arts… these are objects which deserve at least as much attention, as the inquiry where we can purchase calicoes cheapest.[49]

The absence of economic diversification resulting from Smith's recommendation must indeed result in a reduced rate of invention and technological change. John Philip Young also affirms this point, noting how highly specialized economies, such as purely agricultural nations and regions, exhibit a diminished capacity for invention. Young thus explains "that the proportion of inventions credited to the South during the antebellum period was very small," and that "a detailed examination of the matter would show that the inventive faculty was almost dormant in those sections of the country which devoted themselves wholly to agricultural pursuits."[50]

Conversely, the American Protectionists believed that greater diversification would augment the inventive capacity of society by giving scope to inventive genius and human ingenuity. Indeed, as has been noted previously, true genius is often the product of nature, and it is likewise the case that particular kinds of genius are suited to particular fields of enterprise. It thus follows that in order to take advantage of this gift of nature, and unlock the full scope of inventive genius, talents, and ingenuity, a diversity of industry needs to be secured, which connects directly to the tariff question. Daniel

Webster illustrates this point quite succinctly by asking, "why is protection... necessary to the country?" The answer, according to Webster, is that a "variety of employments is a matter of great importance to society, for it gives scope to every degree of ingenuity."[51] In other words, tariffs, as John Philip Young explains, have the effect of "calling into play... the inventive faculties of man by diversifying industries."[52]

It is therefore clear that the American Protectionists had a systematic understanding of the relationship between Man's individuality, economic diversification, and the inventive and entrepreneurial capacity of the economy. In short, a varied and diversified economy aids entrepreneurial discovery by affording a greater range of opportunities by which different individuals can exercise their unique talents and inventive genius. This would, in turn, further augment the inventive and entrepreneurial capacity of the nation, producing an even greater degree of diversification through which the great variety of talents can be exercised.

Entrepreneurial Profit as a Migratory Force

Although the American Protectionists saw that the motivation for invention and innovation as extending well beyond the profit motive, profits were still seen as playing an important role in coordinating and maintaining invention in the economy. In fact, profits and inventions were seen as indispensable to one another. Inventions, in the first place, were seen as necessary for maintaining national savings and will thus influence the level of national investment. This relates to the fact that society's willingness to save and invest is dependent upon the expected returns or the expected profitability of investments. Without inventions, however, the return on investment would steadily diminish and capital accumulation would cease as the economy is deprived of new investment opportunities. Indeed, "it is invention," explains John Rae, "which show[s] how profitable returns can be got from [investments]." It can therefore "be esteemed the cause [of investment]."[53] Inventions, therefore, give rise to national savings by creating profitable investment opportunities. Yet, the rate of profit itself also exerts an influence on the pace and direction of invention.

Even though it has been established that entrepreneurial profit will inevitably fall short of the benefits which the invention bestows upon society, the entrepreneur is still nevertheless motivated by profit. In the words of George M. Steele:

> That a benevolent man [i.e., the inventor or entrepreneur] will delight to confer upon society every such boon of which he has been the creator... But, on the other hand, it must be evident that a majority of the inventions which aid in the multiplication of wealth involve sacrifices which would never be incurred but for the hope of reward; and that, even in the case of those who are mainly moved to their undertakings by public spirit, this hope adds a stimulus without which, in many instances, the enterprise would fail.[54]

Thus, in spite of the fact that entrepreneurs are generally motivated by factors which extend beyond the pursuit of profit, profits nonetheless represent an important motive for the entrepreneur. Because of this, entrepreneurs will tend to seek out new industrial pursuits which afford, or which they perceived will afford, higher returns. This pursuit of profit serves as a migratory force within the market system which steers resources into new industries. As more mature industries become saturated with producers, profit rates will tend to stagnate or even decline due to competitive pressures. It is this stagnation, however, which motivates the more entrepreneurial members of society to seek out and discover new sources of profit. This pursuit of new sources of profit provides an impetus to inventions and innovations. As Van Buren Denslow explains:

> All profits tend constantly toward an equality of return on past efforts, but an inequality and exorbitance of return on all new efforts which achieve a larger measure of satisfaction to human desires from a smaller expenditure of effort. Hence profits are the migratory or steering principle in industry, whose guidance, rent, interest, and wages all await and follow. Profits impel to the great inventions, discoveries, innovations, economies, improvements.[55]

This also has important implications for the long-run trajectory of capitalism. Throughout the history of economic thought, the belief has persisted that there exists a general tendency in capitalism for the rate of profit to fall. The American Protectionists held that no such tendency exists. What Classicals, Marxists, and later Neoclassicals mistook as a falling general rate of profit simply reflects the stagnation of specific industries. The Protectionists did not deny that a stagnation or decline in profits could occur, but if the economy is continually diversifying itself with the emergence of new and profitable industries, there is no general tendency for profits to fall. In fact, a falling rate of profit represents an endogenous and migratory force within the capitalist system which compels entrepreneurs to seek out new inventions and industrial pursuits. In the words of Van Buren Denslow:

> A good deal of effort has been expended to prove what Mr. [John Stuart] Mill calls "the tendency of profits [to fall] to a minimum"... As [this] relates to each particular enterprise in which profits are won, this is more than true, indeed, [but] it is inadequate to the truth. Profits may be said to begin at unlimited figures, and to recede rapidly until... they totally disappear. Each particular mode of investment of capital invites a competition from others, [and] a rise [in] wages, rent, and interest, until these swallow up all the returns [profits].
>
> *If this were not so, profit would not be the migratory force which pioneers the way to new fields, processes, and modes.* But when this doctrine... is stated as a "tendency for profits to fall as society advances"... it is a palpable absurdity.... All observation indicates that as large profits are arising in the new industries [, the same] as [when] the old gave rise to [large profits] when they were new, or, to use the old adage, there are "always as good fish left in the sea as ever were caught out."[56]

Thus, rather than capitalist production grinding to a halt through an exhaustion of investment opportunities, capitalist production perpetually reinvigorates and diversifies itself through the actions of the entrepreneurial class of producers with their actions being guided, at least to some degree, by the pursuit of profit. This contrasts with the standard view that profits represent a signal to the entrepreneur to move the economy back into equilibrium. In the first place, high profits are a signal to entrepreneurs to move resources out of equilibrium and into newly established modes of production, but equally important is how the falling rate of profit in stagnating industries sends a signal to the entrepreneur to seek out and discover new inventions, innovations, and industrial pursuits.[57]

Notes

1. Meardon, "Yankee *Ingenuity*," 42.
2. Reed, *The Tariff*, [1888] 7.
3. Patton, *Political Economy*, 17.
4. Porter, *Protection*, 28.
5. Rice, *Philosophy*, 68, 176.
6. Whilst John Stuart Mill acknowledges the role of invention, this insight was borrowed from Rae, and is certainly less of a feature in Mill's thought, see O'Brien, *Classical Economists*, 265
7. Smith, *Wealth of Nations*, 409–410.
8. Rae, *Statement*, 15.
9. Hamilton, *Report on Manufactures*, 11.
10. Rae, *Statement*, 321–322.
11. Hoyt, *Protection*, 411.
12. Rae, *Statement*, 19–21.
13. Carey, *Manual*, 87.
14. Bigelow, "Labor and Capital," 479.
15. Patton, *Political Economy*, 35.
16. Seaman, "Human Progress," 410.
17. Hayes, *Woollen Tariff*, 11.
18. Hayes, "Nationalistic and Cosmopolitan," 150.
19. Coxe, *Memorial*, ix.
20. Greeley, *Essays*, 48.
21. Colton, *Public Economy*, 405–406.
22. Smith, *Manual*, 74.
23. Hayes, 'Solidarity,' 136.
24. Rae, *Statement*, 211, 216.
25. Denslow, *Principles*, 72.
26. Rae, *Statement*, 22.
27. Phillips, *Propositions*, 226.
28. Rae, *Statement*, 31.
29. Rae, *Statement*, 253.
30. Phillips, *Propositions*, 42.
31. Rae, *Statement*, 365.
32. Ware, *Notes*, 41.
33. Coxe, *Essay*, 32.
34. Denslow, *Principles*, 186–188.
35. Denslow, *Principles*, 627.
36. Rae, *Statement*, 222–223.
37. Patton, *Political Economy*, 35.
38. Wilson, *Principles*, 71.
39. List, *Natural System*, 105.
40. Hamilton, *Report on Manufactures*, 16.
41. Ware, *Notes*, 134.
42. Rae, *Statement*, 253.

43. Hayes, "Customs Duties," 13.
44. See Frith, "Protectionist Thought," 179f.
45. Seaman, "Human Progress," 410.
46. Stebbins, *Manual*, 13.
47. Hamilton, *Report on Manufactures*, 12.
48. Reed, *On the Tariff*, [1896] 19.
49. Bowen, *American Economy*, 494–495.
50. Young, *Protection and Progress*, 202.
51. Webster, "Andover," 242.
52. Young, *Protection*, 112.
53. Rae, *Statement*, 31.
54. Steele, *Rudimentary Economics*, 180.
55. Denslow, *Principles*, 294.
56. Denslow, *Principles*, 194–195.
57. For a more detailed discussion, see Frith, "Denslow."

Chapter Seven

THEORY OF DISTRIBUTION AND SOCIAL MOBILITY

Although the American Protectionists concerned themselves primarily with production, they also made significant and original contributions to the domain of distribution. In doing so, the American Protectionists would assume a pioneering role in developing a productivity theory of distribution. This emphasis on productivity then went on to shape their distinctive approach to social mobility, and this emphasis on social mobility represents a sharp break with the Classical and Marxist schools. Against the Classical and Marxist tendency of treating the class structure as seemingly fixed and monolithic, the American Protectionists emphasized the importance of social mobility in allowing workers to become capitalists themselves. Indeed, to the extent that the American Protectionists concerned themselves with distribution, they understood that social mobility was a far more important factor for promoting national prosperity. Thus, rather than stoking class antagonism, the American Protectionists saw capitalists as a role model that workers could and should aspire toward. In this sense, they fundamentally conceived society as consisting of individuals building an economic surplus together, as opposed to classes in conflict over a given amount of economic surplus.

A Harmony of Interests

On the question of distribution, the American Protectionists developed one of the earliest and most systematic explanations for how industrial development culminates in class harmony. Their system of distribution can be seen as the antithesis of that put forth by Ricardo, Malthus, and Marx. Whereas Ricardo and Malthus portrayed class relations as antagonistic, and Marx portrayed them as exploitative, American Protectionists viewed class relations as fundamentally harmonious and mutually beneficial. This position is best put by Robert Ellis Thompson, who explains that:

> Labor and capital in conflict are in an unnatural state; harmony is their true relation… Capital finds its account in the cheerful service of labor, not in its discontent. To labor, capital is a benefactor in the highest sense; were the whole class of capitalists with all their accumulations to be annihilated, labor would be reduced to indigence and a struggle for existence more severe than can easily be conceived.[1]

In emphasizing this harmony of interests, the American Protectionists rejected what is known as the "Ricardian surplus principle" and the "iron-law of subsistence wages" developed by the English Classical School—both concepts that would be later incorporated into Marxist economics. According to the so-called Ricardian surplus principle, the profits of capitalists and wages of laborers are both paid out of the residue surplus leftover after rents are paid to the landlord, with the implication that profits and wages will vary inversely with one another.[2] Ricardo, for instance, asserts that "in proportion as less is appropriated for wages, more will be appropriated for profits, and *vice versa*" and "there can be no rise in the value of labour without a fall of profits."[3] The interests of capitalists and laborers are thus necessarily opposed in the Ricardian model. Higher wages would only serve to exhaust the surplus, thereby reducing the profits received by the capitalist, and similarly, a rise in profits will necessarily reduce the wages paid to workers. The American Protectionists mockingly rebranded this doctrine as the "see-saw theory of wages."[4]

In contrast to the zero-sum implications of the Ricardian surplus principle, the American Protectionists viewed wage determination as a dynamic and positive-sum game between labor and capital. Their emphasis was on labor and capital working together in the creation of wealth from which they would both benefit, as opposed to fighting over the distribution of a given amount of wealth. This positive-sum thinking is even implicit as early as the writings of Alexander Hamilton, which states that "so far as the dearness of labor [or high-wages] may be a consequence of the greatness of profits in any branch of business, it is no obstacle to its success."[5] The American Protectionists thus considered the interests of capital and labor as fundamentally aligned. As Henry Carey explains:

> The interests of the capitalist and the labourer are thus in perfect harmony with each other, as each derives advantage from every measure that tends to facilitate the growth of capital, and to render labour productive, while every measure that tends to produce the opposite effect is injurious to both.[6]

The second pillar of the Classical-Marxist theory of wages is the iron-law of subsistence. This law posits that wages are fixed at the level of subsistence, or, in the words of Ricardo, "the natural price of labour is that price necessary to enable labourers… to subsist and to perpetuate their race."[7] In renouncing the subsistence theory of wages, the American Protectionists would develop a theory of wage determination predicated on productivity growth. The American Protectionists argued that productivity growth and technological change meant that society could escape the misery and class antagonisms which the English Classical School prophesied to be the economic destiny of mankind. Man's destiny was instead one of growing prosperity and harmony. The iron-law of subsistence wages also relates another important difference between the Classical-Marxist position and that of the American Protectionists. Unlike the Classicals and Marxists, the American Protectionists rejected the view that there exists a natural rate of wages which is fixed and uniform. Wage rates are instead varied across the economy with rates being at least as numerous as employments are diversified. Peshine Smith thus sneered at the suggestion of a uniform rate of wages, noting that "the economists of the shop-keeper [Classical] school think there is what they call a *natural* rate of wages…

The writers who adopt this view of 'natural wages' are constrained by their instinctive ense of justice to try to reconcile the diversity of wages."[8]

Finally, in any discussion of the harmony of interests, it would be remiss not to nention the importance of that other original factor of production: nature. It should e recalled from earlier that nature represents a free gift. Thus, even before profits and vages are divided between the capitalist and the worker, the process of distribution neans that both will receive an unearned return from nature. Indeed, it is precisely ecause nature is a free gift that economic activity represents a positive-sum game or both workers and capitalists. Since the American Protectionists fundamentally onceived of distribution as mutually beneficial to both, this should caution against he standard caricature that protectionism means zero-sum thinking. In fact, it was he English Classical School, not the American Protectionists, who were more often teeped in zero-sum thinking, despite being heralded as refuting the mercantilists on his basis. In any event, it is clear that American Protectionists conceived of harmony f interests between workers and capitalists, and in line with this harmony of interests, he American Protectionists expounded a theory of wages whereby wages would pproximate the growth in productivity.

Theory of Wages

n the nineteenth century, a major contention between the Classical economists and he American Protectionists was the cause of high American wages relative to those of urope. The English and American Classicals asserted that high American wages were ue to a limited population and an abundance of unsettled land in the west, and this orestalled the onset of diminishing returns and subsistence wages, as prophesized by Aalthus and Ricardo. For pragmatic reasons, early American Protectionists, such as Iamilton, Clay, and Mathew Carey, tended to downplay the height of American wages. Iigh wages meant that labor was dear, and it was alleged that this would be an obstacle o the development of manufactures. Yet, progressing further into the nineteenth entury, the American Protectionists saw that wages were not universally high across he United States, but were concentrated primarily within the more industrial and ensely populated Northeast. Wages could thus not be the result of a relative scarceness f labor and the relative abundance of land, but was seemingly somehow connected vith the level of industrialization. With this view in mind, the American Protectionists roceeded to develop a theory of wages centered on industrial progress and productivity rowth.

Whilst the American Protectionists' theory of wage determination revolves around roductivity, the American Protectionists did not endorse a theory of wages based n "marginal productivity." Unlike the traditional marginal productivity theories of istribution whereby wages are determined by the exact marginal amount which a factor ontributes to total output, and is arrived at in a monocausal manner, the American rotectionist writers characterized wages as loosely approximating productivity through ne convergence of multiple different mechanisms. Wage determination is thus seen s a multi-causal, yet mutually reinforcing, process by which wages move in tandem with productivity growth over the long run. Although perhaps more critical than other members of the School on the issue of wage determination within certain employments in a firm, Horace Greeley provides a good example of this thinking:

> While I hold Wages in general the fair equivalent of the services [of labor]… I see clearly that they are at best a rude approximation… in their application to individual cases. Here are one hundred employees in a shop or factory, each working for an established and uniform rate of weekly or monthly pay. But their work is not of uniform value… One is a skilful, thoroughly instructed craftsman, who… turns out none but the best products; another comes to work late and irregularly, wastes time in every way, can barely pass muster as an artisan, and his handiwork narrowly escapes condemnation. These men's services are not of equal value, and probably never will be… [but] their remuneration is equal.[9]

Even though the remuneration of the individual worker or capitalist does not reflect their respective marginal productivity in a precise manner, they still broadly share in the overall profitability and productivity of the firm or industry. Afterall, both the capitalist and laborer are joint producers of wealth, so both share in the exploits accompanying productivity growth. What is also inherent in this thinking is the view that more productive firms and industries, and even nations as a whole, will thus tend to experience higher wages.

The American Protectionists highlighted four mechanisms which tend to increase real wages over the long run, and all of which were in some way connected with productivity. The first mechanism emerged as a logical extension of Henry Carey's reproduction cost theory of value. According to the reproduction cost theory of value as productivity rises, the cost of reproduction diminishes. When this law is applied to the production of capital goods, this means that rising productivity must also reduce the reproduction costs of capital goods themselves, as it would for any other commodity. This renders capital goods less expensive relative to labor. As capital goods become less expensive, it follows that more capital can be combined with labor, and this renders labor increasingly productive. As a result, the capitalist can provide laborers with higher compensation for their superior productivity. In the words of Henry Carey:

> The quantity of labor required for *reproducing* existing capital, and further extending the quantity of capital, diminishing with every stage of progress. Past accumulations tend steadily to decline in value—labor rising not less steadily when compared to them [capital goods]…
>
> Both [the capitalist and laborer] thus profit greatly by the improvements which have been effected. With every further movement in the same direction, the same results continue be obtained—the proportion of the laborer increasing with every increase in productiveness of effort.[10]

Likewise, Carey points out that in the process of reproducing capital goods, incremental improvements or innovations are also incorporated into the newly reproduced goods further enhancing productivity at every step.

The relative remuneration of capital and labor does, of course, depend on the particular employment relationship. If the laborer operates as an independent contractor, who assumes the role of the entrepreneur and hires out capital goods, then the laborer is assured to benefit from the reduction in the price of capital goods. If the laborer is employed by the capitalist then the degree to which he benefits is more complicated, but the capacity for higher remuneration still necessarily increases. As William Elder explains:

> The laborer must receive his share, or wages, out of the product to which he contributes. That share depends upon the quantity of such product. The larger this is, the greater the fund on which he draws. When he hires the capital, his share is the residuum after paying the capitalist his interest, or profit… This is certain when the laborer is his own employer; and his profit is found in the enhanced productiveness of his labor due to the aid of capital. When the capitalist hires the labor, which is the more general state of the case, a like equitable division of profits is *possible*, or in other words the fund is created for such equitable dividend, and it is made possible for him to receive the due advantage of his cooperation in the enlarged yield of his industry.[11]

The American Protectionists identified several other mechanisms, however, that would compel and incentivize the capitalist within the individual firm to remunerate labor for this increase in productivity. Yet, even in the absence of these additional mechanisms, the general decline in reproduction costs for both consumer and capital goods means that the purchasing power of existing wages will have a tendency to increase with economic progress, and this operates regardless of whether the individual workers receives higher remuneration from their capitalists. In other words, productivity growth has the effect of increasing wages in real terms since the reduction in reproduction costs means a lower price of commodities relative to existing wages. Or as William Elder explains, "the increase of accumulated capital… lessens the value in labor of products already existing and brings them more easily within the purchasing power of present labor." [12]

The second mechanism which produces higher real wages concerns the accumulation of intellectual capital by the worker. Virtually all American Protectionists had some conception "that wages," as Henry Carey observes, "are the reward of human labour [and] of the exertion of skill or talent."[13] Capitalists would thus be willing to pay more for workers possessing a higher degree of intellect and skill in exactly the same manner as they would pay a higher price for more productive capital. This likewise means that employments that require comparatively higher skill will tend to yield comparatively higher wage. This can be seen in the following statement by Horace Greeley concerning industrial and agricultural wages:

> Manufactures requiring greater intelligence, rarer skill, more delicate manipulation, than Agriculture, it is inevitable that the recompense of Labor therein should be proportionally higher. Even though an equality should be maintained in the lowest grades of service, the comparative value of skill, experience, ability, is far greater in Manufactures, and must be paid for accordingly.[14]

In addition to the above, the accumulation of skill and intellect also means that workers possess a greater bargaining position in the negotiation of employment contracts on account of their superior productivity. Jacob Harris Patton explains, for instance, that intelligent labor "stand on a plane of political equality with their employers, and their intelligence, when connected with integrity of purpose and self-respect, gives them influence."[15] Indeed, it should be recalled from earlier that Calvin Colton went so far as to declare that skilled workers are masters over capitalists.

The third mechanism concerns the introduction of labor-saving machines. The importance of labor-saving machinery represents a key feature of the wage doctrine of American Protectionists extending all the way back to Alexander Hamilton. Although Hamilton never developed a systematic theory of wages, his writings imply that the introduction of labor-saving machines would lessen wage costs as a concern for domestic manufacturers. As the productivity of labor becomes amplified by the introduction of labor-saving machines, this would make industry better able to accommodate higher wages. Hamilton saw, for instance, that labor cost in per unit terms "is diminished in proportion to use which can be made of machinery." Indeed, "MECHANIC POWER introduced… [and] performing half the necessary labor, leaves only half to be done by hand." Thus, "it is evident that…the cost of fabrication of the article in question… as far is it is connected with the price of labor, will be reduced from ten to five, in consequence of the introduction of that power."[16] This logic was later echoed and elaborated upon by Henry Clay, who explains that:

> The argument [that high wages makes industry unviable] assumes, that natural labor is the principal element in the business of manufacture. This [is an] ancient theory… valuable inventions and vast improvements in machinery, which have been made within a few past years, have produced a new era in the arts. The effect of this change in the power of production… [means that] we must no longer limit our views to… the price of wages… Capital, ingenuity in the construction and adroitness in the use of machinery, and the possession of raw materials, are those which deserve the greatest consideration… The state of our population is peculiarly favorable to the most extensive introduction of machinery. We have no prejudices to combat, no persons to drive out of employment.[17]

There are several elements involved in this labor-saving mechanism of wage growth. In the first instance, the introduction of labor-saving machines will enhance productivity and, as implied above, this will tend to improve wage rates, or at the very least, would make higher wages increasingly viable for the firm or industry in question. This introduction of labor-saving machines was also seen as working in combination with the accumulation of intellectual capital, with the two amplifying the effect of each other. As Van Buren Denslow observes:

> The introduction of labor saving machinery has some tendency to enhance wages… wherever extraordinary rates of profit are being made [from labor-saving machinery], there capital will forego a part of its profits in the form of increased wages, in order to increase its output rapidly and to "make hay while the sun shines."… As the successful working on new forms of machinery nearly always involves some degree of skill, it is often better economy to enlarge

> the wages of those who have some degree of skill than to take on new and unskilled hands. Probably every labor-saving invention has witnessed the increase of wages to labor, through the increased profits to capital obtained by saving labor-cost in the production of commodities.[18]

Indeed, high wages and the introduction of labor-saving machines were even seen to produce a compounding effect through positive feedback. In other words, the American Protectionists observed that high wages themselves tended to spur the introduction of labor-saving machines since capitalists would be incentivized to substitute labor with machinery. John Philip Young explains, for instance, that the "extraordinary development of labor-saving inventions in the United States is probably largely due to the great cost of American labor… In a country where wages are low the incentive to resort to labor-saving devices is never very strong and their use is always resisted, passively or actively."[19] Thomas Brackett Reed makes a similar observation, explaining that "on account of higher wages, there are greater inducements to substitute labor-saving devices for costly labor."[20] The substitution of labor with machines means that wages can be further advanced through an increase in productivity, which in turn, would promote further substitution of labor for capital.

The American Protectionists also saw that this capital-substitution effect would have an additional, but equally powerful effect on national wage rates. The introduction of labor-saving machines would result in the outright elimination of unskilled and hence low-wage employment. In the long-run, this has the effect of raising the national wage rate. This is best explained in the following passage by Robert Ellis Thompson:

> Furthermore, machinery supersedes muscle but not brains, force but not intelligence. It drives men from low-priced, mechanical work, to employments that demand a higher capacity and command higher pay. Increasing the productiveness of labor, it increases also the workman's share of its results. And this share is not to be conceived as lying idle in the hands of those that earn it. It is again expended in employing other workmen by purchasing necessaries and comforts.[21]

Whilst labor-saving machinery could conceivably result in transitory disruptions in economic activity in certain instances, as will be elaborated upon later, the general effect in the long run would be to create more employment and raise the national wage rate by expanding productive capacity. It is for this reason that Erastus B. Bigelow rejected the term 'labor-saving machines' all together, arguing that "the advance in wages which has taken place concurrently with the increasing use of labor-aiding machinery is conclusive proof that such machinery, in the long run, increases rather than diminishes the demand for labor" and "hence the term 'labor-saving' as applied to inventions is a misnomer."[22] In due course, labor-saving machines would raise wages within the firm by raising productivity, but also the general rate of wages nationally by eliminating low-wage employment.

The fourth mechanism involves the capitalist raising wages in order to render labor more productive. This was seen as working independently of the productivity gains bestowed by capital investment. The American Protectionists maintained that in order to have a productive work force, laborers require wages and living standards far above the subsistence levels assumed by Malthus and Ricardo. High wages are necessary to keep workers in optimal health and properly nourished, but most importantly well trained and educated. As Henry Carey explains:

> The higher degree of intellect applied to the work of production, the larger will be the return to labour, and the more rapid will be the accumulation of capital… The colonial [free trade] system looks to low wages, necessarily followed by an inability to devote time to intellectual improvement. Protection looks to the high wages that enable the labourer to improve his mind… To increase the productiveness of labour, education is necessary. Protection tends to the diffusion of education, and the elevation of the condition of the labourer… To raise the intellectual standard of man… our object can be accomplished only by raising the value [i.e., wages] of man.[23]

This also connects to the important issue of international trade. Protectionists maintained that highly remunerated labor, with their superior productivity, would be able to undercut and outproduce cheaper foreign labor. In the words of Peshine Smith:

> The American System rests upon the belief that in order to make labor cheap [for the capitalist], the laborer must be well fed, well clothed, well lodged, well instructed, not only in the details of his handicraft, but in all general knowledge that can in any way be made subsidiary to it. All these cost money to the employer and repay it with interest… In raising up a body of such labourers… they can … [produce] to the last degree of manufacture, more cheaply than it has ever yet been done elsewhere.[24]

This fourth mechanism highlights that nominal wage costs in isolation mean little to the capitalist. What matters is the relation between compensation and productivity. If higher wages lead to productivity growth which more than offsets the cost of the higher wages, then capitalists will find it in their own interest to provide higher remuneration for their workers as a form of capital investment.

However, the implication that productive high-wage labor can outcompete foreign low-wage labor, should not imply that the American Protectionists supported flooding foreign markets with cheap commodities to drive out foreign producers and foreign workers. Rather, it means that the home-market can be secured by domestic producers for domestic producers by outcompeting foreign imports. Horace Greeley captures this view, declaring that:

> The true and ultimate relation of the Laboring Class of one country to that of another—is not that of underworking rivals, seeking to take the bread from the mouths of each other's children… If it were practicable… through invention, machinery, the aggregation of capital, talent, experience, and skill, for the artisans of my country to undersell and run out the artisans of all other countries, so that all manufactures should be gradually transferred to and thenceforth prosecuted only on our soil, I would not speak the word that would insure such transfer.[25]

Even aside from improving nutrition, health, and education, there was another important effect of capitalists voluntarily raising wages. By raising wages, this would elp motivate workers, and would align their interests more closely with that of the apitalist, thereby fostering greater harmony. As Giles B. Stebbins remarks:

> [High] wages as give possibility for comfort and taste, for accumulation, education, and the hope of a larger life, tend to good feeling and to harmony and equality of rights and condition. The fairly paid artisan or laborer feels less a slave and more a co-operative helper of the employer, with common hopes and interests. He is a man and not a human machine.... [A] reduction of wages in this country... is far from desirable, and is not wished for by a large majority of employers. They know and feel that the conditions of trade and production which enable them to pay our present rates are better for all.[26]

)f course, the American Protectionists did not view this as an iron-law of wages that nvariably leads every capitalist to increase wages endlessly, and they acknowledged hat there were clearly limits to the logic. However, if it is in the interest of the capitalist or workers to be more highly remunerated through the mechanisms highlighted bove, then there is an underlying economic incentive for them to do so. Robert Ellis Thompson thus explains that "against the English School generally," the American 'rotectionists "showed that [their] doctrine... is a delusion resting on no facts; that here is no natural necessary rate of wages, while there are necessary upper and lower imits to the rise and fall of wages... the employer finds his interests promoted by high vages more than low."[27]

It should finally be noted that these four mechanisms—(1) the declining reproduction osts of capital goods, (2) the accumulation of intellectual capital and skill, (3) the ntroduction of labor-saving machinery, and (4) capitalists being incentivized to raise vages for productivity gains—operate not in isolation, but in a mutually reinforcing vay to sustain wage growth over the long run. Indeed, because labor-saving machines xperience declining reproduction costs, improvements in productivity (and hence real vages) tend to be cumulative. Thus, when labor-saving machines are first introduced, hey command a high price due to the high initial cost of production, but as production xpands and becomes more efficient, the reproduction cost of such machines gradually iminishes. This means that more machines can be added to production, and because hese machines themselves improve productivity, this further reduces the reproduction osts of goods over time. The increased capital accumulation thereby improves vorkplace wages through enhanced productivity, meanwhile the lower reproduction osts raise real aggregate wages by improving purchasing power. Capitalists are also ncentivized to raise wages since doing so improves worker productivity through better utrition, education, and motivation. Both effects thus give workers greater capacity o invest in their own education and skills, rendering their labor more productive. The ise in wages also spurs the substitution of expensive labor with increasingly affordable nachinery, further accelerating productivity growth and capital accumulation.

The American Protectionists thus developed a productivity theory of wage, but ne which sees wages as approximating productivity, rather than a precise marginal roductivity theory. Indeed, the American Protectionists recognized that because capital nd labor are joint producers, their contributions cannot be precisely disentangled, which is a problem modern economics continues to grapple with. Perhaps the closest answer was that given by Henry Carey. Carey argues that whilst capital and labor would both benefit in absolute terms, labor's share of industrial income would increasingly grow relative to capital. That said, unlike many other Protectionists, Carey defines capitalist profits (as opposed to entrepreneurial profit) very narrowly as that "paid for *the aid of things*" and wages as that paid "for *the services of men*."[28] However, since most capitalists combine the roles of capital provider and manager, this definitional precision does not resolve the practical question of distribution, since managerial tasks, let alone entrepreneurial premium for discovery, are treated by Carey as a form of labor. Yet, when the capitalist is viewed in the conventional sense, as embodying both roles, the precise breakdown between returns to capital and returns to labor remains indeterminate.

Whilst the general tendency is for wages to rise over time with productivity growth the American Protectionists acknowledged that determining the exact distribution at any given moment is marred with difficulties. The exact distribution would be influenced, for instance, by institutional factors, bargaining power, and fluctuations in the profitability of the enterprise. In the latter case, even though the general trajectory was one of wage growth over time, the relative distribution was seen as oscillating between the capitalist and laborers depending on business conditions. Part of this also relates to the issue of risk, uncertainty, and potential losses on the side of the capitalist which makes it virtually impossible to determine relative sacrifice, and thus relative contribution. In the words of Van Buren Denslow:

> It is not clear, however, yet in what definite relation profit-making stands to wages-earning… For profit-making includes also loss-incurring, and the means of estimating the totality of losses, incurred by the profit makers, are very defective.[29]

Because of this, many American Protectionists saw that the process of distribution was necessarily disjointed. Whereas the capitalist typically advances the laborer's wage before final distribution occurs, the return to the capitalist is always uncertain until the production and final sale of commodities have taken place. In this sense, workers who receive a fixed wage will benefit from having forgone the risks and uncertainty involved and are thus shielded against possibility of losses. The American Protectionist therefore cautioned against attributing instances of high profits relative to wages to exploitation. As Jacob Harris Patton explains:

> In relation to their respective incomes the employed may be inclined to ignore some of the most influential items in enumerating the conditions under which the dividends of the employer are obtained. The latter include the salary of the owner; the interest on his money invested (the result of former labor); the risks that he runs… and the uncertain conditions of the market—all these unknown quantities must be met and provided for before he can draw his dividends. On the other hand, the workman has something sure in his wages… without the responsibility of the management, or the contingency of financial failure that might involve him in debt and blight his prospects for life. Under such conditions, is not the workman remunerated in proportion to the value of his capital fully as much as the employer?[30]

Yet, ultimately, for the American Protectionists, the relative distribution of a fixed amount between capital and labor represents a secondary concern. What matters is that labor and capital both advance through ingenuity and the mastery of nature. In other words, there was no class struggle, but only labor and capital struggling for mastery over nature.

Theory of Social Mobility

As much as the American Protectionists were champions of high wages, it must be said that for them, the far more important feature of capitalist development was the expansion in the opportunities for workers to climb the social ladder and become capitalists themselves. In fact, one of the reasons higher wages were applauded by the American Protectionists was because it helped to facilitate workers becoming capitalists. This theory of social or class mobility represents the centerpiece of their theory of distribution, and this feature distinguishes the American Protectionists from other nineteenth century schools of economics, which tended to view class structures as highly rigid. The view that workers have the capacity to transcend their class designation is well put by Jacob Harris Patton:

> [T]he original workman, who in the course of time, by being industrious, temperate and economical, [is] enabled to invest in such manner that he himself [becomes] a capitalist and an employer. The path to success was open to him, and a similar one is now open to the workman whom he employs. In the divine arrangement, each one has his chance... In the end such principles of integrity may lead them to positions even higher than the one to which he himself aspired.[31]

The first element of this theory of social mobility relates to the issue of reproduction costs. Similar to that described in their theory of wages, the American Protectionists saw that there exists a general tendency in capitalist production for prices to diminish over time, and they also saw this tendency as extending to the production of capital goods. The second element of the theory relates the tendency for wages to rise with productivity growth. Because of this dual tendency for the reproduction costs of capital goods to decline and for wages to rise, the American Protectionists saw that the capacity for laborers to acquire capital goods would gradually and persistently improve over time. The third element concerns the capacity for laborers to acquire and accumulate intellectual capital. This was seen as the outgrowth of high wages, which allows workers to invest in their education, in addition to the skills and knowledge acquired in their respective employments. Within industrial capitalism, therefore, there is a gradual expansion in the capacity for laborers to become capitalists themselves. As Henry Carey explains:

> It is evidence that the labors of the present are becoming daily more productive—that the value of all commodities, as measured by labor, is steadily declining—[and] that the [wages of the] laborer is rising... with constantly increasing facility for becoming himself a capitalist.[32]

The third element mentioned above, namely the expanding capacity for workers to accumulate intellectual capital, should also not be understated. Since discovery and invention was seen as vital to entrepreneurship, if workers desired to become an entrepreneur, in the capacity as a capitalist, intellect and skill is required. President William McKinley explains, for instance, that:

> We must have more concern for the man, for his welfare, his improvement and development, [and] the enlargement of his opportunities… These conditions will ultimately secure cheaper commodities, not through harsh and unnatural exactions placed upon labor, but through that skill and craft and invention which are the sure outcome of intelligent, thoughtful, independent, and well paid labor. The mind will not invent, will not discover, new and better and more economical processes and methods of production, if the body is used as a mere "creature of burden."…
>
> It must be conceded that the protective system has accomplished much in this direction [of improving the condition of labor]; certainly more than any other system… It has opened to him every gateway to opportunity. We observe its triumphs on every hand: we see the mechanic become the manufacturer, the workman [become] the proprietor, the employee [become] the employer. It does not stifle, but it encourages, manly effort and endeavor.[33]

Virtually all American Protectionists were of the view that social mobility improved with capitalist development, but there were differing views as to the extent. Their theory, after all, emphasizes a growing tendency towards greater social mobility, but it was not seen as a fixed rule. Even though there is an expansion in the opportunities to become a capitalist, this does not imply that everyone has equal ability or capacity to seize such opportunities. Because Man is defined by his individuality, this necessarily implies that certain individuals tend to make better capitalists or possess a unique flare for entrepreneurialism—although there was not always agreement on exactly what these qualities were.

Indeed, even before this theory of social mobility became firmly established, Hamilton cautioned against "dispositions… attracted by the mere novelty of an undertaking. [as] these [individuals] are not always those best calculated to give it success." Hamilton stressed instead "that the confidence of cautious, sagacious capitalists… should be excited."[34] Ezra Seaman, in contrast, emphasized the risk-seeking entrepreneur, which in some ways anticipates Schumpeter's conception of the entrepreneur. In the words of Seaman:

> Their minds are more full of schemes, and projects often ill digested; and they have more enterprise, but less stability of character, as a general rule… They are more daring and hazardous, but less safe; and their operations frequently partake of the character of gambling speculations. But even their wildest visions, such as the constant search of mechanics after principles upon which to construct a perpetual motion, have often resulted in the discovery of mechanical principles which have been of the greatest value to mankind.[35]

Nevertheless, there was a recognition among most members of the School that it took a certain character to become a successful capitalist or entrepreneur. It is perhaps for this reason that Hamilton argued that "inequality would exist as long as liberty existed, and that it would unavoidably result from that very liberty itself."[36] The idea that not everyone possesses the capacity to become a capitalist was also expressed by Erastus B. Bigelow, who explains that "the number of persons possessing [the] organizing and administrative faculty [to run a business] is comparatively small; hence a large amount of human effort is wasted by misdirection, and failures are nearly as numerous as successes."[37]

Perhaps the most optimistic position on social mobility was expounded by Horace Greeley. Indeed, Greeley implies that through protected industrialization all workers have the capacity to become capitalists themselves, whether this be a traditional enterprise, small independent proprietors, or workers pooling their capital to establish voluntary cooperatives.[38] Most American Protectionists, however, were far less optimistic about the prospect of cooperatives than Greeley, but at the same time, they had no objection to them operating freely within a private enterprise system. Henry Carey explains, for instance, that "among the numerous attempts at manufactures by co-operative societies, we scarcely know of one that has had success… [since] instead of the capitalist… there is no one [in charge] whose peculiar interest is to see to the profitable employment of [the cooperative]."[39] A similar view was also held by Robert Ellis Thompson, who explains that if cooperatives are "intended to supersede the wages system entirely, cooperation is open to serious theoretical and practical objections." Yet, Thompson still accepts that "in spite of many failures, cooperation," in the sense of individual cooperative enterprises, "has an honorable record of successes."[40]

In any event, the American Protectionists understood that there exists a variety of avenues through which workers could become capitalists, whether this be by establishing a traditional business enterprise, becoming an independent contractor, or forming a cooperative. Moreover, even though there was a spectrum of views ranging from Hamilton to Greeley concerning the ultimate degree of upward social mobility, none accepted the view implicit in Classical and Marxist thought that individuals are invariably locked into their existing economic class. The opportunities and capacity for workers to become capitalists was seen as constantly expanding.

Preconditions and Obstacles to Wage Growth

The American Protectionists assumed that certain preconditions were necessary to allow for the expansion in wages, and the expansion of opportunities for individuals to climb the social ladder. With respect to wages, it was argued that competition for the purchase of labor was necessary, or at the very least desirable, to keep upward pressure on wage growth. Likening competition for the purchase of labor to that of purchase of commodities, Henry Carey saw that:

> Two men competing for its [a product's] purchase, its owner becomes a freeman. The two competing for its sale, become enslaved… The man who finds a purchaser for his labor, competes for the purchase of that of others…. [Hence] the greater the competition for the purchase of labor, the more perfect is the power of the laborer to select for himself the pursuit in which his powers shall be employed.[41]

Calvin Colton made similar remarks explaining that "it should be observed that labor is never *independent*, when it has no *alternatives;* that is when it is not strong enough in its own position to accept or reject the wages offered to it in a given case."[42] Workers, therefore, require sufficient employment opportunities for the process of wage growth to be sustained. This necessarily meant that a greater amount and variety of capitalists was required, and the American Protectionists saw this as being insolubly connected with economic diversification. In the words of Robert Ellis Thompson:

> The more openings there are for the laborer to invest his capital (which is his labor), and for the capitalist to invest his (which is the accumulation of past labor), the better each will be remunerated. Hence the connection between varied industry and fair wages, as well as fair profits. In any country… in which that is wanting, labor will be but poorly paid, and especially so, if agriculture is the only pursuit open to the great body of the people… With the rise of a varied industry, the number of workers rises to a maximum, that of idlers sinks to minimum.[43]

An economic environment conducive to industrial diversification means more opportunities for individuals to become capitalists and this creates greater competition for the purchase of laborers. Since there are natural limits to the demand for specific commodities, the only true way to have generalized competition for the purchase of labor is to have a highly varied and diversified economy. Moreover, this connects the concept of individuality to the question of wage growth. Since different individuals are naturally predisposed to different employments and pursuits, a diverse range of industrial activities will tend to maximize the productivity of the population, and this would therefore contribute to wage growth.

Market structure also represent an important element concerning wage growth, since monopoly pricing is an obstacle that could conceivably reduce the tendency for reproduction costs to fall, thereby suppressing one of the crucial mechanisms that propels real wage growth. However, since the success of labor depends on the success of capitalists, the American Protectionists generally objected to anti-trust policies designed to bust up large firms. They were, of course, concerned about the monopolization of industry, as they favored a decentralized system of producers, but they understood that it is virtually impossible in the long run for monopolies to exist (or rather for them to maintain monopoly pricing) if internal markets are kept free from excessive governmental barriers to entry and interference. Indeed, "one thing is certain," remarked Albert Clarke, "extortion will not be submitted to. No company that practices [extortion] can live long."[44]

In fact, it was not completely apparent that trusts and monopolies under internal free market conditions necessarily led to higher prices. Robert Ellis Thompson observed, for instance, that "nor have [trusts], as a rule, put up prices of the articles they produce. Coal oil was cheapened by the Standard Oil Company and made safer for the public [and] sugar fell heavily when the sugar trust got under way."[45] Generally speaking, monopoly pricing was only seen as sustainable through government sanction. The American Protectionists were thus far more concerned about the State instilling monopolies through regulatory barriers and taxes that prevented new capitalists from entering the market. Albert Clarke thus cautions that "the remedy [i.e., anti-trust laws] would be worse than the disease" and "in spite of legislation… aimed to prevent these combinations and *smash* these trusts, the consolidation or absorptions are here as a fact, more numerous… than ever before."[46]

In fact, most American Protectionists contended that one reason as to why English wages were suppressed, compared to the United States, was due to the system of special privileges, licensing laws, excessive taxation, and other legislated barriers to entry which sustained the monopolization of British industry that had been built up under royal charters. This suppressed the necessary preconditions for wage growth. Francis Bowen explains, for instance, that "in England… government, by excessive taxation and regulation… have ultimately the effect of giving a monopoly to the great capitalist."[47] Indeed, Orrin Skinner contrasts the system of privileges contained the English System with that of the American System, explaining that:

> Strictly speaking, monopolies have no existence whatever in the United States. A monopoly is a vested right to accomplish certain ends by all possible means. It is absolute exclusion. Such monopolies, in a relative sense, were incident to the early English law, but have… been regarded as foreign to the genius and spirit of our institutions… protection neither creates nor fosters [monopolies]… [Protection] opens the door to… avenues of industry beyond [which] *all parties must be subject to the law of universal competition.*[48]

Indeed, protectives tariffs were even seen as necessary to guard the domestic market against such foreign monopolies. Whilst the American government could eliminate special privileges within the domestic market, preventing such concentration domestically, they have no authority to dictate how foreign governments regulate their internal markets, and thus cannot eliminate special privileges awarded to foreign competitors. This feeds into what the American Protectionists saw as the true remedy against trusts and monopolies: the cultivation of a greater number and a greater variety of producers. Even in the case of domestic monopolies, the cultivation of different kinds of industries would create functional substitutes (alternate goods that serve similar purposes) which consumers can purchase in place of the monopolized goods. As David Rice explains:

> To all commodities which we are capable of producing in economy and quantity to regulate their prices in our market, we must establish and extend our industries, to produce them in that degree. Hundreds of manufactories of a given commodity, widely spread throughout the nation, will not only render the formation of a domestic trust in their production and distribution to the consumer, impossible, but they will also render the exactions of foreign trusts, which send us the like articles, equally impossible. He who can procure the needed commodity from a hundred widely different sources, over a score of more of different commerce, cannot be subject to the exactions of a trust which could close only a part of those sources or avenues of supply… Protection… surely creates the conditions antagonistic to monopolies… [it] diversifies the sources of domestic supply and the avenues of access to them.[49]

Indeed, foreign monopolies posed dangers beyond simple price hikes. They could engage in "dumping," or selling below cost to eliminate domestic competition, only to raise prices once their domestic rivals are destroyed. Protective tariffs prevented such strategies by ensuring domestic producers could survive temporary bouts of dumping or excessive overproduction. Moreover, state-backed foreign monopolies often benefit from subsidies and other paternalistic policies that allow them to undercut domestic producers regardless of their true level of efficiency. Thus, rather than the baseless claim often peddled by free traders that "the mother of all trusts is the customs tariff," the American Protectionists saw tariffs as actually guarding against monopolies when domestic markets are kept free of excessive regulation.[50]

The Role of Protection

It should be clear from the analysis presented in the sections above that protectionism was not viewed as a means of preserving low-wage employment, but for the purposes of securing high wages and upward social mobility. Of course, the American Protectionists did not view tariffs as possessing a direct mechanism that can elevate wage rates in and of itself. Robert Ellis Thompson himself notes that "it can not be asserted, of course that a protective tariff works directly to raise wages."[51] Indeed, it is even conceivable that one could accept the American Protectionist theory of wages without necessarily accepting their protectionist conclusions. In any event, the American Protectionists did conceive of indirect mechanisms through which protective tariffs could aid the process of wage growth.

The indirect linkage between protection and wage growth most clearly relates to the preconditions outlined above: industrial diversification and the competition for the demand for workers. By diversifying industry through protective tariffs, this creates more congenial employment opportunities for labor, which, in turn, boosts productivity and thus wages. Likewise, by creating more entrepreneurial opportunities for emerging capitalists, protection directly improves social mobility. This improvement in social mobility is more powerful than first appears. By achieving greater social mobility and thus creating a greater number of capitalists, this produces more avenues of demand for workers, as there are now a greater number and variety of capitalists competing with one each other for the employment of workers. In the words of Van Buren Denslow:

> Protection… by increasing the number of occupations and enterprises that can be carried on… compete for the hire of labor, and so raising the rate of wages… [Whilst] many workingmen imagine that it is the… capitalists who cause their wages to be as small… it is to these that they owe the fact that they can earn any wages at all. But, in fact, it is the competition of the enterprisers [for labor] with each other that advances wages. It is the extent and number of the enterprises that… that increases the competition of the enterprisers [for labor], and protection determines the extent and number of the enterprises that can be made profitable…
>
> If, therefore, there… be 1,500 *nuclei* of industry at which new employers are bidding against each other for the employment of workmen; [there are] hence 1,500 centers of increased demand for labor from which higher wages for labor radiate.[52]

This is part of the reason why social mobility was seen as far more important by the American Protectionists than the question of distribution *per se*, as greater social mobility will sustain higher wages over time.

However, there were several other reasons for why protection indirectly reinforces wage growth. The first of these relate to the higher degree of certainty afforded by protective tariffs concerning the profitability of private enterprise. Van Buren Denslow again explains that "wages are dependent on profits, in the sense, that no employer will continuously pay wages unless he can make a profit by doing so." Therefore, "if protection promotes profits it cannot avoid in equal degree promoting wages… [as] whatever promotes the cause promotes the effect."[53] Indeed, it must be recalled that the American Protectionists saw distribution as a disjointed process due to the fact that the entrepreneur advances wages to the worker prior to the final amount of profit being realized. This is where protective tariffs come in. Similar to how infant-industry protection affords a higher degree of confidence in the success of a new enterprise, tariffs also provide entrepreneurs and capitalists with a higher degree of confidence in their profitability. With the position of the entrepreneur being less precarious, the entrepreneur can therefore advance higher wages to workers. David Rice thus explains that:

> Capital must be ensured a certain reward for the enterprise, else we shall have no enterprise; and the more certain the reward, the smaller the amount of it which will satisfy capital, and the larger the portion of the product which it will concede to labor. Protection performs one of its chief functions in rendering this reward of capital certain. It consequently lessens it… which leaves a greater share of the product to be devoted to increasing the wages of labor… for nothing is more certain than that both the reward of capital and the wages of labor must be derived from the product, in the long run… But, although capital must… concede a much larger portion of the product to labor than under other economic systems, it is not without its compensation for the sacrifice.[54]

As a closely related point, by enabling capitalists to extract higher profits and for the government to collect revenue, tariffs would tend to facilitate investment in private capital and public investment in infrastructure. In doing so, labor would be rendered more productive and thus better remunerated. The capitalist would, likewise, receive higher profits due to the superior productivity of the worker and through the use of more productive infrastructure. Moreover, the substitution of direct taxes with import tariffs would allow the capitalist to retain greater means to either invest in his laborers or capital goods. Likewise, by foregoing the burden of internal direct taxation, the wages of the labor would, in effect, be higher in real terms, giving them greater means to invest in themselves (i.e., intellectual capital) or to purchase capital goods. It is for this reason that Alexander Everett notes that:

> The wages of individual labor with the latter [United States] are much higher than the former [Europe]; because in the United States… every individual enjoys the entire fruit of his own labor [i.e., productivity], with scarcely any diminution either from the taxes or the state of property.[55]

These sentiments are also affirmed by Stephen Colwell, who explains that "laborers whose physical powers are not unduly taxed, whose minds are properly cultivated, and whose labors are duly requited, are the happiest men of this world."[56] In any event, the positive feedback between industrial profits, capital accumulation, productivity, and wages would serve to reinforce this process and establish a virtuous cycle.

Another argument relates to the fact that by raising the price of imports, protective tariffs would lessen the temptation for capitalists to engage in wage competition. Or to put it differently, capitalists would be less likely to reduce wages in order to gain a price advantage over producers from abroad. Tariffs would instead incentivize the capitalist to compete through investing in new technology and productivity-enhancing improvements. Van Buren Denslow explains, for example, that:

> Whenever low prices, obtained by importation, involve the destruction of a domestic production, which both countries have equal natural facilities for producing, the first interest of the importing country is to encourage the application, by its own people, of the artificial facilities to which the rival country owes its temporary superiority, and consequent lower prices.
>
> These may consist of inventions, machinery, discoveries, capital, skill, low rates of interest, low rates of wages or the like. All of these any country can more wisely adopt than the low rates of wages, since a descent in rates of wages involves a degradation in the standard of living, which may react on the productivity of the labor itself, by making it less efficient, and may involve an inhumanity from which the conscience of society would revolt.[57]

When faced with competition from abroad, the capitalist may be tempted to gain a short-term price advantage by lowering wages, when in the longer term, this would have the effect of disenfranchising workers, and thereby lowering productivity. A more sustainable source of competitiveness would be to invest in skills, inventions, and labor-saving machines. The protective tariff would lessen the need to compete through the former (competition based on wages) and incentivize the latter (competition based on technology and productivity). It is for this reason that Ellis H. Roberts declared that "nor is it necessary… to reduce wages in order to secure a share of foreign commerce." Indeed, the "alternative is to increase the efficiency of labor." It is "the aim and purpose, as well as the direct consequence, of the protective policy is to maintain and develop this superior efficiency."[58]

This argument also relates to what some American Protectionists considered to be destructive competition, that is, competition predicated exclusively on driving prices down to unsustainably low levels. Contending with this point, Stephen Colwell notes that in terms of economic welfare, what really matters is the purchasing power of workers and capitalists, not the nominal prices of goods *per se*. In the words of Colwell:

> The most important consideration… is not the nominal prices or rates at which their exchanges are made, but the efficiency and skill of the labor, the obtaining the largest quantity of commodities, and of the best quality…
>
> In such a system [of domestic industry], if the rates of labor are high, the prices paid for commodities may appear high compared with those paid for corresponding articles in other

> countries; but the criterion of the benefits enjoyed by the inhabitants of two countries, is not the price of the articles they consume, but *the quantity* of articles they consume; the *price of labor* and the price of goods must be taken together. That system of industry is the best which affords the largest consumption to the masses, and the best opportunities of moral, mental, and physical improvement.[59]

In short, what matters is the growth of productive, and thus purchasing power. If protective tariffs were to lead to nominally higher prices, yet purchasing power is advanced through increased productivity and higher wages, than tariff protection would still be justified. That said, it is important not to exaggerate the logic of this particular argument, as most American Protectionists argued that protection would lead to lower real prices in the long-run through falling reproduction costs, and these low prices were seen as necessary for the enhancement of purchasing power and upward social mobility.

Whilst the American Protectionists were primarily focused on supply side considerations, they also connected their ideas to the demand side of the economy. There was the understanding that within a relatively closed or protected economy that capitalists would be more willing to increase wage rates, as these higher wages would tend to recirculate as expenditures within the home market, rather than leaking out into foreign markets. David Rice again explains that:

> Likewise capital, when under protection it concedes a larger share of the product to wages, which gives superior vitality to labor, finds itself in turn invigorated by the circumstance that our laboring men spend more of their earnings to procure those commodities which capital, invested in our industries, produces, and thus they add to the aggregate of the returns of capital, even though its proportion derived from a given amount of commodity be diminished. Thus capital, by first benefiting labor, receives in turn a reciprocal benefit.[60]

This insight alone was not seen as a sufficient reason to increase wages, since the capitalist would nevertheless stand to benefit if they simply retained the income for further investment. Yet, when combined with the productivity mechanisms discussed previously, a protected home market would be more conducive to higher wages than an open economy, since the capitalist class as a whole would stand to benefit from the increase in domestic consumption, and thus reinforces the mechanisms of wage growth outlined earlier.

Notes

1. Thompson, *Elements*, 235.
2. The term 'Ricardian surplus principle' was coined later by Kaldor, "Alternative Theories," 84–87. See also Harcourt & Kriesler, "On Ricardo," 150–167.
3. Ricardo, *Principles*, 500, 31.
4. Thompson, "Henry Charles Carey," [1879] 819.
5. Hamilton, *Report on Manufactures*, 19.
6. Carey, *Political Economy*, 1:339.
7. Ricardo, *Principles*, 86.
8. Smith, "Notes: Chapter 7," 79.

9. Greeley, *Essays*, 87.
10. Carey, *Social Science,* 3:111–113.
11. Elder, *Questions,* 88.
12. Elder *Conversations*, 52.
13. Carey, *Political Economy*, Vol. 1, 338.
14. Greeley, *Essays*, 167.
15. Patton, *Political Economy*, 105.
16. Hamilton, *Report on Manufactures*, 18–19.
17. Clay, 'American Industry', 279.
18. Denslow, *Principles*, 299.
19. Young, *Protection,* 480.
20. Reed, *The Tariff,* [1888] 9.
21. Thompson, *Elements,* 127.
22. Bigelow, "Labor and Capital," 486.
23. Carey, *Harmony*, 209–213.
24. Smith, "Protection," 42.
25. Greeley, *Essays*, 170.
26. Stebbins, *Manual,* 130–131.
27. Thompson, "Carey," [1883] 720.
28. Carey, *Political Economy*, 1:336.
29. Denslow, *Principles*, 295.
30. Patton, *Political Economy,* 107–108.
31. Patton, *Political Economy*, 107.
32. Carey, *Social Science,* 3:114–115.
33. McKinley, "Value," 743–744.
34. Hamilton, *Report on Manufactures,* 16.
35. Seaman, *Essays*, 146–147.
36. Hamilton, "Constitutional Convention," 218–220.
37. Bigelow, "Labor and Capital," 480.
38. Greeley, *Essays*, 273.
39. Carey, *Political Economy*, 2:425.
40. Thompson, *Elements*, 137.
41. Carey, *Manual*, 427.
42. Colton, *Rights of Labor*, 7.
43. Thompson, *Elements*, 129.
44. Clarke, "Trust Insanity," 4.
45. Thompson quoted in Clarke, "Trust Insanity," 3.
46. Clarke, "Trust Insanity," 4.
47. Bowen, *American Political Economy*, 236.
48. Skinner, *American Politics*, 417.
49. Rice, *Protective Philosophy*, 158–159.
50. Harry Havemeyer quoted in Irwin, *Clashing,* 314.
51. Thompson, "Protection," 819–820.
52. Denslow, *Principles*, 624–627, decapitalized for readability.
53. Denslow, "Why a Protectionist?," 7–8.
54. Rice, *Philosophy*, 140–141.
55. Everett, *New Ideas,* 116.
56. Colwell, *Claims of Labor*, 6.
57. Denslow, *Principles*, 124.
58. Roberts, *Government Revenue*, 304–305.
59. Colwell, *Preliminary*, ixxi–ixxii.
60. Rice, *Philosophy*, 141.

Chapter Eight

THEORY OF POPULATION, ASSOCIATION, AND AGGLOMERATION

The American Protectionist theory of population represents the antithesis of Malthusian economics. In contrast to the Reverend Thomas Robert Malthus, who expounded the view that population growth results in scarcity, the American Protectionists argued that population growth has a tendency to produce abundance. In fact, the American Protectionists were staunch defenders of population growth well prior to Malthus penning his *Essay on the Principle of Population* in 1798. As early as 1791, William Barton had already declared that:

> There is not, perhaps, any political axiom better established… that a high degree of population contributes greatly to the riches and strength of a state. In fact, the progressive increase of numbers, in the people of any civilized country, is reciprocally the cause and effect of its real wealth.[1]

Indeed, once Malthus' theory reached American shores, it would soon encounter fierce opposition from the American Protectionists. As the first member of the School to respond directly and explicitly to Malthus, John Melish would declare "be fruitful, and multiply and replenish the earth, the opinions of men of *the Malthus School, to the contrary, notwithstanding*."[2] This invocation of biblical imagery captures the defiant optimism that would characterize the American Protectionist theory of population, as well as their subsequent views on association, agglomeration, and urban–rural balance.

Theory of Population

In responding to the ideas of Malthus, the American Protectionists were not simply critical. They were also constructive. They sought to develop an alternate doctrine that would supplant Malthusian economics. This doctrine rests on two key pillars. The first is that population growth is ultimately self-regulative, and the second is that an increase in population typically results in a higher rate of productivity growth. Both of these taken together would dismantle the Malthusian theory of population, for if population is self-regulative then there is no inherent tendency for population, as assumed by Malthus, to increase geometrically. Further, if an increasing population leads to higher productivity growth then this also dispels the Malthusian claim that the means of subsistence only tends to increase arithmetically. Thus, when taken together, the American Protectionists argued that there is no inherent tendency for population to outpace the means of subsistence.

The view that population growth is ultimately self-regulative is rooted in the American Protectionist view of Man. Unlike the Malthusian worldview which appeals to Man's brutish impulses, the American Protectionists looked to Man's higher-order faculties, such as intellect and moral restraint. Because of these higher-order faculties, the American Protectionists envisioned that humans would naturally limit their rate of procreation in the event that population were to press upon the means of subsistence. In the words of Henry Carey:

> [Human] procreation must not, in contradistinction to every other animal function, be assumed to be a fixed, invariable action, ruled... with mechanical rigor, entirely independent [of human will]... the ratio of reproduction is not so fixed and limited, that figures can express it... That this flexibility [in procreation] has been provided... under a self-adjusting law... to the necessities of the race, and in harmony with the surroundings.[3]

Indeed, John Rae similarly notes that "the inferior animals... led by pleasure, may be said to be under the necessity of multiplying... Man, knowing the consequences of the act, may... refrain from procreation."[4] The view that population growth is ultimately self-regulatory also came from empirical observation. The American Protectionists saw, for instance, that birth rates tended to be higher in poorer parts of the world or even in poorer parts of society in order to compensate for high rates of infant mortality and low odds of survival, rather than some inherent tendency to outpace the means of subsistence.

Yet, as development proceeds, birth rates have a tendency to slow down through self-regulation. Protectionists thus sometimes stated that "the power of reproducing life is in inverse proportion to the power of maintaining it."[5] In capturing this view that a declining birth rate corresponds with increased development, William Elder remarks that:

> The whole of natural history demonstrates the rule that, where mortality is largest, fecundity [fertility] is greatest... The facts to be considered are broadly contrasted in the excessive fertility of the drudges of Europe and of the slaves of America on the one side, and the less fertility of the highest grade of society everywhere on the other.[6]

This can be viewed in direct contrast to the Malthusian view of population. Whereas Malthus assumed that an increase in the means of subsistence causes fertility rates to increase, the American Protectionists argued that the opposite tended to occur. As the means of subsistence increases, which subsequently improves the chances of survival, the tendency instead is for Man to regulate and thus reduce the number of offspring produced. Hence, fertility rates will tend to moderate with economic development. However, this tendency toward self-regulation and moderation in birth rates also extends beyond the decline in infant mortality and reflects a more general rise in Man's intellectual culture. Robert Ellis Thompson explains, for instance, that while population growth improves civilization and intellectual culture through the process of association and concentration (discussed later), the subsequent rise in Man's intellect would also moderate birth rates. In the words of Thompson:

> A high degree of civilization and mental culture imposes an immediate and natural check upon the growth of numbers. The growth of mind and growth of numbers are two balancing forces, two tendencies counteract each other… Thus we find that population is self-regulative. Its multiplication brings the civilization, that is the one effectual and all efficient check to all undue multiplication.[7]

The second and more important pillar of the American Protectionists' theory of population corresponds with the view that population growth produces abundance as opposed to scarcity, which is the opposite of that put forth by Malthus. In short, even in the absence of Man's self-restraint in procreation, population growth would not pose a problem since it has a tendency to produce a more than proportional increase in wealth creation. In other words, population growth causes wealth and subsistence to grow in per capita terms. The American Protectionists thus identified what they saw as the fundamental flaw of Malthusian economics. Whereas Malthus viewed the growth of population and of subsistence as being determined independently of one another, the American Protectionists recognized how procreation tended to augment the growth in the means of subsistence. Alexander Everett, for instance, explains that Malthus "views every individual added to a society as an additional consumer, without appearing to reflect, that he is also at the same time an additional laborer."[8]

American Protectionists recognized, of course, that an increase of the population would increase the demand for subsistence, but since individuals tend to produce more than what they can consume individually, it follows that even a proportional increase would invalidate Malthus's theory. Indeed, Robert Ellis Thompson makes this point emphatically, noting that Malthusian "theory is discredited by the experience of the past… The pressure… upon subsistence is characteristic of the periods and the places where population is most sparse —not of those where it is densest."[9] American Protectionists went further than this though, arguing that the means of subsistence would experience a more than proportional increase due to invention and rising productivity. In other words, population growth tends to promote increasing returns. Alexander Everett explains, for instance, that:

> It is sufficiently notorious, that an increase of population on a given territory is followed immediately by a division of labor; which produces in its turn the invention of new machines, an improvement of methods in all the departments of industry, and a rapid progress in the various branches of art and science. The increase effected by these improvements in the productiveness of labor is obviously much greater in proportion than the increase of population, to which it is owing.[10]

Virtually all American Protectionists agreed that productivity growth tended to outpace the growth of population. They saw that Malthus was ignorant of the operation of inventive growth within the economy, and thus how a larger population sows the seeds of abundance through the multiplication of the inventive faculty. Indeed, even independent of the increase in population, an increase in invention and productivity growth would still tend to occur due to the natural tendency for technological improvement over time, which in isolation would increase wealth per capita. However, the American Protectionists saw that population growth would itself contribute positively to productivity growth and invention. Robert Ellis Thompson notes, for instance, how "the more the numbers… the greater [the] people's mastery over nature, and the larger the share of the good things that will fall to each individual."[11] In a similar vein, Ezra Seaman remarks that "the increase of population… has progressed step by step, in all civilized countries, with the inventions and improvements in the mechanic arts, the increase of productive industry, and the extension of commerce."[12]

That said, the full scope of factors contributing to this increase in productivity relates more so to rising population density and the process of agglomeration, than population growth in the abstract, and will thus be expanded upon later. In any event, the American Protectionists had a clear conception of how population growth tended to produce abundance, as opposed to scarcity. Hence, even if the first aspect of their theory hypothetically fails and population growth was not self-regulative, there would still be no cause for concern since the means of subsistence would still tend to outpace the rate of population growth.

The pessimism of Malthus was therefore controverted by the American Protectionists and was supplanted with an optimistic and ultimately more realistic destiny for mankind. George B. Curtiss explains, for instance, that "the pessimistic forebodings of Malthus and his followers have been proved by experience to be without foundation… That the world is large enough, and its resources [are] sufficient if properly utilized, to furnish an abundance for all; there cannot be the slightest question."[13] Indeed, rather than being concerned about overpopulation, the American Protectionists were actually more concerned about the prospects of fertility rates declining too dramatically. John Rae declares, for instance, that whatever tends "therefore to weaken or destroy those social instincts which tend to generate love of offspring, is a crime against society."[14] Robert Ellis Thompson, likewise, remarks that "history shows us also that a vast decrease in the population of a country, through the sweeping operation of Mr. Malthus's positive and preventive checks, is a dangerous possibility."[15]

The above represents the basic theory of population put forth by the American Protectionists. But population growth in isolation is one thing. The American Protectionists went beyond this simple model and connected their theory of population with an analysis of population density and the economics of agglomeration. However, before discussing these ideas, it is important to introduce the principle of association which represents the foundation of the American Protectionists' views on population density, as well as their economic system more broadly.

The Principle of Association

Central to understanding how population density generates prosperity is the principle of association. In fact, the principle of association is foundational to the broader economic system of the American Protectionists. At its most basic, the principle of association views Man as a social creature. Because of this, Man has a need to associate with his fellow man, and this typically occurs within a community and within close geographical proximity to one another. Although coined by Henry Carey, the basic concept can be seen in American Protectionist thought as early as the writings of William Barton. According to Barton:

> The very nature of man, necessarily constitute him a social animal: And, in the very origin of society, their mutual necessities, with the various talents, means and opportunities of individuals for supplying them, must have produced a reciprocity of services, and an occasional interchange with one another of that property, which each had acquired by his own exertions.[16]

Because individuals are limited in their capacities, it follows that each individual has a mutual dependence on their fellowman. From this, individuals must utilize the services of others on a reciprocal basis. They must therefore associate with one another.

This principle of association is intrinsically connected with Man's individuality. As discussed previously, the American Protectionists placed a heavy emphasis on Man's individuality, postulating that every individual is different and unique, and that there exists an immense variety in individual talents, aptitudes, and dispositions. Yet, in spite of this individualism, the American Protectionists rejected the more extreme individualism which views Man in an atomistic manner, preferring instead to treat Man as part of a community. In other words, they saw that individuals must associate with other individuals, and thus cannot be treated in isolation to one another. Indeed, it is precisely because there are these individual differences that association comes about. It is also why association is essential for mankind. In the words of Henry Carey, "association depends upon INDIVIDUALITY. There can be no association without differences."[17] The American Protectionists thus considered individualism as properly and intimately connected with the community, and by extension, the nation. Both were essential to one-another. George M. Steele provides perhaps one of the best renderings of this position:

> Not only is association essential to man, but individuality is equally essential. A superficial thinker might regard these two characteristics as antagonistic. The fact is so far otherwise, that each of them is actually dependent on the other. No man would associate with another unless the one had something which the other wanted. But for this, there would be no commerce. Two hatters making the same kind of hats would neither of them have anything which the other would want. Men of the same mental habits and requirements could not benefit one another. Men must differ, or they will not associate; and the greater the difference, the greater the association.[18]

Therefore, unlike many other nationalist ideologies, which subordinate the individual to the nation or nation state, the American Protectionists saw individualism and nationalism as complementary ideologies, with individualism fitting neatly within nationalism. The process of association would allow for the expression of the unique characteristics possessed by different individuals to an increasing degree through the creation of a diversity of pursuits. This expression of individuality would likewise enable further association by creating a greater range of products through which commerce and further association can occur. William Elder thus explains that "the operation of these two forces—Association and Individuality... are thus reciprocal and corroborative in enhancing each other and in promoting the progress of the man, the community, and the race."[19] Indeed, because of this reciprocal relationship between association and individuality, association was seen as necessary component for achieving industrial freedom. In the words of Robert Ellis Thompson:

> The growth of the power of association is, at the same time, growth in individual freedom. The more closely men are thus united, the more free each one is to give full play to the bent of his own character. He is not forced to make his living by an employment for which he may have no taste, and in which he can therefore never use his natural gifts to the best advantage.[20]

This reciprocal relationship between association and individuality provides the foundation for understanding the American Protectionist theory of agglomeration.

Theory of Concentration and Agglomeration

Before Alfred Marshall pioneered the subfield of agglomeration economics, the American Protectionists had already developed their own theory of agglomeration. This was known as the theory of concentration.[21] The principle of association discussed in the previous section represents the starting point of the theory of concentration. In short, concentration refers to the concentration of the population within towns and cities, which is necessarily tied to an increase in the density of the population. In fact, the benefits arising from population growth relate more to the increase in population density than population growth in the abstract. This view is well illustrated by Robert Ellis Thompson who explains "man's 'power over nature' continues to grow with every advance in the compactness of society."[22] Or as Francis Bowen puts it "cities and towns are the great agents and tokens of the increase of national opulence and the progress of civilization."[23]

The American Protectionists outlined roughly nine reasons why concentration and rising population density tends to improve productivity and economic welfare. These reasons include: (1) the growth of individuality and association; (2) an increase in the division of labor and the diversity of pursuits; (3) a reduction in transportation costs; (4) the stimulation of new wants; (5) the diffusion of knowledge and ideas; (6) technological diffusion and spillovers; (7) tighter linkages between different industries; (8) an increased provision of training and educational institutions; and (9) an improved affordability of internal improvements. William D. Wilson, for instance, identifies at least four of these factors, explaining that there are "distinct causes affecting the... increase in wealth, which are dependent upon the density of the population: (1) division of labor, (2) savings in the cost of exchanges, (3) stimulation of new wants, (4) production of new commodities."[24]

Individuality and association connect closely with the increase in the diversity of employments and the division of labor, both of which were seen as dependent, to some degree, on the concentration of the population. Indeed, more than anything else, the process of concentration was applauded by American Protectionists due to its ability to facilitate the maximization of individuality. Francis Bowen explains, for instance, that "to concentrate the people" is "to give full scope to all the varieties of taste, genius, and temperament." This scope allows for the greatest capacity to exercise such a diverse range of individual attributes, and this "can only be found in cities and large towns."[25] John Rae makes a similar observation, noting that when:

> A territory is scantily peopled, and its inhabitants spread over it at a great distance from each other, they can never subdivide themselves into different trades and employments, and each devoting himself to a particular business and art, exercise his whole ingenuity to bring that particular occupation to perfection; and that hence arts are in general in the most flourishing condition, where the population is the most dense.[26]

In other words, the concentration of the population allows for a greater variation and diversity of pursuits, which facilitates the maximization of individuality. Henry Carey thus explains that as "population further augment[s]" and "employments became diversified... the more [the individual] becomes individualised."[27]

From this, it follows that, by enabling a greater diversity of employments and pursuits, the process of concentration also tends to promote new discoveries and inventions by allowing individuals to concentrate their mind and effort more fully on the pursuits that are most suited to their natural talents. Indeed, Ezra Seaman provides a clear rendering of this connection between concentration and inventions and improvements, explaining that:

> Where men are congregated together by commerce, manufactures, and the mechanic arts, in cities and large towns, they see more objects to stimulate them to activity and enterprise... their intellectual passions are more stimulated... [and] the division of employments being more complete, and their minds more concentrated for years upon one department of industry or business, they are generally enabled to attain a much higher degree of science... Hence the minds of... persons become more active and acute in their respective employments, more original, more inventive, more inclined to seek after new discoveries, and inventions, and new modes of enterprise.[28]

This tendency for concentration to increase the rate of invention and entrepreneurial discovery also relates to the concept of technological diffusion and information spillovers. It should be recalled that the American Protectionists considered technological spillovers to be bounded geographically. Given this geographic boundedness, the process of concentration will thus facilitate the diffusion of technology and information. Recognizing this tendency, Willard Phillips observes that the geographic concentration of a variety of different industries would be far more conducive to invention and improvement than a single industry in isolation. Indeed, "you cannot have a few isolated, solitary arts, in high perfection," explains Phillips. "Each art, in order to its success, needs the near and ready aid of a thousand others. Easy and familiar communication between artisans… keeps the inventive faculties in lively exercise."[29]

The necessity for varied and diverse industry also extends to the ease of communication between different firms within the agglomeration, which itself can be considered as an information or knowledge spillover. In criticizing the Classical view that nations should specialize in the production of a specific commodity, Phillips affirms the importance of communication between different industries in close proximity, explaining that:

> One is, therefore, struck with the simplicity and conceited levity of teachers of economical philosophy, who take for granted that a solitary art can be… carried on successfully, in competition… with a competitor who is surrounded with all the auxiliary arts and trades. Besides cheapness, there is an advantage to the artisan in the quality of the articles supplied to him by others in his own vicinity. He will, in the long run, be supplied with those better adapted to his particular business, than he possibly could be by workmen three thousand miles off…. You will readily see about you, proofs enough that the nearer you are to the place whence your tools and materials are supplied, and the more intimate your communication is with it, the better adapted to your wants they will be.[30]

Indeed, Henry Carey placed a similar emphasis on how concentration facilitates communication and the dissemination of knowledge, noting that:

> The greater the tendency to association [and concentration], the greater is the facility for the dissemination of new ideas in regard to modes of thought or action, and for obtaining aid in carrying them into practical effect. The object of the [free trade] monopoly system is that of separating men from each other, and depriving them of this advantage. The object of protection is to enable them to come together.[31]

Another important benefit arising from the concentration of population relates to the reduction in transportation costs. By bringing the consumer to the side of the producer the American Protectionists saw that the process of concentration would reduce or eliminate the costs involved in transportation. Henry Carey explains, for instance that "the nearer the parties to the exchange, the smaller is the proportion absorbed by the parties engaged in the works of trade, transportation, or conversion—that the smaller that proportion, the more rapid must be the accumulation of wealth."[32] Indeed since this reduction in transportation represents a saving to producers and consumers it has the indirect effect of aiding capital accumulation by promoting savings. It is for such reasons that the American Protectionists often referred to transportation costs, particularly when the commodities are hauled long distances, as the "tax on transportation."[33] In fact, as will be discussed in a later chapter, foregoing the tax on transportation would represent a crucial argument in support of the compensatory effects of infant-industry protection.

The process of concentration also contributes to the accumulation of intellectual capital. Since the provision of universities, libraries, and other educational institutions is only viable once the population of towns and cities reaches a critical mass, it follows that through the process of concentration, there is a gradual development in the capacity to accumulate intellectual capital. As Henry Carey explains:

> With increased power of association [and concentration], there is a steady improvement in the provision for the development of the intellectual faculties…. [accompanying concentration] are numerous [schools, universities, and] other institutions devoted to particular branches of education, some of which are provided for by government, while others are supported by the contributions of individuals.[34]

In a similar vein, the American Protectionists also linked concentration and rising population density with an increase in the provision of internal improvements. Tench Coxe perceived, for instance, that "a scattered population requires a greater extent of roads, than can be kept in any decent repair." In contrast, the creation of larger towns and cities, with a higher population density, means that "good roads may be made without oppressive taxation" by spreading the costs over a larger population.[35] Robert Ellis Thompson adds to this observation, noting that as internal improvements and other similar services are rendered more viable through an increase in population density, this results in a greater economizing of labor and economies of scale. Using the example of water infrastructure, Thompson explains that "when the density of population [has] made it worth while to carry the water in pipes through the streets of our city, it [the water] was obtained with far less outlay of labor than when every man carried his bucket to the river's bank, or even to the pump."[36]

It should therefore be emphasized that since the benefits of concentration all contribute toward rising productivity in some way, the American Protectionists argued that a rising population density has a tendency to raise wage rates. Indeed, as Ellis H. Roberts states, "low wages are not caused by density of population… on the contrary, with the growth of population labor receives better pay and higher consideration."[37] This contrasts sharply with the Ricardian-Malthusian-Marxian view of population, which argues that an increase in population would only serve to reinforce subsistence levels of wages by suppressing the wage rates further.

Finally, it is important to acknowledge that the American Protectionists understood that trade-offs exist between the benefits of concentration and achieving sufficient economies of scale. Where a product could not be sourced locally, the American Protectionists understood that commerce should proceed on a regional (regions within the nation) or national basis. This position is illustrated by the American Protectionists' commitment to a strictly national policy of protection and is also demonstrated by Horace Greeley's response to the question: "If the United States should be fenced about by a tariff, why not Illinois or Rhode Island?" In response, Greeley declared that whilst "such logic may provoke a smile, [it] can hardly require serious refutation." Indeed, "the fact that every industrial pursuit, and especially every one that requires a heavy concentration of capital, skill, [and] machinery… to ensure its successful prosecution, must have 'room to turn itself'." Thus, "a reasonably capacious area upon which to find customers and consumers… is too obvious to require demonstration"[38]

Indeed, according to the logic of the American Protectionists, regional and national commerce would still exhibit some of the beneficial effects associated with concentration and association, albeit in a diminished magnitude. To put it differently, the closer the proximity, the more the benefits accrue, with this diminishing as the proximity lessens. Localized production and exchange is thus seen as the foundation for regional and national commerce, just as national commerce serves as the foundation for international trade.

Forces of Attraction and Dispersion

The writings of the American Protectionists not only identify the process of concentration, they also provide a detailed explanation of the forces which give rise to these centers of concentration, and conversely, the forces which inhibit or lead to their disintegration. In explaining the rise of centers of concentration, the American Protectionists introduced two concepts referred to as "forces of attraction" and "forces of dispersion." Attraction represents the force which gives rise to centers of concentration, whereas dispersion is a force which inhibits the creation of such centers.

In explaining the operation of the forces of attraction, the American Protectionists used the analogy of gravitational forces in the solar system. Similar to how gravity pulls together material from space to form celestial bodies, the American Protectionists observed that masses of individuals would exhibit a similar gravitational or attractive force, leading to a concentration of the population, and thus the formation of towns and cities. In the words of Henry Carey:

> The greater the number [of people] collected in a given space the greater is the attractive force there exerted... Gravitation is here, as everywhere else in the material world, [operates] in the direct ratio of the mass, and in the inverse one of the distance... Such being the case, why is it that all the members of the human family do not tend to come together on a single spot of earth? ... We are surrounded by [cities] of various sizes, and some of these are themselves provided with satellites, each having its local centre of attraction, by means of which its parts are held together... Small as are the asteroids, each has within itself a local centre of attraction enabling it to preserve its form and substance, despite the superior attraction of the larger bodies by which it is everywhere surrounded.[39]

Indeed, as William Elder similarly notes:

> This associative attraction is analogous to the material law of gravitation, which groups the atoms of the universe in planets, solar systems, and constellations; ordering and collocating them around their several centers; the local centers by counter attraction, holding each group in its own sphere and office, and every individual of each group in its appropriate position.[40]

The need for association, as well as the associated benefits of concentration discussed previously, constitutes the attractive force which leads to the creation of industrial town and cities. This was also seen as contingent upon the establishment of industrial arts and manufacturing industries. In fact, the American Protectionists emphasized the existence of positive feedback between the process of association, concentration, and the establishment of industry. Concentration would, for instance, promote a diversity of pursuits, but this diversity of pursuits would also promote a further concentration of the population.

A particularly important aspect of this process relates to the clustering of support industries and linked industries. Even as early as 1804, Tench Coxe developed an early concept of clustering and is perhaps even the first writer to apply the term "cluster" to the study of economics. In doing so, Coxe reveals how certain groups of industries tend to emerge as clusters, whereby a key industry gives rise to support industries. Using the example of an agricultural cluster, Coxe observes that "In a country *devoted to agriculture*, the cluster of arts and trades which minister to its wants spring up of course, and almost from necessity."[41] In spite of Coxe's example of agriculture, as will be shown, agriculture in isolation was typically seen as exhibiting an insufficient force of attraction to give rise to larger agglomerations.

The forces of dispersion represent an opposing force to that of attraction. In identifying these dispersive forces, however, the American Protectionists differentiated between detrimental and benign forces of dispersion. The detrimental forces of dispersion were seen as those which inhibit the development of local centers of association and concentration. They were thus detrimental in the sense that they prevented the expression of individuality, and it also meant that the nation's populace would forego the other benefits associated with association and concentration highlighted previously. These detrimental forces of dispersion are also inversely linked with industrialization. If the economy fails to industrialize and instead specializes in agricultural production, then individuals will tend to disperse and scatter across agricultural lands. It also follows that any movement toward deindustrialization would tend to produce similar results due to the disintegration of linkages between different industries and employments. Tench Coxe explains, for instance, that:

> Agriculture *alone* will never concentrate the population, so as to form a town of any considerable magnitude. There can only be a country where a few neighbouring proprietors are collected… which instead of being the centre of trade and industry is often the focus of dissipation.[42]

Francis Bowen would later echo this view, explaining:

> The interfusion of manufactures and commerce with agriculture, favors the increase of national capital… by concentrating the population in cities and towns. Agriculture [in isolation] is necessarily diffusive in its effects; the laborers must be distributed over the whole face of the territory which they cultivate.[43]

This detrimental form of dispersion is also linked to a concept known as centralization (not to be confused with concentration). Centralization refers to the centralization of industry and the domination of trade by a particular nation or major trading port. This concept can be seen as analogous to that posited in the theory of comparative advantage whereby a nation specializes in industrial production with others specializing in agriculture or raw material to supply the foreign industrial center. This industrial center, which in the nineteenth century was seen to be Britain, represents a centralizing force which inhibits the formation of local centers of concentration in agricultural-exporting economies by disintegrating local linkages between industry and agriculture, causing a dispersion of the population across agricultural lands. As Henry Carey explains:

> The object of the English [free trade] system is to promote centralization, and its necessary consequence is that of compelling the dispersion of man...The proclaimed object of [this] monopoly system is that of producing a necessity for scattering ourselves over large surfaces, and thus increasing the difficulty of association… The object of protection is that of bringing the consumer… to the side of [the] producer… the consumer of cotton to the side of its producer… and the shoemaker to the side of the farmer and planter… If we look westward, it is the same. Centralization produces depopulation, and that is followed by poverty and crime.[44]

Centralization and concentration were thus seen as having an inverse relationship with one-another. Centralization inhibits forces of attraction and promotes dispersion, whereas association and concentration exhibits forces of attraction which inhibits detrimental dispersion. This relationship was also linked closely with the distinction made by American Protectionists between commerce and trade. Henry Carey explains, for instance, that:

> Commerce promotes the development of the treasures of the earth, and enables men to come nearer together to find instant demand for all their faculties and to accumulate wealth and power to be used in the peaceful pursuits of life. Trade causes the exhaustion of the soil and the dispersion of men… Centralization and dispersion are the necessary consequences of the growing supremacy of trade [over commerce].[45]

Thus, the American Protectionists saw free trade, by preventing industrialization domestically, as a detrimental dispersive force. Carey explains, for instance, "that of the system falsely called free-trade is [there] to promote dispersion," whereas "the object of protection is to enable men to remain at home… which cannot exist where the tendency to dispersion exists."[46] Hence, tariff protection was seen as a necessary check against centralization and detrimental dispersion which arise from specializing in agricultural production. By promoting manufacturing, protectionism would allow for the creation of local centers of industry, allowing for concentration and association.

Crucially, however, dispersion is not strictly detrimental. Whereas specializing in purely agricultural production promotes a detrimental form of dispersion, there are also benign forces of dispersion which are seen as a natural outgrowth of concentration. The chief factor which impels this benign tendency toward dispersion results from rising rents and land prices associated with the increasing population density within more established industrial towns and cities. Rising rents, according to the American Protectionists, represents a price signal or dispersive force which causes the population o disperse outwards and establish new centers of economic activity. Van Buren Denslow hus explains that:

> Rent [is] a Dispersive Force on Population. Essentially, therefore, rent is a natural social force operating to disperse population, and economize working space, by imposing a tax upon the occupation of the more valuable localities, proportionate to their value for working purposes.[47]

This tendency toward dispersion resulting from rent was seen as benign since the result vould not be a scattering of the population, but a tendency to establish new industrial :enters or satellite cities. This force therefore operates in both a dispersive and attractive nanner. "In this point of view," explains Denslow, "rent is the centrifugal force, vhich disperses men from the centers toward which commerce and exchange attracts hem, and obliges them to form new and smaller centers."[48] The creation of these new ndustrial centers would then neutralize the attractive forces of the larger cities through he presence of counter-attractive forces.[49] In the words of Henry Carey:

> The establishment of a local attraction [will tend] to neutralize the attraction of the capital, or great commercial city; and where such local centres must exist, there, invariably, is found the greatest tendency to the development of individuality, and the combination of action—and the most rapid progress in knowledge, wealth, and power.[50]

Rent thus plays an important role in the theoretical system of the American Protectionists since it coordinates population movements and the geographical listribution of industry. In the words of Denslow, "rent, therefore, is just a beneficent orce in economics as is wages or commerce, for it is as essential to disperse as to .ttract mankind."[51] This is part of the reason why the American Protectionists rejected he likes of Georgist-style rent and land taxes, land nationalization programs, and ent controls. By distorting land prices, such policies would only serve to inhibit the eeding of new industrial centers and would lead to situations analogous to that of entralization by creating overpopulated centers, or what would now be called "mega-ities." Indeed, the American Protectionists, whilst in favor of concentration, imply hat there are certain diseconomies associated with overconcentrated cities, such as ırban slums. Henry Carey, for instance, describes "great cities" as "great sores," and /an Buren Denslow similarly notes that in these great cities, the "pecuniarily helpless warm in greatest numbers," albeit conceding that this is "not because they are here educed by competition to poverty, but because they are here enabled to survive longest n the smallest endowment of productive energy."[52]

For the American Protectionists, the ideal system was not the creation of mega-cities, ut a clustering of medium-sized industrial cities throughout the continent, which is ırgely reminiscent of the experience of the United States. Indeed, whilst some secondary ources have argued that the American Protectionists rejected Manifest Destiny and estward expansion, this is not strictly true.[53] What the American Protectionists rejected vas the premature dispersion and westward expansion which accompanied free trade nd specializing purely in agricultural production. The American Protectionists were not opposed to westward expansion if it represents a natural outgrowth of concentration and leads to the sowing of new industrial centers throughout the country-side. Indeed, Giles B. Stebbins captures this wider vision of Manifest Destiny extolled by the American Protectionists:

> The "manifest destiny" of this country is not to be simply a great agricultural nation, but to build up the richest and most beneficent varied industry and commerce in the world. We cannot have the best farming until we have the best manufacturing, in varied forms and materials, near the farm, each an indispensable help to the growth and perfectness of the other. Give us both, and the blending of these varied experiences and vocations, the meeting and mingling of these many life-currents, tinged and shaped by such wide mastery of man over nature's forces and materials, is full of benefit.[54]

In any event, the American Protectionists developed a sophisticated explanation of the forces which lead to the formation of industrial cities and towns. What is more, is that this theory predates the development of agglomeration theory within the economics mainstream. Indeed, it is quite telling that the forces of attraction and dispersion are even referred to by the American Protectionists as centripetal and centrifugal forces, which is consistent with the terminology now employed in new economic geography and modern agglomeration literature.[55] This more than illustrates that the American Protectionists were far ahead of their time on the question of agglomeration economics and can thus be considered pioneers in the field.

Urban–Rural Balance

As alluded to in the previous section, the American Protectionists envisioned a clustering of medium-sized industrial cities and towns along the countryside. This vision was underpinned, in no small part, by the need to form a balance between the urban and rural sectors of the economy. By concentrating large towns and cities alongside agricultural production, the American Protectionists saw that agriculture would also accrue many of the benefits accompanying association and concentration. Indeed, Oliver Putnam explains that "agriculture, in [an isolated] state, contributes little to the augmentation to national wealth. But as population becomes denser and other occupations and employments arise, it grows more productive."[56]

Similar to how manufacturing industries would tend to experience increasing returns and rising productivity through concentration, the American Protectionists saw that this would apply equally to agricultural industries, assuming they are located within proximity to centers of industrial activity. This point is well put by Friedrich List who explains that:

> Manufacturing industry and agriculture, being regarded as a whole, prosper in the proportion of their proximity, and in proportion as they are less disturbed in the reciprocal influence which they exercise upon each other… Agricultural power is productive likewise in proportion as agriculture is more strictly united… with a manufacturing industry complete in its various branches.[57]

This geographic interfusion of agriculture and manufacturing connects directly with the need for tariff protection with Henry Carey declaring, for instance, that "the object of protection is to accomplish all these objects, by bringing the loom and the anvil to take their natural places by the side of the plough and the harrow, thus making a market on the land for the products of the land."[58]

In positing this view, the American Protectionists reaffirmed their assault on the Ricardian assumption of constant returns to scale. With respect to agriculture in particular, the American Protectionists took aim at the Ricardian notion of "the original and indestructible powers of the soil," which presupposes that soil fertility and agricultural productivity are intrinsically fixed.[59] According to this view, agricultural land was subject to neither improved fertility through the application of manure or fertilizer, nor depletion through the exhaustion of the soil. The rejection of Ricardo's assumption of permanent and indestructible soil productivity can be seen as early as 1837, with Henry Carey posing the question of "what are indestructible powers? The most fertile soil, if not renewed, will have its powers destroyed."[60]

This rejection of the original and indestructible powers of the soil led to the development of a theory which contemporary critics of American Protectionism labelled as the "manure argument," with the term seemingly appropriated by the American Protectionists themselves.[61] This manure argument builds upon the previously discussed law of the endless circulation of matter and force which posits that nothing can be created or destroyed, but can only be changed in form. Similar to how the American Protectionists characterized economic activity as Man's transformation of matter and energy into goods and services fit for human use, agricultural production involves the transformation of nutrients and elements from within the soil into agricultural produce. However, in the case of agricultural production, these transformations must necessarily involve the depletion of nutrients and elements. As Henry Carey explains:

> Each and every plant requires for its nourishment certain elements, by the continual extraction of which the earth is impoverished; and thus do the exhaustion of the land, and the dispersion of men, in one year, prepare for further exhaustion and dispersion in another one. Such having been the case with cotton and sugar cultivation in the Southern States, and that of wheat and tobacco in the more Northern ones, the consequences are seen in the fact, that the impoverishment of the soil and the dispersion of population proceed from year to year at a constantly accelerated pace.[62]

Indeed, this depletion of productive soil represents a negative temporal externality not factored into the present exchange value of agricultural production. The implication of this is far-reaching as it means that agricultural production will tend to experience diminishing returns, as the nutrients and elements become increasingly exhausted, thus rendering the soil less fertile. The novel response to this problem elicited from the American Protectionists was to replenish the soil and offset the loss of nutrients by allowing manure from the urban and industrial sectors to be recirculated and reapplied to agricultural land. This would only be practical, however, if agriculture were situated within the vicinity of larger towns and cities. Peshine Smith explains, for instance, that only "centres of population, however, supply manures which may be made immediately available by the individual farmer, with no other assistance than that of his own carts and horses.[63] Robert Ellis Thompson explains, likewise, that "the creation of a varied industry enables the farmer to enrich himself without impoverishing the soil. It does so by bringing the farmer and the artisan into neighborhood, and giving the former facilities for making returns to the soil that he would not otherwise possess."[64]

Of course, the American Protectionists recognized that realizing these benefits often depended upon certain local policies and institutions. Thompson notes, for instance, that "the existence of the means and the power to make adequate returns to the soil is no guarantee that these will be fully employed. Through the sewers of our great cities, and the rivers into which they empty, immense quantities of fertilizing matter are poured into the sea, and are thus utterly lost." This clearly implied support for amending local government policies to enable the economic use of such manures. In any event, the process of concentration made the use of manures possible and practical, even if institutional reforms were needed to fully capture these benefits. In any case, it is important to stress that the American Protectionists considered the term "manure" in a broader sense than its conventional usage. For the American Protectionists, manure would refer to any organic and inorganic urban waste, as well as agricultural and industrial by-products, that could be used as fertilizer.[65]

The manure argument focuses on the implications of urban-rural balance with respect to soil fertility. However, this constitutes only one aspect of agricultural productivity, and one which largely involves the prevention of diminishing returns in agriculture. An equally important aspect of urban-rural balance concerns the role of technological spillovers from the industrial to the agricultural sectors. Indeed, John L. Hayes explains that whilst inventions and improvements in manufacturing have historically tended to spillover onto other forms of manufacturing, agriculture has increasingly developed the capacity to capture and absorb technological spillovers from manufacturing industries. In the words of John L. Hayes:

> For a long time the mechanical arts reacted chiefly upon each other. The inventive and constructive power invoked by manufactures reached tardily, but at length, the fields of husbandry. The labor-saving machinery of the farm, the harvesters, reapers, mowers, and planters at the last two decades, came into existence. Agriculture, now doubled in its productive capacity, not by improvements properly its own, but through the auxiliary forces of the mechanical arts, presents the final and triumphant demonstration of the solidarity of the industries.[66]

The American Protectionists thus conceived agriculture as fully capable of exhibiting increasing returns through the application of technology, but this was seen as contingent upon it being situated alongside manufacturing. Henry Carey explains, for instance, that "agricultural improvement waits upon, and never precedes, industrial development." Hence, "the application of new manures, the discovery of improved modes of applying power, and the invention of machines… [is] consequent upon that diversification of pursuits, by means of which, the various human faculties are stimulated into action."[67] This view is also supported by Friedrich List, who remarks that agricultural production in isolation is always unproductive as "the new processes, new implements, the improved modes of culture scarcely ever reach remote places."[68] The presence of spillovers from the industrial sectors onto agriculture also culminates in what the American Protectionists termed "scientific agriculture." It is only through the presence of a diverse array of industrial pursuits in close proximity that agriculture achieves its productive potential and ascends to the rank of scientific agriculture. As David H. Mason explains:

> [No] pursuit calls to its aid such a diversity of knowledge [than agriculture]... The whole circle of the sciences and the arts is made tributary to its successful prosecution; yet a country devoted to the production of... raw materials for export to foreign countries can not possess, in an advanced state, the sciences and auxiliary arts most essential to its own industry [of agriculture]...
>
> We can not have a few isolated, solitary arts in complete excellence. They are social and gregarious. Each, in order to its success, requires the near and ready assistance of a hundred others. Only a manufacturing people can develop and sustain that diversity of the arts and the sciences which culminates in and is inseparable from a scientific agriculture.[69]

Another important point raised by the American Protectionists in support of clustering urban centers alongside agricultural communities concerns the costs of transporting agricultural commodities. Agricultural commodities were seen as especially prone to the so-called "tax of transportation," since many such commodities are disproportionately bulky and heavy. Thus, situating towns and cities alongside agricultural land would be particularly beneficial for farmers and agriculturalists. As Friedrich List explains:

> Compare, for instance, the state of agriculture in the vicinity of a populous city with that in remote districts.... [the cost of transportation] is applied only to commodities which bear distant carriage.... [and] a considerable portion of the proceeds of sale is absorbed in expenses of transport. The capital expended in reproduction of a crop is with difficulty replaced by any disposition which can be made of it.[70]

Indeed, by reducing or foregoing transportation costs, farmers and agriculturalists would have greater savings which they can then reinvest into their farms and agricultural land. Henry Carey thus explains that "being at market, and saving all the cost of transportation and commission, he [the farmers] is enabled to improve his machinery of cultivation."[71]

This theory of urban-rural balance represents the final nail in the coffin of the Malthusian theory of population. Instead of a higher population density bringing about shortages of food, the American Protectionists explained how the clustering of densely populated industrial towns and cities alongside agricultural land would bring about rising agricultural productivity and thus increasing returns in food production. The American Protectionists demonstrated therefore that mankind's destiny was not one of scarcity and starvation, but would be one of opulence and abundance.

Notes

1. Barton, *Observations*, 1.
2. Melish, *Geographical Description*, 269, emphasis in original.
3. Carey, *Social Science*, Vol. 3, 267–269.
4. Rae to Mill, c. 1854, 430.
5. Elder, *Questions*, 77.
6. Elder, *Conversations*, 86.
7. Thompson, *Elements*, 65–66.
8. Everett, *New Ideas*, 21.
9. Thompson, *Elements*, 57.
10. Everett, *New Ideas*, 26.
11. Thompson, *Elements*, 66.
12. Seaman, *Essays*, 189.
13. Curtiss, *Protection*, 794.
14. Rae to Mill, c. 1854, 437.
15. Thompson, *Elements*, 60.
16. Barton, "True Interest," 3.
17. Carey quoted in Steele, *Outline Study*, iv.
18. Steele, *Outline Study*, 7.
19. Elder, *Questions*, 9.
20. Thompson, *Elements*, 220.
21. The term originates with Henry Carey, but allusions can be traced to Coxe, *Memorial*, xi.
22. Thompson, *Elements*, 69.
23. Bowen, *American Political Economy*, 79.
24. Wilson, *First Principles*, 117.
25. Bowen, *American Political Economy*, 495.
26. Rae, *Statements*, 35.
27. Carey, *Social Science*, 3:209.
28. Seaman, *Essays*, 146.
29. Phillips, *Propositions*, 227.
30. Phillips, *Propositions*, 222–223.
31. Carey, *Harmony*, 27.
32. Carey, *Social Science*, 2:70.
33. Carey, *Political Economy*, 407; Baird, *Protection*, 9; Thompson, *Elements*, 263; Dudley, *Farmer Freedeth*, 3.
34. Carey, *Social Science*, 2:122.
35. Coxe, *Memorial*, ix–x.
36. Thompson, *Elements*, 69.
37. Roberts, *Government Revenue*, 366–367.
38. Greeley, *Essays*, 38.
39. Carey, *Social Science*, 1:42–43.
40. Elder, *Questions*, 10.
41. Coxe, *Report of the Committee*, xvi.
42. Coxe, *Memorial*, ix.
43. Bowen, *American Political Economy*, 77.
44. Carey, *Harmony*, 203–208.
45. Carey, *Social Science*, 2:238–240.
46. Carey, *Harmony*, 147, 202.
47. Carey, *Social Science*, 1:190.
48. Denslow, "American Economics," 22.
49. Carey, *Social Science*, 1:57; Elder, *Questions*, 10.

50. Carey, *Social Science*, 1:190.
51. Denslow, 'American Economics', 22.
52. Carey, *Harmony*, 203; Denslow, *Principles*, 122.
53. Hudson, *Protectionist Take-off*, xiii.
54. Stebbins, *Protectionist's Manual*, 16.
55. In addition to Denslow, Carey (*Social Science*, 3:312, 415) refers to centripetal and centrifugal forces.
56. Putnam, *Tracts*, 18.
57. List, *National System*, 232–234.
58. Carey, *Harmony*, 190.
59. Ricardo, *Principles*, 54.
60. Carey, *Principles*, 1:189.
61. Denslow to Carey, February 12, 1867, box 12, folder 6, HCCP.
62. Carey, *Social Science*, 1:218.
63. Smith, *Manual*, 206.
64. Thompson, *Elements*, 243.
65. Thompson *Elements*, 47.
66. Hayes, "Solidarity," 136.
67. Carey, *Social Science*, 2:272.
68. List, *National System*, 238.
69. Mason, *Western Farmers*, 82.
70. List, *National System*, 238.
71. Carey, *Social Science*, 1:279.

Chapter Nine

THEORY OF THE BUSINESS CYCLE

Before John Maynard Keynes pioneered the subfield of macroeconomics, the American Protectionists grappled with the question of what causes the business cycle. Their explanation, however, differed from both the Classical economists and the later Keynesians. Unlike the Classical economists who attributed recessions to entrepreneurial miscalculation, and later Keynesians who attributed them to deficient aggregate demand, the American Protectionists identified technological change as the primary cause of cyclical disruptions in economic activity. In positing this theory, the American Protectionists produced one of the first technological theories of recessions in the history of economic thought.

The Classical Consensus: No Such Thing as a General Glut

The Keynesian Revolution fundamentally transformed business cycle theory, and in doing so, what became known as Keynesian macroeconomics would eclipse the prior consensus shared by both Classicals and American Protectionists. Whilst it is true, of course, that the theory of the business cycle put forth by the American Protectionists differs significantly from the Classical understanding, both were essentially in lockstep in their rejection of what would become known as the Keynesian theory of business cycle: that recessions are the result of deficient aggregate demand or generalized overproduction. Of course, this pre-Keynesian consensus was not originally posed in opposition to Keynes himself, but against a group of economists loosely known as underconsumptionists. These underconsumptionists included the likes of Thomas Robert Malthus, Jean Charles Léonard de Sismondi, Thorstein Veblen, and even Karl Marx, who like Keynes, had advanced similar theories of the business cycle predicated on aggregate-demand deficiency.

According to the consensus affirmed by both Classicals and American Protectionists, however, recessions can never be the result of generalized overproduction or underconsumption. In other words, production in aggregate terms could never possibly exceed willingness to buy. Instead, both the Classicals and American Protectionists emphasized what they saw as misalignments in the structure of demand relative to the structure of supply. For the Classical economists, in particular, recessions were the result of entrepreneurs making mistakes when it comes to forecasting the future demand for certain products.[1] This explanation is perhaps most succinctly expressed by

David Ricardo, in his reply to Malthus, that "men err in their production, there is no deficiency of demand."[2]

The American Protectionists deemphasized errors in entrepreneurial forecasting, but they accepted the central premise that recessions could never result from deficient aggregate demand, and that slumps were transitory in nature due to misalignments between the structure of supply and the structure of demand. Peshine Smith explains, for instance, that "the proposition that any good thing has ever been produced in excess of the wants of humanity, will not bear a moment's examination; nor is there the slightest reason to apprehend that such an event is likely to occur."[3] This position is similarly echoed by Francis Bowen who responds explicitly to the underconsumptionists, noting that:

> Some distinguished Economists, among whom are Sismondi and Malthus, have maintained that there may be a general over-production of wealth… We are all familiar with the fact, that there is often, in the market, a glut of a particular commodity, or of several commodities at once… But the doctrine of these Economists is, that there may be a general glut… [our] reasoning is quite conclusive against the possibility of a general glut.[4]

Ellis H. Roberts likewise remarked that it is not "possible to produce too much in the aggregate."[5] Indeed, even the simpler Classical explanation that recessions are the result of entrepreneurs erring in their production causing transitory oversupply in specific commodities was supported by some individual American Protectionists, as demonstrated by Jacob Harris Patton:

> [There] often lurks a temptation to increase the production beyond the wants of the community; and the lack of prudent foresight in the owners of capital often causes them to yield to the tempter… When there is a sufficient amount of woolen cloth made to supply the wants of the consumers, and the capital in that branch of industry pays a fair dividend, and the workpeople receive fair wages and continuous employment, the owners, it may be, wish still larger incomes, and they invest in that business more capital and correspondingly increase the production. They thus show defective business capacity, if they do not take into consideration the wants of the consumers who are already sufficiently supplied by the output of the present mills…
>
> [In this] case a glut in both markets occurs, and the loss of profit on the stock on hand that cannot be sold, causes a depression in the industry, and, perhaps, stoppage for a time of the mills, with loss of money to the owners and loss of employment and wages to the workpeople. It would have been better if this extracapital had been invested elsewhere.[6]

In any event, it is clear that the American Protectionists rejected the notion of general overproduction. Yet most American Protectionists went further than the traditional Classical explanation by highlighting the role of inventions in bringing about miscalculations in production. The American Protectionists would therefore arrive at a distinct explanation of the business cycle whilst still affirming many of the fundamentals put forth by the Classicals.

A Technological Theory of the Business Cycle

The American Protectionists went beyond the Classical economists by identifying technological change as the underlying mechanism behind the business cycle.[7] Productivity-enhancing inventions, it was argued, would bring about temporary disruptions in production by creating sudden bouts of overproduction in specific sectors of the economy. The basis of this theory originates in a manuscript written by Tench Coxe. Writing with respect to the Panic of 1819, Coxe posits that crises emerge due to advancements in labor-saving inventions which result in the overproduction of specific commodities. Indeed, "the most serious matters, affecting the United States in the form of depression of the value of the productions of its industry," explains Coxe, are "the wonderful power of machinery" and the "wonderful power of inventions of a scientific kind."[8] In the case of the Panic of 1819, Coxe identified the introduction of labor-saving inventions in cotton manufacturing as the root cause of the crisis. In the words of Coxe:

> [Cotton manufacturers using] hand work ... made [cotton cloth] at 10, 8, 9 & 6 cents per yard, while their neighbours were introducing the steam, water or power loom, which makes a good cloth of cotton... at the cost of a single cent!
>
> From the superior perfection of our own machinery and scientific means, in various branches, many of our Manufacturers, who too long worked by means of human hands, have been subjected to an accumulation of excess goods, occasioning a dead mass of capital to some: ruin to others.[9]

Similar sentiments were also later echoed by James G. Blaine, who states that:

> An argument much relied upon and strongly presented by the advocates of free-trade is the alleged tendency to over-production of protected articles, followed uniformly by seasons of depression and at certain intervals by financial panic and wide-spread distress...
>
> The assailants of protection apparently overlook the fact that excessive production is due... to causes beyond the operation of duties either high or low. No cause is more potent than the prodigious capacity of machinery set in motion by the agency of steam. It is not strange that, with this vast enginery, the power to produce has a tendency to outrun the power to consume.[10]

The adoption of labor-saving machines by multiple producers at the same time within a particular industry, therefore, has the potential to lead to overproduction in that particular industry. The American Protectionists were thus not denying the existence of overproduction. In fact, it was their explanation for why recessions occur. They saw, however, that overproduction is related to the adoption of specific inventions and tended to be isolated to a particular sector or a particular range of sectors within the economy. Henry M. Hoyt thus explains that "we have seen how... overproduction for a given market breaks down exchange values," for in that industry "alone resided superior efficiency of production."[11] The American Protectionists were not disparaging technological change of course. They were adamantly in favor of encouraging technological improvements through protective legislation, but they recognized that such developments could indeed create transitory dislocations in production.

The question of how overproduction in specific sectors can lead to a more or less generalized disruption in economic activity (i.e., a clustering of business failures) relates to the role of linkages in the economy. It should be recalled that the American Protectionists considered industrial linkages as serving a valuable function in the economy, and these linkages underscored the need for a diversified national economy with the varied sectors of industry forming into one harmonious whole. Conversely, linkages also represent the mechanism by which overproduction in a specific sector or specific sectors can unravel into an economy-wide recession. In short, because of the presence of linkages, overproduction and distress in a particular industry will tend to produce distress in linked industries. Henry Carey explains, for instance, that:

> The producer of coal suffers because the furnace is closed, and the producer of iron suffers because the factories are no longer built, and the maker of cloth suffers because labour is everywhere being wasted, and the power to buy cloth is diminished.[12]

This tendency was also recognized by Tench Coxe, who notes that businesses who "have operated on immense scales… spread injury around them in every direction by their failures."[13] One of the more important linkages, however, which can cause what would be an otherwise localized crisis to become generalized are the linkages which industry has with the banking sector. In Coxe's example, for instance, the collapse of the banking sector could be traced to the failure and subsequent defaults among producers within the oversupplied cotton manufacturing industry. As the localized crisis spreads to the banking sector, there is then a further tendency for it to ripple throughout the rest of the economy due to the myriad of linkages between the banking and virtually every other kind of industry. Thus, Coxe, returning to his example, explains that:

> From such a state of things [i.e., overproduction and subsequent bankruptcies] requisite on, suddenly made, upon the whole body of borrowers and credit purchasers in town & country… a vast proportion of the present difficulties among the land holders, cultivators, merchants, bankers, manufacturers, dealers, and improvers undoubtedly arise.[14]

This distinctly American Protectionist explanation also explains why growth sometimes behaves in a cyclical manner with linkages amplifying both upswings and downswings in economic activity. Since the prosperity of a specific sector or a specific range of sectors will produce a tendency for banks to extend credit into such sectors, this means that if overproduction occurs, as the result of technological improvement, something which typically accompanies the expansion of a particular industry, the subsequent impact upon the banking sector, and hence the rest of the economy as a whole, will be more pronounced due to the presence of linkages. This means that periods of expansion in particular industries will sometimes be followed by transitory slumps in economic activity, as business failures spread through the economy.

Diversification as a Stabilizing Force

Since recessions and depressions are the result of technological improvements that produce an overproduction of specific commodities, or a specific range of commodities (as opposed to generalized overproduction), the American Protectionists did not endorse the use of counter-cyclical public spending as a cure. Creating an artificial stimulus to encourage the consumption of goods already in excess would only act as a perverse incentive for businesses to continue overproducing commodities in oversupply. In fact, crises were often seen as a necessary correction to the chronic oversupply of specific commodities, and would thereby force entrepreneurs to abandon their existing modes of production and to seek out new industrial pursuits. Van Buren Denslow saw, for instance, that:

> Commercial… crises perform, in certain ways, a useful function in industry, and tend ultimately to promote production, while at first discouraging it. They correct a tendency of industry to continue in given channels… Commercial crises, in these instances, are a means of correcting undue persistence in the beaten ways of industry, and of turning labor and capital into the new and unbeaten ways where they are more needed… All conductors of industry and employers of labor, whose position is weak, are weeded out and must look for "something new." In the universal search for "something new" those new industries are found and developed, in which society is chiefly interested because in them lie eventually the great profits and the great utilities.[15]

Even though American Protectionists rejected the notion that governments could cure recessions via stimulus spending or other direct means, they did contend that recessions could be mitigated against. Since recessions are the result of the overproduction of specific commodities, and because there is no such thing as generalized overproduction, both the prevention and the cure is to greatly increase the variety and diversity of production. This way, idle workers and resources can move from the oversupplied to the undersupplied areas of production. Peshine Smith explains, for example, that:

> Some writers have been bewildered, of a general over-production of commodities… [But] the truth of the matter may be quite as correctly rendered by the statement, that the supply of other commodities is deficient, as that any particular one is redundant… The true remedy for what is called over-production, in any article, is an increased production of other things.[16]

Ellis H. Roberts likewise remarks that:

> Too many may crowd into a single vocation, or its product may lose its profitable ratio to the general demand. Then new occupations must be substituted, and the sphere of production must be enlarged.[17]

This emphasis on economic diversification as both a guard against and a remedy for sector-specific overproduction was widespread across the School. George B. Tibbits applied this principle to agricultural specialization, observing that "the cause of this great depression of agriculture is obvious. *That branch of business, compared with every other, is overdone.*"[18] Robert Ellis Thompson similarly notes that while "over-production… has characterized some branches of manufacture… there are still plenty of openings for the investment of new capital in [other] manufactures."[19] Likewise, Thomas H. Dudley articulated the problem with respect to overconcentration of capital in overworked industries, emphasizing the need for a more diverse range of investment opportunities for capitalists. In the words of Dudley:

> No civilized country has been or ever will be prosperous and great without a diversity of industrial pursuits… If an excess of capital should be thrown into one industry there would be an over production in that industry, and prices would fall, and loss ensue; and all the other industries would be to a greater or less extent affected by this loss. If, however, capital should be so distributed as to stimulate and develop all the industries alike, and in this way give employment to all the people, there would be gain instead of loss.[20]

Indeed, even John Philip Young, who represents an outlier in the School due to his pessimism about "systematic overproduction," rejects policies designed to boost aggregate demand, arguing that the best approach is to "concentrate… efforts upon the promotion of domestic industry… by stimulating the people in manifold directions… [and] to provide a greater field of the exercise" of enterprise and industry.[21]

In any event, by cultivating a greater variety of pursuits and allowing resources to move from the oversupplied to the undersupplied areas of production, this also has the effect of stabilizing those sectors in oversupply. As entrepreneurs and workers move out of the oversupplied areas, overproduction will cease, the competition within that particular industry will be lessened, and profitability will gradually return. Rufus Choate explains, for instance, that manufactures "do [a] good service to agriculture by lessening the number that pursues it, and giving them a nearer and better market."[22] Likewise, William Jennison also saw that "a variety of productions will have a tendency to check that excessive competition now prevailing among the agricultural class, the cultivators of grain, of tobacco and cotton" to name a few examples.[23]

Moreover, the cultivation of these new industries will also tend to stabilize established industries by creating new sources of demand. The best rendering of this can be found in George B. Dixwell, who declares that:

> Each new commodity, convenience, and amusement furnishes a new market for the existing industries, and enlarges the effective demand… [Thus] the introduction of a new industry finds ample unemployed capital for its development, and in which its products immediately enlarge the market for the products of the old industries, and enable them to increase their production.[24]

In terms of creating a more diverse and varied economy, the American Protectionists saw that this could only be achieved by creating conditions conducive to inventive and entrepreneurial activities. In their eyes, this was best achieved by enacting and sustaining the American System. Indeed, Orrin Skinner explains that the American

System "relieves the crowded and overworked avenues of industry by opening a way to the prosecution of new industrial pursuits."[25] This thinking is also well expressed by Daniel Webster, who explains that "reasonable protection… multiples the modes of employment. It prevents any channel from being filled and choked up. One of the secrets of prosperity is, that there shall be a considerable variety in pursuits."[26]

In this way, the approach of the American Protectionists differs from the more activist Keynesian response in that their approach is very much hands off and passive in nature. Government was only seen as shaping the conditions necessary for diversification and entrepreneurship, but it is ultimately the inventive and entrepreneurial function of private enterprise which led recovery. Ellis H. Roberts captured this vision of an entrepreneurial-driven recovery most fully:

> The champion of commerce [domestic exchange] discovers a Gorgon in the form of overproduction. He tells us we must beware of developing home industry because the markets will not take our commodities. In no country where population is so great and soil so various and occupations so diverse as with us is it possible to produce too much in the aggregate… [rather] the equation of commodities to each other may be temporarily amiss… Instead of curtailing production, what we need is greater variety of manufacture, a more diversified industry. The trouble is that the supply is not in sufficient variety… The folly of putting all one's eggs in one basket has passed into an axiom… In this branch or that, an excess has doubtless been created, but the trouble has been that labor has not been sufficiently diversified…
>
> The cure for apparent overproduction is not to stop work and moan over excess of commodities. On the contrary, the secret of prosperity is to create new manufactures, and to afford occupation to more people, and thus provide them with means to buy enjoyments with which they are not yet familiar… with every new industry a field is found by individuals who have played the idler, or have waited for their opportunity.
>
> Men have special tastes and aptitudes. A witty scholar has defined idleness to be ill-directed industry. Beyond question the idle singer of a summer day may have in him the qualities which will conquer success in some occupation which enlists his tastes and his genius. Every invention enlists fresh recruits in production. Every new vocation rallies some men who have stood idle in the market place.[27]

n particular, invention needs to be in the form of product inventions or the discovery of new fields of industry, as opposed to process inventions or productivity enhancing improvements. Product inventions allow for variation and diversification of industrial pursuits which thereby lessens the tendency for overproduction in specific sectors; whereas process inventions increase the likelihood for transient overproduction to occur in specific sectors.

The other crucial point of this theory of the business cycle is that highly specialized and undiversified economies are more susceptible and vulnerable to recessions than diversified ones. Indeed, if the nation specializes in one particular sector, and overproduction occurs in that particular sector, then for all practical purposes, this industry-specific crisis constitutes a general crisis because that particular sector constitutes such a significant portion of the economy. Although overproduction in particular sectors will be inevitable in certain instances, the economy as a whole will be more readily able to withstand recessions if it is more diversified since the undersupplied sectors can act as a shock absorber for the economy by absorbing the idle workers and resources from the oversupplied sectors. Justin Smith Morrill captures this logic, explaining that "diversified employments" and "industries are mutual insurers, and when disaster befalls any special branch the loss is made up from the better fortune of all other branches," but such is not the case for "those nations confined to a single venture."[28] In other words, economic diversification, as opposed to the specialization advanced by the Classical economists, is necessary to mitigate recessions and depressions.

Notes

1. For a more thorough treatment of the Classical theory of the business cycle, see Kates, *Say's Law.*
2. Ricardo to Malthus, 173.
3. Smith, *Manual*, 247.
4. Bowen, *American Political Economy*, 225.
5. Roberts, *Government Revenue*, 183.
6. Patton, *Political Economy*, 62–63.
7. Some American Protectionists held to monetary theories of the business cycle, albeit ones that do not necessarily rule out non-monetary causes.
8. Coxe, *Inquiry*, 8.
9. Coxe, *Inquiry*, 5–6.
10. Blaine, *Twenty Years*, 1:213–214.
11. Hoyt, *Protection*, 158.
12. Carey, *Harmony*, 49.
13. Coxe, *Inquiry*, 5.
14. Coxe, *Inquiry*, 6.
15. Denslow, *Principles*, 396.
16. Smith, *Manual*, 247.
17. Roberts, *Government Revenue*, 183.
18. Tibbits, *Memoir*, 7.
19. Thompson, *Elements*, 360–361.
20. Dudley, *Best for Farmers*, 12.
21. Young, "Economic Aspects," 87, 82.
22. Choate, *Speech*, 42.
23. Jennison, *Outline*, 3.
24. Dixwell, "Bastiat," 22–23.
25. Skinner, *American Politics*, 416.
26. Webster, "General Effects," 534.
27. Roberts, *Government Revenue*, 180–186.
28. Morrill, *Protective Tariff*, 13.

Chapter Ten

THEORY OF INTERNATIONAL TRADE

The greatest heresy committed by the American Protectionists was their rejection of free trade. Described by William Stanley Jevons "as a fundamental axiom of political economy," no doctrine commanded more near-universal assent among nineteenth-century political economists than the theory of comparative advantage and the benefits of unrestricted exchange.[1] Yet in challenging this orthodoxy, the American Protectionists would demolish the theory of comparative advantage, one assumption after another—supplanting it with their own distinct explanation of trade. Where the Classicals saw fixed and original differences in productivity rates as forming the basis for trade, the American Protectionists considered how productivity changes through the act of production itself. Where the Classicals looked to abstract factors of production, American Protectionists understood that factors are naturally suited to different pursuits. Where the Classicals preached international specialization, the American Protectionists championed protected diversification. Indeed, Henry Carey said it best when he declared that "two systems are before the world… One is the English system; the other we may be proud to call the American System."[2]

At its base, the American Protectionist theory of international trade concerns the influence of diminishing and increasing returns in economic production. As mentioned previously, the American Protectionists viewed manufacturing as subject to increasing returns. This occurs through the application of inventions, labor-saving machines, human capital, and the learning by doing nature of industry. As a result, industrial production has a natural tendency towards increasing returns or—to use the vernacular of the American Protectionists—tends to experience diminishing costs of reproduction over time. This view is well expressed by William D. Wilson:

> Hence in every stage of an advancing civilization human labor becomes more effective, and avails more and more, in the production of those articles… And with each such advancing stage, therefore, the price, the actual labor-cost of nearly every article, should be less than in any preceding stage.[3]

In contrast to industrial economies, it was argued that exporters of raw material will almost always witness a perpetual deterioration of trade performance over time as the country's productive soil becomes increasingly exhausted. Indeed, since raw material exporters would and, according to the theory of comparative advantage, should sell their raw materials to industrial nations, only to buy it back as finished goods, this means that the already existing trade imbalances will grow increasingly wider and unsustainable over time. George M. Steele explains, for instance, that "unless manufacturing centers exist in the midst of agricultural areas, products of the soil must be conveyed to a great distance. But *this implies virtually an exportation of the soil,* and this is a diminution of the capital of the farmer."[4]

Raw material exporters would thus become increasingly impoverished relative to industrial nations. Yet, it goes much further than this. Because productive soil is essentially exported from raw material exporters to industrial economies, this also results in a net exportation of productive power. This, in turn, results in a net productivity transfer from the agricultural industries of raw material exporters to advanced industrial economies. Henry Carey thus explains that "the reverse of… what we are told in English [economics] books" is true. "Limiting the latter [agricultural exporters] to the work of scratching out the soil and selling it in distant markets, [is] thus preventing the growth of agriculture," rather than enhancing it.[5] Peshine Smith echoes these concerns, noting this tendency for free trade to culminate in diminishing returns for agricultural producers. In the words of Smith:

> The system of foreign trade… itself, necessarily tends to impoverish the land already under cultivation, to reduce it to a lower grade of fertility, or what is [in effect] the same thing, [as] to require a greater outlay of labour and capital, in order to maintain its rate of production.[6]

However, this tendency towards decreasing returns only holds for nations that specialize in agricultural production. Or to put it differently, it only occurs when agricultural production is divorced from manufacturing. Whilst agriculture will tend to experience diminishing returns in a pre-industrial setting, the opposite is the case in developed industrial economies.

Through advancements in technology, chemical science, and through the application of machinery, the American Protectionists observed that agriculture, like manufacturing, is completely capable of experiencing increasing returns. They therefore argued that agriculture must be situated within proximity to industrial centers. This allows agriculture to capture technological spillovers, to benefit from the application of machinery, and it also allows productive soil to be returned to the land.

The American Protectionists thus repudiated the Ricardian assumption that trade performance is the result of fixed and permanent differences in productivity between nations as conditioned by factor endowments. Instead, trade performance must be viewed in light of how production, and hence how trade itself, alters the productivity of different industries both within and between nations. It was thus conceivable, and indeed very probable, that domestic and international trade affects productivity in different ways. Peshine Smith expresses this point well, noting that "we must inquire, therefore, whether domestic exchange has any advantage over foreign trade, in rendering a given amount of labour more productive."[7]

The recognition that internal and external trade—and by extension protection and free trade—can produce different rates of productivity growth is a hallmark of the American Protectionist analysis of trade. This will be demonstrated more thoroughly throughout the rest of the chapter. Yet one of the most explicit illustrations of this pproach comes from David Rice, who explains how protection, by giving greater scope r entrepreneurial experimentation and discovery, produces a comparatively higher ıte of inventive growth than free trade. In the words of Rice:

> Another economic law which affects the comparative producing capacity of protective nations, as against the free-trade tariff nation… is that which we may term the energized inventive faculties of the former. When business is exceedingly brisk in any general branch of manufacture, the inventive faculties of millions of people are continually and actively at work to improve upon its agencies… They will… [undertake] experiments in numbers of directions to gain one success, which, but for these experiments, would have lain dormant… So in the protected nations, their inventors and their business men are alert and bold… [Under free trade, however,] the inventive faculties of the people become dormant, and capital becomes timid and refuses to invest in new experiments or appliances to promote and cheapen production.[8]

'he Infant-Industry Argument

'he oldest argument presented by the American Protectionists in support of rotectionism is the infant-industry argument, which also happens to be the argument ıey are most well known for. Whilst Hamilton's *Report on Manufactures* is most commonly ted as the source of this argument, the basic argument dates to roughly a decade prior ı Hamilton's *Continentalist* essays. In the words of Hamilton:

> There may… [through the protection of industries] be a possibility of opening new sources, which, though accompanied with great difficulties in the commencement, would in the event amply reward the trouble and expence of bringing them to perfection. The undertaking may often exceed the influence and capitals of individuals; and may require no small assistance… from the authority of the state.[9]

'he infant-industry argument argues that since foreign producers in more developed ations received a head start in development, and are thus more productive, it follows that ıfant industries will be smothered in the cradle if they are forced to compete with their ıore developed foreign counterparts. Indeed, "manufactures" explains George Tibbits cannot, without great efforts, and the strong protection of government in their infancy… e introduced, domesticated, and established… while foreign manufactured articles are still eely admitted, and allowed to be brought into competition with home manufactures."[10]

It is for this reason that George M. Steele declared that protection is "the only sure efence of new and feeble industries against the unequal competition of those long stablished in other communities."[11] Protectionism is thus necessary to allow infant-ıdustries to catch-up to their more advanced rivals. This position is well put by John .ae who explains that:

> The legislator effects his purpose… by duties on that imported from abroad… [It is] sufficiently apparent that nothing prevents the branch of industry in question being established, but the difficulties attending new undertakings, the want of skilled labor, and a sufficiently accurate

> knowledge of the properties of the materials to be employed in the formation of the new instruments, it is then proper to proceed to direct and general encouragements by bounties or duties. In this way real capital, and healthy enterprise are directed to the art, the difficulties attending its introduction overcome in the shortest possible space.[12]

The infant-industry argument can thus be juxtaposed to the Classical theory of comparative advantage. Whereas the gains-from-trade described in Ricardo's theory of comparative advantage can be identified at a given point in time by comparing the relative cost of production between two nations, the American Protectionists saw that a simple comparison of static production costs represents a dubious criterion on which to formulate trade policy. Static production costs are largely meaningless since costs of production are always liable to change, and in the case of developing economies, liable to fall. Indeed, because industry is marked by the process of learning by doing and by falling costs of reproduction as industry expands, the American Protectionists looked to what industry would become instead of what it presently is.

The American Protectionists were adamant, however, that the promotion of infant-industries should not be pursued through coercive and heavy-handed government policies. As David Rice explains, "it must be remembered that capital cannot be coerced into investing in any branch of industry. It must be led, but it cannot be driven."[13] In fact sometimes the case for infant-industry protection was presented on purely psychological grounds. As noted previously, since individuals tend to be creatures of habit, they are often reluctant to engage in new industrial pursuits. Hamilton thus explains that "the apprehension of failing in new attempts is perhaps a more serious impediment" to the establish of new industries. Hence, the use of protection is often necessary so "that the confidence of cautious, sagacious capitalists… should be excited."[14] In short infant-industry protection was there to provide entrepreneurs with the opportunity the confidence, and the breathing room to experiment and engage in new industrial undertakings without being crushed by foreign producers.

Historical analysis also formed a part of the infant-industry argument. The American Protectionists noted that whilst more advanced economies often preached free trade they themselves almost always employed protectionist policies to develop their infant industries. It was only after their industries reached a degree of development where they were unmatched in terms of productivity that they then espoused the universal adoption of free trade. This led Friedrich List to explains that:

> It is a vulgar rule of prudence for him who has reached the pinnacle of power to cast down the ladder which he mounted, that others may not follow. In this lies the secret of Adam Smith's theory, and its cosmopolite tendencies… A nation which by protective duties… has built up a manufacturing industry…. to such a point of strength and power as not to fear the competition of any other, can pursue no safer policy than to thrust aside the means of elevation, to preach to other nations the advantages of free trade.[15]

In its original context, the infant-industry argument was seen as being temporally bounded, that is, applicable to a certain place and time. However, later American Protectionists saw that the logic behind the infant-industry argument was applicabl more broadly to established and mature industries. They thus argued that infant-industry protection was the rule, rather than the exception, and this lent itself to a perpetual and permanent policy of protection. This is due to the fact that there are always new entrants and infant firms within established industries. This position is well expressed by John L. Hayes:

> The view that protective duties in this country have now accomplished their mission implies the vague, indefinite, and unpractical notions commonly held by revenue reformers… It contemplates them as a whole [as opposed to them as individual manufactures], without discrimination in regard to the infinite variety of conditions, circumstances, and wants in manufacturing industries. It implies that our manufactures, as totality, once in their infancy have now passed into the stage of manhood; whereas as manufactures advance, the buds and seedlings in new branches of manufacture increase, so that portions of manufactures are always in their infancy.[16]

Moreover, whilst some industries will reach a relatively higher state of maturity than others, it is nonetheless the case that all industries are, in a sense, infant, as they are always going through a process of change and development. In short, there is never a point where you can clearly isolate and identify an industry as having reached maturity. This logic is well captured in Willard Phillips' response to the staunchly free-trade Walker report:

> If by the inquiry "when will our arts cease to be infant?" be meant… "when will they come to the point of perfection where nothing can be added or changed for the better?" We may well hope that this never will be. This would be the stand-still point… Arts can never advance to the utmost bounds of human invention, and exhaust all possibilities of improvement… They will advance by one improvement giving rise to another, so as to propagate infant arts in an infinite series. Theorists seem to think it possible… to pass from rudeness to the ultimate perfection in any and all arts, at a step… [Yet] the arts do not… instantaneously spring into existence in complete maturity and perfection. "Life is short and art is long;" that is, long in comparison with human life.[17]

This also links to their analysis of individual versus national wealth discussed in previous chapters. Because human life is finite, whereas the life of the nation is potentially infinite, it follows that since industry is in a continuous state of development, producing in its stride permanent and diffusive benefits to society, it will be successive generations of the nation's populace who will reap the majority of the benefits from new industrial undertakings in the present day. The encouragement of infant-industries and new industrial pursuits is therefore predicated, in no small part, on the view that it will contribute more to the wealth of the nation than the wealth of any given individual entrepreneur bringing it into existence.

The Preservation of Mature Industries

Although the American Protectionists never used the term the "mature-industry argument," there is a clear line of thought within the School which emphasizes the preservation of mature industries. This passing from infant-industry to the mature-industry argument came most explicitly with Alexander Dallas' *Report on the General Tariff.* The argument is, however, more of a general collection of arguments. In short, the mature-industry argument holds that even after an industry reaches a relatively mature state of development, it still makes sense to maintain protective tariffs, since the adoption of free trade would risk the loss of the nation's productive resources. In fact, in its original context, Dallas argued that the protection of mature industries is defensible even at the expense of revenue, explaining that "government will surely deem it better to sacrifice a portion of its revenue, than to sacrifice those institutions which private enterprise and wealth have connected with public prosperity and independence."[18]

A key element of the mature-industry argument revolves around the concept of heterogenous factors of production. Indeed, this conception would naturally lead to the conclusion that foreign competition is fundamentally different in nature to competition among domestic firms. Since factors of production are heterogenous, it follows that trade induced deindustrialization would constitute a loss to the nation's productive resources. Indeed, in the case of a domestic firm losing out to domestic competitors, productive resources are not wholly lost, as they have the ability to shift and to be absorbed by their competitors. Yet, such is not the case if domestic firms lose out to foreign competitors. In this scenario, the entire stock of productive resources within a particular industry cannot simply be sold as an industry declines since there must be buyers within that industry willing to purchase and employ them. Stephen Colwell thus explains that:

> There are not merely difficulties in the way of a national change from one department of industry to another, according to the phrase so flippantly employed by the [Classical] School… there are utter impossibilities in the way…. [When] individuals have changed occupations… the national industry has undergone no change: one manufacturer has given place to another, and one agriculturist to another. [However,] manufacturing capital is chiefly invested in immense factory buildings… and in machinery and implements fit for nothing else; this capital cannot, by any possibility be applied to agriculture.
>
> [Thus] when a whole nation can no longer manufacture… the capital invested in buildings, machinery, and implements, is wholly lost. And even when men skilled in working in iron and cotton, wool and silk, are compelled to find labor in other branches of industry, an immense productive power is lost, because all their skill, experience and facility, becomes useless.[19]

Thus, when viewed through the lens of national wealth, it becomes clear that the failure of a private business in isolation does not necessarily detract from the wealth of the nation, yet the failure of an entire industry does. Indeed, the failure of an isolated business may indeed contribute to national wealth if these resources are absorbed and better utilized by its domestic competitors, but no such mechanism exists if an entire industry is lost.

Tariffs were thus not only viewed as a means of encouraging the development of infant-industries, but also as a preventative measure to preserve existing industries and to maintain the nation's productive capacity. American Protectionists likened protection to a levee which guards industries against temporary bouts of excessive foreign production. John L. Hayes explains, for instance, that:

> The objection here arises that this enormous development of manufacturing power shows that our protective duties have performed their work and may be safely dispensed with… The duties, however, still perform a most important service. Though they may have ceased to stimulate, they defend. They are like the levee, which must be high enough to resist the highest tides and the occasional inundations.[20]

A similar position is also espoused by Nathanial A. Ware, who declares:

> We are asked, why keep on the old tariff if the goods become as cheap as the foreign? I answer, that the tariff becomes a dead letter as to fair and honest prices, but is useful as a preventive [measure].[21]

Indeed, as elaborated upon in the next chapter, American Protectionists argued that domestic consumers would forego the tax burden of tariff protection once industries reach a relative state of maturity. According to this view, the protection of mature industries only involves a cost to consumers during periods in which international markets are temporarily flooded with foreign goods. The costs of keeping these industries afloat during such periods of inundation were thus temporary and necessary. In the long run, these costs would be more than offset by preventing the loss of productive resources. The logic of maintaining tariffs as a means of preservation is not too far removed therefore from the standard infant-industry argument. Infant-industry protection is predicated on the view that the short-term costs of protecting infant industries is justified by the long-term benefit which those industries will bestow upon the economy. Likewise, the temporary cost to the consumer of preserving mature industries during periods of excessive foreign production is justified by the longer term benefits of retaining these industries and preventing the loss of the nation's productive resources.

The Home-Market Argument

The home-market argument represents another key argument expounded by the American Protectionists. This argument, in particular, concerns the indirect benefits accruing to agriculture from the protection of manufacturing industries. At its most basic, the home-market argument rests upon the view that production is the cause of consumption. Or to be more precise, for an individual to be a consumer of a particular commodity, the individual must first be a producer of another commodity. Since there are natural limits to the production of specific commodities, it thus follows that the creation of another class of producers, such as manufacturers, will enable greater consumption of these commodities. In this case, greater consumption of agricultural commodities. Indeed, as George Tibbits writes, "it is from the great variety and plenty of other products made within the same country, that the rude product of the land finds its advantage, by furnishing values in other articles for which it can be exchanged in the home market."[22] Or as Oliver Putnam puts it, "manufacture[s], in the multiplication of its products, increases the demand for the products of the other branches of industry."[23] Indeed, although the home-market argument was typically employed with respect to enlarging the demand for agricultural commodities, the logic extends to all kinds of goods and services. However, in the case of agricultural commodities, the argument is relatively simple. The encouragement of industrial production would constitute a new source of demand for agricultural production. This position is well put by Richard W. Thompson, who explains that:

> Every manufacturing establishment in the United States... helps to build up a home market in its own vicinity. Such establishments, considered as a whole, furnish employment to many thousands of laborers, who have to subsist themselves and their families out of our surplus agricultural products.[24]

The view that the production of commodities constitutes the demand for other commodities in the home market also formed a counterargument against the view that the cultivation of new industries through protectives measures diverts capital from, and thus hurts, existing industries. In responding to Bastiat of the French Liberal School, George B. Dixwell argues that:

> Bastiat imagined that a new industry would be established by capital drawn from the old industries, which would be thus cramped and diminished... [but the] products [of the new industry], when established, constitute an additional market for the products of the old industries, enabling them all to increase their production.[25]

The above also connects closely to another key aspect of the home-market argument which concerns the creation of linkages between different sectors within the economy. As discussed previously, the American Protectionists held that establishing a domestic manufacturing industry within the national economy, would create linkages with, and thus demand for, domestic agricultural inputs. This thinking is well again exemplified by Oliver Putnam, who explains that "in consuming cotton goods of foreign manufacture, we encourage the cultivator of foreign cotton; whereas in consuming cotton goods of domestic manufacture we encourage only our own [cotton agri]culture."[26]

Another crucial element of the home-market argument concerns the superiority of the home market in terms of the certainty and reliance which it bestows upon the nation's farmers and agriculturalists. In short, the national government has no direct control over the policies of foreign governments, and thus cannot guarantee continued access to foreign markets. It only has sovereignty over the home market. It is therefore riskier for a nation of agriculturalists to be reliant on foreign demand as compared to home demand. Alexander Hamilton captures this thinking perfectly, explaining how:

> There appear strong reasons to regard the foreign demand for that [agricultural] surplus as too uncertain a reliance, and to desire a substitute for it in an extensive domestic market. To secure such a market there is no other expedient than to promote manufacturing

> establishments. Manufacturers, who constitute the most numerous class… are for that reason the principal consumers of the surplus of their labor.[27]

In addition to its certainty and reliability, the home-market was also seen as superior when factoring in the transportation costs involved in shipping agricultural produce to foreign markets. By creating a home market through the establishment of manufactures, this means that the farmer would be able to forego the "tax of transportation." In the words of Thomas Haines Dudley:

> He [the farmer] also wants a near market. The heaviest tax on a farmer is that which he pays for getting his crops to market; therefore, the nearer the market the less the cost. The home market is nearer than a foreign market, hence less expensive.[28]

The American Protectionists therefore differ from the mercantilist doctrine of encouraging manufactures and forcing colonies or trading partners to supply raw materials and agricultural production. For the American Protectionists, the establishment of manufacturing was also seen as a means of supporting domestic agriculture through a harmony of interests. Such sentiments are well put by Andrew Stewart who explains that:

> It is the great object therefore to take care of agriculture, make this prosperous and the whole country will prosper; and how is agriculture to be made prosperous but by building up and sustaining home markets. It is therefore not for the manufacturers, but for the mechanics and farmers, yes, sir, for the farmers, that I advocate the protective policy.[29]

It should be finally noted that the home-market argument is not an argument for outright autarky. It is instead an argument for the primacy of internal over external trade. The American Protectionist accepted some role for foreign trade, albeit subject to protective tariffs, but they understood that a strong home market must always be the foundation on which foreign trade is sustained. This position is well put by John Phillips Young who explains that "the internal trade of a country, in the nature of things, will always be its most important trade, and that under any rational system of economics external trade must be relegated to the second place and become, as it were, merely an incident of national progress."[30] Or, as Giles B. Stebbins explains, "the home market for our home workers is the foundation; the export of our growing surplus is its result."[31]

Industrial Diversification versus Trade Specialization

The American Protectionists saw industrial diversification as producing numerous benefits ranging from linkages to technological diffusion. However, whilst these are incredibly important to their system, they can be largely viewed as secondary benefits. The more important benefit of industrial diversification is how it creates greater scope for different individuals to exercise their unique talents and aptitudes by undertaking pursuits that are most congenial. Indeed, it should be recalled that the most significant divergence between the Classicals and the American Protectionists relates to their treatment of human nature. Whereas Classical economics treats individuals as uniform and homogeneous, the American Protectionist thought sees individuality as the distinctive feature of mankind. This divergence has profound implications for international trade and underpins the American Protectionists' strongest argument against the Classical trade theory and its conclusion that nations should specialize.

To recognize the scope of their argument, it is important to delve into the assumptions underpinning Classical trade theory. Since the Classical economists assume that a unit of labor is simply a unit of labor, it is perfectly reasonable to accept the conclusion that specializing in a single commodity, or a narrow basket of commodities, under free trade would represent a prudent policy. The Ricardian line of thinking, in particular, underscores this view. According to Ricardo, "under a system of perfectly free commerce, each country naturally devotes its capital and labour to such employments as are most beneficial to each." Indeed, "by using most efficaciously the peculiar powers bestowed by nature, it distributes labor most effectively."[32] Thus, according to Ricardo, labor is distributed to the most efficient area of production, not because of the individual characteristics of the laborers themselves, but on the basis of natural resource endowments. Because labor is abstract and homogenous, the Ricardian logic implies that mobility of labor between industries is costless. Moreover, since Classical economics more broadly assumes that individual differences arise from the division of labor, it follows that all laborers will become equally accustomed to whatever narrow line of production the theory of absolute or comparative advantage dictates.

In contrast, the American Protectionists completely rejected the idea that nations should specialize, and instead, espoused diversification and championed the cultivation of all industries, and not just manufacturing. This represents an argument from fundamental axioms. Because individuals are naturally different, diversification is necessary to accommodate these differences. As Andrew W. Young explains:

> It is erroneously assumed by the opponents of protection, that its object is to promote the manufacturing interest in particular… Protectionists, on the contrary,… believe that the labor of a country should be diversified… The reasons for favoring this diversity of human industry are, first, that all men are not fitted by inclination or natural faculty for the same pursuit.[33]

Indeed, since individuals possess different talents, abilities, dispositions and interests, cultivating a greater scope and variety of employments and pursuits would maximize the productive potential and welfare of the nation's citizens. In contrast, if a nation were to specialize in a narrow range of economic pursuits, as implied in the theories of absolute and comparative advantage, this means that a great bulk of the nation's citizens would be locked into employments unsuitable and uncongenial to their individual qualities. Classical trade theory is thus completely mistaken, and its conclusion that nations should specialize, would diminish the nation's productive potential, rather than enhancing it. In the words of George M. Steele:

> In every considerable community there are a great number of diverse tastes and aptitudes, many of which cannot be easily adjusted except to particular employments; and unless these [particular employments] exist, a large proportion of the labor-force will be either unapplied, or so applied as to lose much of its legitimate effect.[34]

Indeed, this view dates back to the very inception of the School, and was first expressed by Tench Coxe, who declared that:

> When the variety of human talent is duly remembered… that minds of the strongest & most active powers for their proper objects, may fall below mediocrity, or labour without effect, if confined to incongenial pursuits, it will appear unwise so to arrange our political oeconomy as to impel to agriculture the whole body of the people… Those who have been peculiarly qualified by nature for the useful arts, should find the encouragement necessary to call forth their various talents. All employment… were doubtless intended to be pursued… [and] attained to facility and eminence in the greatest variety.[35]

The American Protectionists thus acknowledged that mankind as a species is uniquely characterized by its high degree of diversity, differentiation, and individuality. Without a diversity of employments, there will necessarily be unique qualities which will remain dormant and unutilized. As such, "[the] American tariff," explains Jacob Harris Patton, "should [be] so… calculated to create a diversity of industries, which are essential… [to] the exercise of different shades of talent and taste."[36]

By creating a variety of different opportunities, a protective tariff would thus allow individuals to seek out modes of enterprise and employment best suited to their unique characteristics, and would thus raise national productivity more than it would if the economy specialized in a particular commodity or narrow range of commodities. This view is well expressed by Horace Greeley, remarking that:

> A multiplication and diversification of pursuits [aids productivity by] giving employment to a wider range of tastes and capacities, and drawing more and more into the walks of systematic industry by proffering more varied incitements thereto. If it seemed more profitable to devote all our energies to tilling the soil, that seeming would be fallacious, because oblivious of the need of a great diversity of pursuits to educe our diverse capacities and incite as well as employ our varied aspirations and faculties.[37]

The benefits would also extend beyond those immediately employed in the newly cultivated pursuits, with these new pursuits exerting positive ripple effects throughout the entire economy. Indeed, if it follows that general productivity is hampered through trade specialization, then even those who are employed in congenial pursuits would witness lower economic welfare than if they lived in a nation with a more diverse range of economic activities. Greeley again underscores this view, noting that:

> A people who have but a single source of profit are uniformly poor, not because that vocation is necessarily ill-chosen [for a given individual], but because no single calling can employ and reward the varied capacities of male and female, young and old, robust and feeble… A diversity of pursuits is indispensable to general activity and enduring prosperity.[38]

The above, of course, establishes how diversification raises productivity rates and economic output. Yet cultivating greater opportunities for individuals to exercise their unique talents and interests was seen as a worthy goal in itself, since it affords more meaningful employment which maximizes human potential. Yet, even when viewed against the criterion of economic efficiency, the American Protectionists provide a compelling argument against trade specialization, and thus against the Classical theories of absolute and comparative advantage.

Agricultural Diversification

An added dimension of the diversification argument concerns the cultivation of diversity of agricultural pursuits. As has been noted earlier, the American Protectionists observed that agricultural production tended to exhaust the soil of nutrients and elements, which necessitated the use of manure to replenish the soil. Yet, manure, strictly speaking, was not the only means of offsetting the depletion of nutrients from agricultural lands. There was another means of replenishing the soil, which further underscores the need for economic diversification, and in this case, agricultural diversification. It was argued by the American Protectionists that a diversity of agriculture would allow for rotational grazing and cropping to take place. This, in turn, could replace the system of monocrop agriculture that pervades agricultural-exporting nations, which exacerbates soil exhaustion. David Rice, for instance, observed this tendency for monocrop agriculture to exhaust the soil, noting how:

> Free-trade advocates advise the farmer to exhaust his soil by continually cropping it with the same cereal crops, wheat and corn, instead of diversifying his crops and recuperating his soil… This exhaustion of the soil is a permanent national loss, as well as an immediate one to the farmer.[39]

Similar to the manure argument, rotational cropping would aid soil fertility by preventing the exhaustion of any particular nutrient. Likewise, by allowing the rotation of a diverse range of different crops and livestock, nutrients could also be fixated and returned to the soil. Robert Ellis Thompson explains, for instance, that "by the absence of any system of rotation of crops[,] year after year men will take the same elements from the soil by growing the same crop upon it, wheat or tobacco, or some other."[40] And Peshine Smith also declares that "nature thus teaches the necessity of a rotation of crops, and the greatest advances in agriculture have been since the lesson has been thoroughly learned."[41]

A system of rotational agriculture was contingent upon, or was at least aided by, the protection of a diverse range of agricultural pursuits. By protecting a range of agricultural pursuits, this would cultivate a wider scope of crops and livestock, allowing the farmer or the agriculturalist to engage in rotational agriculture. This led Van Buren Denslow to declare that "protection may help prevent a wasteful exhaustion of soils by inducing a more diversified system of [agri]culture and rotation of crops."[42]

This position connects closely with the home-market argument. By maintaining a more diverse home market near the door of the farmer, it promotes a variety of different agricultural commodities needed to supply such a market, allowing rotational agriculture to take place. Horace Greely explains, for instance, "that the farmer who has an ample market at his door may and will diversify his products, improve or at least retain the better qualities of his soil by a rotation of crops, and return to that soil the elements which cultivation has exhausted, is plain."[43] Indeed, following the logic of the home-market argument, an increased variety of agricultural production would also help stabilize the existing agricultural markets, with Henry Carey observing that "steadiness and regularity in the returns to agricultural labor grow with increase in the variety of commodities to the production of which the land may be devoted."[44]

Of course, not all American Protectionists advanced the cause of direct agricultural protection, but by the late nineteenth century, this was emerging as the consensus position. This is perhaps best put by Robert Ellis Thompson:

> Special objection is made to the imposition of Duties on the raw material of a manufacture. This objection is sustained by such good Protectionist authorities as Alexander Hamilton and Professor Bowen. I confess that even this high authority has not enabled me to see much force in the objection. The Protective Tariff has not for its object the promotion of manufactures only, but the development of the national industry in every direction… In this view the protection of the woolgrower, for instance, is as legitimate as is that of the woolen manufacturer.[45]

In light of the above, it can be seen that the American Protectionists rejected the Ricardian theory of trade with respect to both industry and agriculture. Whilst the American Protectionists accepted that natural endowments play a role in agricultural production, they rejected the implication that this meant that the nation must specialize in the particular agricultural commodity dictated by such endowments. The American Protectionists recognized that the original powers of the soil were not indestructible, as Ricardo argued, but that production itself conditions the productive potential of the soil. A diversified system of agriculture was therefore necessary to maintain this productive potential. Of course, agricultural diversification was also justified on the basis of individuality, but the added need for rotational agriculture presents a further need for diversification within agricultural production.

Maximizing Producers and Minimizing Exchangers

So there is no confusion, it should be stressed that the American Protectionists did not accept the Classical and Marxist delineation of productive (labor which produces a physical surplus) and unproductive labor (labor which produces services). To the American Protectionists, all forms of labor were, in essence, productive. Henry Carey, for instance, calls out the mistaken Classical view of classifying a "painter as productive when he paints a picture, but [as] unproductive, when he teaches hundreds of others to make pictures equal to his own."[46] Friedrich List goes even further, observing that "those who raise pigs, and those who manufacture bag-pipes or pills, are indeed productive; but the instructors of youth [teachers] … are productive in a much higher degree," noting that "the former produce exchangeable values; the latter, productive power."[47] This view was long-standing among American Protectionists with Hamilton refuting a similarly specious claim made by Physiocrats that only agricultural labor was productive, explaining that "the establishment and diffusion of manufactures have the effect of rendering the total mass of useful and productive labor in a community, *greater than it would otherwise be*."[48]

Whilst the American Protectionists rejected the clumsy distinction between made between productive and unproductive classes, they were still of the view, however, that production supersedes exchange or trade in its value to the economy. This view was presented along the lines of opportunity cost, whereby labor employed in the process of exchange or transportation meant that the opportunity for these laborers to engage in production is foregone. This is not to say that transporters and exchangers were unproductive pursuits in themselves, as they very often do contribute to the productiveness of the economy. Indeed, this view is revealed in the following passage by William Elder:

> Whatever power may be exerted over matter, in form or place, is production, and, therefore, is productive labor. The agriculturist is no more a producer than the miner, *the transporter*, or the manufacturer. The greater part of the agriculturist's products owe all their serviceableness to the labor which changes their form and place.[49]

The fact remains, however, that transportation and exchange cannot take place without production. Production is the bedrock of wealth creation with transportation and exchange emerging downstream of it. In terms of wealth creation, there are thus limits to the usefulness of transporters and exchangers, particularly if they diminish the opportunity to engage in production. William D. Wilson captures this point well, noting that there are:

> Limits beyond which trade, or rather transportation, cannot increase the wealth of the world… It is no uncommon thing to hear persons speak of trade and commerce, as that which makes the wealth. Within the limits spoken of, trade does add to the wealth of the world, but no farther. It is indeed true that without trade there can be no great amount of wealth, none, or not many, accumulated fortunes, no large or wealthy commercial cities.[50]

This is intimately connected with the American Protectionists' theory of concentration and agglomeration. If producers can be brought closer to one another, and consumers closer to producers through the process of concentration, this would diminish the need for exchangers and transportation workers, and would thus free up more individuals to undertake production. At the very least, if production and exchange was to take place nationally, this will increase the proportion of laborers engaged in production, and would thereby diminish the amount engaged in global shipping. It is for such reasons that many American Protectionist likened protectionism to a labor-saving machine. By making exchange more direct and nearer to the point of production, it frees up labor engaged in transportation, allowing them to be employed in the production of goods and services. As expressed by Horace Greeley:

> Protection is another name for labor saving… by bringing producer and consumer nearer each other, enabling them to interchange their respective products directly and cheaply, instead of circuitously, through several intermediates, and at great cost. In thus

> reducing the proportion of exchangers and increasing that of producers in a community, it inevitably increases the aggregate product of human effort, and thus enhances the recompense of labor.[51]

Indeed, the American Protectionists held that protection, as opposed to free trade, would lead to a more efficient use of resources, even on purely static grounds, let alone their more dynamic arguments against Classical trade theory. Peshine Smith likewise notes how protection economizes labor, explaining that "internal trade is the more advantageous, because it admits of a greater saving in the labour required to be applied to conversion and transportation, and thus increases the quantity that may be given to production."[52]

This insight forms the basis of an important critique of David Ricardo's theory of comparative advantage. As an uncontroversial proposition, the American Protectionists observed that the opportunity cost of consuming an import is the consumption of a domestically produced good. However, since labor is required for both production and transportation, it means that the opportunity cost of domestic labor engaged in production is labor engaged in both transportation and foreign production. In this case, the transporter is merely engaged in the transfer of wealth, and not the production of it. If imports could thus be substituted with domestic production through the use of tariff protection, this would free up labor which could be employed in the production of wealth in both countries. Or to put it simply, the opportunity costs of global shipping is domestic production. In the words of Henry Carey:

> The whole basis of [the free trade] system is conversion and exchange, and not production, yet neither makes any addition to the amount of things to be exchanged. It is the great boast of their system that the exchangers are so numerous and the producers so few and the more rapid the increase in the proportion which the former bear to the latter, the more rapid is supposed to be the advance towards perfect prosperity. Converters and exchangers, however, must live, and they must live out of the labour of others: and if three, five, or ten persons are to live on the product of one, it must follow that all will obtain but a small allowance of the necessaries or comforts of life, as is seen to be the case.[53]

The theory of comparative advantage therefore misrepresents the true "gains from trade". It only considers labor engaged in production, and completely omits labor engaged in the transportation of said production between national borders. The American Protectionists therefore provide a far more realistic analysis than that put forth in Ricardo's theory of comparative advantage. By allowing production to take place within local centers of concentration and association, or at the very least, within national borders, the American Protectionists understood that protection promotes a more efficient use of labor than free trade. Indeed, the argument extends even beyond labor costs. John Philip Young observed, for instance, how free trade leads to the wastage of fuel and energy through global shipping, which could be applied to domestic production. In the words of Young:

> The exponents of… *laisse-faire*, when considering the subject abstractly, invariably assume that… free interchange in commodities must result in permanently advancing the material welfare of mankind. [But] it is manifestly the duty of economists to point out

> the consequences of waste… In making this examination, facts will be discovered which bear out the assumption that protection is an enormous conservator of energy and that it has a constant tendency to reduce fuel waste to a minimum by bringing the producer and consumer closely together.[54]

The American Protectionists were, of course, not dogmatic in their view of minimizing exchange and maximizing production, and they understood that transportation within certain limits was necessary and even desirable. In this degree of nuance, the American Protectionists were also seeking to avoid what they saw as the Classical-Marxian fallacy of designating certain categories of labor as unproductive.

Notes

1. Jevons, *Methods*, 181.
2. Carey, *Harmony*, 228–229.
3. Wilson, *Principles*, 4.
4. Steele, *Rudimentary Economics*, 87.
5. Carey, *Unity*, 146.
6. Smith, *Manual*, 203; See also Hudson, "Peshine Smith," 210.
7. Smith, *Manual*, 190.
8. Rice, *Philosophy*, 67.
9. Hamilton, "Continentalist 5," 76.
10. Tibbits, *Essay*, 3.
11. Steele, *Rudimentary Economics*, 83.
12. Rae, *Statements*, 368.
13. Rice, *Philosophy*, 141.
14. Hamilton, *Report on Manufactures*, 16.
15. List, *National System*, 139.
16. Hayes, "Customs Duties," 141.
17. Phillips, *Propositions*, 217–218.
18. Dallas, *General Tariff*, 24.
19. Colwell in List, *National System*, 316f.
20. Hayes, "Customs Duties," 140.
21. Ware, *Notes*, 70.
22. Tibbits, *Essay*, 10.
23. Putnam, *Tracts*, 23.
24. Thompson, *Tariff Laws*, 463.
25. Dixwell, "Bastiat," 255–256.
26. Putnam, *Tracts*, 31.
27. Hamilton, *Report on Manufactures*, 13.
28. Dudley, *Farmer Feedeth*, 3.
29. Stewart, *American System*, 110.
30. Young, *Protection*, 173.
31. Stebbins, "Colonial Policy." 8.
32. Ricardo, *Principles*, 139.
33. Young, *National Economy*, 409.
34. Steele, *Outline Study*, 43.
35. Coxe, "Second Draft," 635.
36. Patton, *Political Economy*, 215.
37. Greeley, *Essays*, 348.

38. Greeley, *Essays,* 19.
39. Rice, *Philosophy*, 117.
40. Thompson, *Elements*, 74.
41. Smith, *Manual*, 36.
42. Denslow, *Principles*, 570–571.
43. Greeley, *Essays,* 140.
44. Carey, *Social Science*, 2:33.
45. Thompson, *Home-Industries*, 102.
46. Carey, *Social Science*, 3:46.
47. List, *National System*, 221.
48. Hamilton, *Report on Manufactures*, 6–7.
49. Elder, *Carey*, 11, emphasis added.
50. Wilson, *Principles*, 68.
51. Greeley, *Essays*, 341–342.
52. Smith, *Manual*, 200.
53. Carey, *Harmony*, 46.
54. Young, *Protection*, 149, 153.

Chapter Eleven
THEORY OF TAXATION

Today, the term "trickle-down economics" is often invoked as a criticism against supply-side economists. Yet few realize that the term actually originated as a smear by progressives against what they called the "trickle-down theory of taxation of Alexander Hamilton,"[1] or what could be considered as the American Protectionist theory of taxation. The American Protectionists, of course, never predicated their system of taxation on the belief that wealth would magically "trickle down" from the rich to the masses. They instead envisioned a system whereby low taxation would remove barriers to enterprise and industry which would create opportunities for individuals to climb the social ladder through their own efforts. Despite this mischaracterization, however, the smear underscores one truth: that the American Protectionists were indeed committed to a philosophy of low taxation. This is perhaps best captured by Ellis H. Roberts' declaration that "taxes are a necessity but not a blessing." Indeed, "the fallacy that heavy taxes are a sign of public prosperity is dangerous. Burdens for which no adequate reason exists are near akin to tyranny."[2]

System of Taxation

In order to properly understand the American Protectionists' system of taxation, it is important to delineate between the three types of import duties: protective, revenue, and revenue-only. As the name suggests, protective tariffs are designed to stimulate and protect domestic production. Although not imposed directly for revenue, they do incidentally raise revenue. When it comes to revenue and revenue-only tariffs, there are similarities, but subtle differences that set them apart. Revenue tariffs are low to moderate duties levied on imports with the expressed goal of raising revenue. When levied on competing imports, these revenue tariffs still have an incidental protective effect, but are far weaker than a protective tariff. Finally, revenue-only tariffs are those imposed on non-competing imports with the sole goal of raising revenue and do not afford any incidental protection at all. Non-competing imports would include the likes of coffee and other crops unsuited to North America's climate and soil. These are goods that cannot, for all practical purposes, be produced domestically. All three forms of tariffs are known as indirect taxes, or taxes on consumption. It was upon this foundation of indirect taxation that the American Protectionists established their system of revenue.

From the very beginning of the School, the American Protectionists argued that indirect taxes, and particularly tariffs, should represent the basis of government revenue.

In the *Federalist Papers*, Hamilton declared that "impositions… under the denomination of indirect taxes, and must always constitute the chief part of the revenue raised in this country."[3] This position was also echoed by Tench Coxe who remarked "that to lay a heavy tax on real property [i.e., direct taxation], and to make it the principal resource of government, ought… to be avoided." Indeed, "many… are of [the] opinion, that an impost will be inadequate to the necessities of government; yet I must think, that most of the money which could be drawn from the people with convenience, might be drawn in this way."[4] In fact, many American Protectionists would even affirm the position known as "Revenue from the Tariff Only."[5]

It should be emphasized, however, that whilst earlier American Protectionists, particularly Hamilton, viewed protection with revenue considerations in mind, this view shifted as the School reached maturity. Whilst tariff protection and revenue are intimately connected, it was argued protection should be established purely on the basis of protection itself. William Elder explains, for instance, that "protection is totally misunderstood, and fatally abused, when it is reasoned upon, or employed, as identical with *taxation*. It means and intends the protection of domestic labor, skill and enterprise, and of the capital which they employ."[6] Of course, this is not to say that tariff protection has no bearing on revenue. Rather, the idea was that the principle of protection should not be compromised by the pursuit of revenue, even though revenue would be generated incidentally. Calvin Colton thus argues that "if, in accomplishing the original and main design of a tariff, revenue can be raised, it is well; but it is incidental… This incidental result does not change the original design and character of the measure," that is, protection.[7] In short, protection, declares Elder, "does not look to revenue, but it does, incidentally, secure it."[8]

It was thus generally seen that protective tariffs would incidentally raise more than sufficient revenue for funding the general operations of government and the provision of internal improvements without compromising the principle of protection in any way. It is for this reason that most American Protectionists after Hamilton rejected the use of revenue tariffs since protective tariffs would incidentally secure sufficient revenue. Hamilton, for his part, straddled the line between protection and revenue, endorsing what later Protectionists would have considered a revenue tariff. Hamilton was, however, acutely aware that "all the duties imposed on imported articles, though with an exclusive view to revenue, have the effect in contemplation… [of possessing] a beneficent aspect towards the manufactures of the country."[9]

If in the event that protective tariffs could not raise sufficient revenue, and assuming that there are no unnecessary government expenditures which could be curtailed, rather than compromising the principle of protection, government should proceed to levy revenue-only tariffs, that is, import duties on non-competing imports. If revenue is still insufficient, government should, in the final instance, proceed to impose domestic consumption taxes, which typically took the form of sin taxes on liquor and tobacco. Indeed, domestic consumption taxes should be limited in scope, with Robert Ellis Thompson arguing that "all internal revenue duties—except on spirits, tobacco, and the like… should… be wiped from the statute books."[10] It is also important to note, in the case of domestic consumption taxes, that American Protectionists argued that these taxes should be levied at a rate lower than the tariff on competing imports. This difference between the domestic tax rate and the tariff rate is necessary to ensure that domestic articles would continue to be afforded protection. In fact, this was the very policy pursued by Alexander Hamilton, who explained that:

> To the manufacture itself, the [domestic] duty is no injury, if an equal duty be laid on the rival foreign article. And when a greater duty is laid upon the latter than upon the former, as in the present instance, the difference is a bounty on the domestic article, and operates as an encouragement of the manufacture. The manufacturer can afford to sell his fabric the cheaper, in proportion to that difference, and is so far enabled to undersell and supplant the dealer in the foreign article.[11]

In broad terms, the notion that domestic taxation should be lower than that imposed upon foreign articles represents a guiding principle of taxation for the American Protectionists. This position stands in sharp contrast to that advocated by the Classical economists who favored tax equalization, arguing that the "protective effect of revenue duties should be balanced by the levying of excise duties at home."[12]

It should be clear from the above that the American Protectionists considered revenue as part of an overall system of taxation and expenditures. Whilst protective tariffs were generally seen as sufficient for generating government revenue, the American Protectionists were, of course, conscious that conflicts could arise between revenue and protection. Rather than compromising the principle of protection for the sake of revenue, the government could always curtail expenditures or resort to other forms of indirect taxation. This dispels one of the arguments put forth by the Progressives that the American System lacked flexibility in relation to revenue.[13] Indeed, the problem, in the eyes of the American Protectionists, was not so much that the American System lacked flexibility. It was rather that Progressives lacked restraint in governmental expenditures, which would necessarily lead to a burgeoning of taxes on domestic producers. On this question, Ellis H. Roberts notes that:

> Taxation weighs only on one side of the scales. However heavy that may be, it will be all too light if expenditures are in excess… Drain production and commerce as much as you may, your treasury will be empty if the expenditures run out like a flood.[14]

Indeed, during the ascendency of the American System in the late nineteenth century, the problem was not so much budget deficits, but excessive surpluses, which meant that individuals were being overtaxed, with Ellis H. Roberts noting that "collections in excess of expenditures have become a rule in this country" and "the protectionist must regard excessive revenues as hostile to his policy."[15] This even led Van Buren Denslow to urge "Protectionists to take the lead of the Tax reducers by aiming to strike off the duties on Tea, Coffee, Spices, foreign wines, Silks, [and] a reduction on Sugar & other non-competing articles."[16]

Indeed, because internal taxes necessarily constitute an obstacle or barrier to entry for domestic producers, government restraint in expenditures was seen as necessary to minimize such barriers. In fact, William D. Kelley argued that within national borders, a reduction of domestic taxes can be viewed in some likeness to infant-industry protection. Since infant industries or infant producers are typically those least able to incur the cost of taxation, the elimination of domestic taxes will tend to be more advantageous to them than their more mature counterparts. Thus, in reference to allowing the South's infant industries to catch up to the North, Kelley explains that "the diversified industry of the South... are in their infancy... They need the fostering care of the Government, and in no way can this be bestowed more acceptably than by the immediate repeal of our internal taxes."[17]

At any rate, the American Protectionists conceived of a system of taxation predicated on tariffs and indirect taxes. The American Protectionists saw many advantages of indirect over direct taxation. In the first instance, the American Protectionists, to put it simply, saw that indirect taxes would be far less difficult and costly to collect. Indeed, all the way back in *The Federalist Papers,* Hamilton rejected direct taxation due to the immense costs and difficulties involved in its collection and enforcement. According to Hamilton, "in every country it is a Herculean task" to administer taxes "of the direct kind," and "the expense of an accurate valuation is, in all situations, a formidable objection."[18] In short, a system of revenue involving direct taxes unavoidably requires the creation and maintenance of large and expensive bureaucracies. This necessarily means that cost of collection is going to be less efficient relative to taxes on consumption. This attitude is summed up well by James G. Blaine, who explains that "Mr. Hamilton... more promptly than any other financier... saw that ten dollars could be more easily collected by indirect tax than one dollar by direct levy."[19]

Indeed, the distinction between indirect and direct taxation was captured elegantly by Abraham Lincoln, who declared that:

> The tariff is the cheaper system, because the duties, being collected in large parcels at a few commercial points, will require comparatively few officers in their collection; while by the direct tax system, the land must be literally covered with assessors and collectors, going forth like swarms of Egyptian locusts, devouring every blade of grass and other green thing.[20]

The cost of collection was even less for customs duties relative to internal consumption taxes, since it would only require the stationing of customs officials along national borders. Ellis H. Roberts thus remarks that:

> The customs system requires officers only on the frontiers of a country, and involves a smaller force than imposts gathered from the citizens in their homes. It has been found in practice the system involving the least expense in administration.[21]

The second advantage of indirect taxes is that they are less intrusive than direct forms and do not violate the privacy of producers. In order to collect taxes on income and property, the State must invariably pry into the affairs of the business or the wage earner. Robert Ellis Thompson explains, for instance, that "objections to the income tax… are very strong" for they are "inquisitorial. It demands of the citizen a statement of his affairs for each current year."[22] This position is echoed by Erastus B. Bigelow who notes that "in marked contrast with taxes on property and income, they [customs duties] involve no annoying inquiry as to the circumstances of individuals and no vexatious interference with the practice of any art or trade."[23] This issue of the State invariably prying into the affairs of business is no small concern with Hamilton observing that "men engaged in any trade or business have commonly weighty reasons to avoid disclosures."[24]

This leads into another important objection to direct taxation, that being, that direct taxes are inevitably arbitrary in nature. Since businessmen and entrepreneurs have weighty reasons not to disclose the true state of their financial affairs, they will often conceal and misrepresent their financial affairs, or they will simply undervalue their earnings or property to evade the tax. Plus, on the side of the tax collector, there is an equally problematic issue involved with ascertaining the true value of income and/or property. This ultimately means that the final rate of taxation is at the discretion of the tax official. Thus, unlike indirect taxes which are clear and uniform in their application, direct taxes are unavoidably arbitrary, and "arbitrary taxes," explains Hamilton, "are as contrary to the genius of liberty as to the maxims of industry."[25] What finally arises from this messy system of taxation are issues ranging from costs of compliance to litigation. In the words of Ellis H. Roberts:

> [Such] changes in the revenue laws are the occasion of annoying and costly litigation. Suits which are grievous and mischievous in every way spring out of new rates and new methods [of taxation]… The present system [of import duties] is cheaply administered, and its results are on the whole satisfactory… Let us do nothing to increase such litigation, which does more than else to render Government obnoxious.[26]

In short, the American Protectionists saw that, in practical terms, a system of direct taxation would be unavoidably messy, bureaucratic, obnoxious, and inefficient.

On less practical and more philosophical grounds, the American Protectionists also argued that indirect taxation would be more conducive to personal liberty and natural law. By their nature, indirect taxes are voluntary since the consumer can always forgo consumption of the particular article being taxed. Direct taxes, in contrast, must invariably and unavoidably come out of the income, savings, or property of the individual. Hamilton thus explains that indirect taxes and tariffs, in particular, are "the most agreeable tax to the people that can be imposed, because it is paid insensibly, and seems to be voluntary."[27] This view is echoed by Daniel Raymond who notes that "indirect is preferable to direct taxation, because the tax is then paid by the consumer voluntarily, and the government does not appear in the odious character of an exacter."[28]

Indeed, it should also be added that tariffs are particularly congenial to liberty even relative to other forms of indirect taxes, since the individual always has the option of buying a domestic substitute, and can thus forego the tax completely if they so desire. It is for this reason that Andrew Stewart likened "[tariff] revenue… [to] a *voluntary* and not *compulsory* contribution paid by those only who choose to purchase and consume foreign, in preference to home productions."[29] This insight also led Ellis H. Roberts to conclude that, through the use of import duties, "government can secure its revenue with certainty upon conditions which come very near to voluntary offerings."[30] Or in the words of Richard W. Thompson:

> It is true that the duties upon imports are in the nature of taxes, but it is also true that they are without the odious element which makes taxes seem oppressive. If they fall upon the consumer at all, they are paid voluntarily and without compulsion.[31]

Indeed, even on the side of the foreign producer, tariffs were likened to a voluntary charge which is paid for the privilege of accessing the home market, and thus does not impinge upon the liberties of foreign producers. As Daniel Raymond explains:

> An *impost* is not strictly speaking a *tax*. Taxes are levied upon citizens and property within the jurisdiction of the government laying the tax. An impost is a bonus which the owner of property is required to pay for the privilege of bringing it within the territorial limits of another government for sale or use. The owner… has no option whether he will pay the tax or not; but the owner of property upon which an impost is laid, has his election, whether he will bring his property within the jurisdiction of the government and pay the impost, or keep it out of that jurisdiction and save the impost.[32]

The argument that indirect taxes and tariffs, in particular, constitute a voluntary form of taxation also has important implications for economic development. Although it has been noted elsewhere that savings, and thus investment, is not the primary cause of economic growth, it still represents an important contributing factor. Since taxes on income must forcibly reduce an individual's savings, this means that income taxes are necessarily injurious to growth and development. Consumption taxes, on the other hand, are voluntary and only reduce saving if one engages in consumption. They therefore do not forcibly reduce savings and hence investment. It is thus "a chief excellence of [indirect taxes]," explains Hamilton, "that it preserves a just measure of the abilities of individuals, [and] promotes frugality [i.e., savings] and taxes extravagance."[33]

The Ideal Standard of Taxation

Whilst there are philosophical statements concerning taxation scattered throughout the writings of the early American Protectionists, it would not be until the post-Carey writers that an explicit philosophical standard on which to formulate tax policy would emerge. To better grasp this philosophy, it is best to compare it with the taxation philosophy of the Classical economists, namely the four maxims of Adam Smith and the additional equality maxim of John Stuart Mill. The last three of Smith's maxims are not particularly controversial and were largely affirmed by the American Protectionists. The American Protectionists took issue, however, with Smith's first maxim and Mill's equality maxim. Smith's first maxim asserts that "the subjects of every state ought to contribute towards the support of the government… in proportion to their respective abilities… [and] in proportion to the revenue which they respectively enjoy under the protection of the state."[34]

The American Protectionists rejected Smith's view that only the subjects of the State ought to contribute to the support of the government, as this necessarily implies that only domestic subjects should be burdened by taxation. This, according to Van Buren Denslow, "ignore[s], at the outset, a cardinal point in the protectionist experience, that not only the subjects of a state, but aliens who seek to do business or sell their wares within its borders, or in any way to get the benefits of its markets… ought to… contribute to the support of its government."[35] Since foreign producers benefit from the privilege of accessing and selling their products in the home country's market, and because this necessarily involves the provision of public goods, such as infrastructure, taxation should not be merely limited to the nation's citizens.

The second issue with Smith's first maxim relates to taxing people according to their "ability to pay" and the "benefits they enjoy." Many American Protectionists saw this maxim as hopelessly muddled because it conflates two separate and seemingly contradictory principles into one maxim. An ability-to-pay principle lends itself to both a tax on labor and capital since, from an American Protectionist perspective, a person's ability to pay is determined by their ability to generate a profit or earn an income.[36] However, these taxes are, as Denslow puts it, distinct from "those which arise from the '[benefits] they enjoy' [principle] for this… is measured by expenditure."[37] The benefits-they-enjoy principle therefore necessarily lends itself to a tax on consumption, ostentation, and luxury. The American Protectionists observed therefore that, in practice, Smith's ability-to-pay/benefits-they-enjoy maxim would produce an exceedingly broad and complex tax system which would violate another maxim expounded by Smith and affirmed by the American Protectionists: that the cost of collection ought to be kept to a minimum.

American Protectionists then turned to Mill's maxim of equality. This maxim posits equal taxation on the basis "of not… taking equal proportions from the incomes of individuals, but in taking equal proportions from their enjoyments."[38] This was rejected purely on practical grounds. It was charged that Mill's criterion was purely "chimerical" and represented an impossible and impracticable standard on which to formulate tax policy. The process of ensuring an equality of sacrifice of enjoyments demands that the incidence and burden of taxation is certain and can be accurately determined. In responding to Mill, Denslow explains that "the notion, that the incidence of taxes should be made certain… demands an impossibility in finance."[39] This view is further echoed by Robert Ellis Thompson, who notes that "experience shows that the incidence of taxation is not determined by laws as rigid as those of hydraulics."[40]

The above describes what the American Protectionists did not see as an acceptable philosophical or practical basis on which to formulate tax policy. Instead, they arrived at the view that taxes ought to be those "the taxpayer bears with most ease."[41] In other words, taxation should create the least amount of burden for the nation's producers. In affirming this philosophy, Van Buren Denslow identifies three conditions which makes taxation consistent with this principle. These conditions were seen as constituting the "ideal standard of taxation." These are taxes:

1. … which indirectly promote the energy of national production, in a degree which more than supplies to the taxpayer the means of paying the tax, so that where a penny is taken out of one pocket in taxes, a shilling is put into the other in the form of better wages, more industries, or higher profits.
2. … of which the returns come into the treasury of his own country, while the taxes are paid by the producers of other countries.
3. … whose first incidence is a temporary scarcity of some product, but whose speedy effect is to greatly cheapen its supply.[42]

To put it simply, taxation should be formulated so that (1) it indirectly promotes national industry, (2) at least some of the tax burden can be shifted onto foreign agents, and (3) so that the tax itself will eventually erode away its own burden.

This ideal standard is clearly at odds with Smith's "ability-to-pay" principle if taken to its logical end, since a tax on capital and income necessarily hurts industry, cannot be shifted onto foreign producers, and because it has no mechanism for eroding away its own burden. This is very much in line with the thinking of American Protectionists starting with Alexander Hamilton. According to Hamilton, "all… taxes… which proceed according to the amount of capital supposed to be employed in a business, or of profits supposed to be made in it, are unavoidably hurtful to industry."[43] This position was also affirmed by Willard Phillips, who notes how the "ability to pay" principle in its completion threatens the development of industry:

> This principle of apportioning the taxation in the ratio of the ability to pay, is one that is liable to abuse in popular governments; and this abuse… injures the whole community, since if you threaten accumulation of property with violence, or plunder, though it be under the guise of taxation, you… check and discourage it, and thus check and discourage the general industry and production.[44]

At any rate, protective tariffs were seen to fulfill all three conditions of the ideal standard: they promote domestic industry, shift some burden onto foreign producers, and tend to erode their own cost over time as domestic production expands. It is therefore apparent that this ideal standard of taxation naturally lends itself to a protective duty. Horace Greeley clearly articulates this view, noting the compensatory effects of an import tariff achieved through the cultivation of new industries, which corresponds with the first criterion:

> The superiority I claim for taxation by tariff or duties on imports over any and all modes of taxing commended as direct is this: Taxation by tariff involves and insures a compensating advantage to the great body of our taxpayers, in that it strongly tends to encourage the planting of new industries, the naturalization of new departments of productive labor, on our soil, and the consequent opening to hundreds of thousands of opportunities for earning a livelihood superior to, and more acceptable than, any which they would else have enjoyed.[45]

Although independent theories in themselves, the two following sections will demonstrate how the protective tariff fulfils the two conditions of the ideal standard of taxation outlined above.

The Tendency for Tariffs to Erode Away Their Own Cost

One of the more important taxation theories developed by the American Protectionists concerns the tendency for protective tariffs to erode away their own costs. In fact, if taken to its logical end, protective tariffs will eventually be more than compensatory, providing a net reduction in costs in the long run. This represents one of the most powerful theories concerning protective tariffs, for if it holds true, it dispels the belief that tariffs create a deadweight loss for society and thus dismantles one of the chief arguments which continues to be employed against protectionism. Like many of the other taxation theories discussed in this chapter, the notion has its origins with the writings of Alexander Hamilton. In the words of Hamilton:

> Though it were true, that the immediate and certain effect of regulations controlling the competition of foreign with domestic fabrics was an increase of price, it is universally true that the contrary is the ultimate effect with every successful manufacture. When a domestic manufacture has attained to perfection, and has engaged in the prosecution of it a competent number of persons, it invariably becomes cheaper. Being free from the heavy charges which attend the importation of foreign commodities, it can be afforded, and accordingly seldom or never fails to be afforded cheaper in process of time than was the foreign article for which it is a substitute. The internal competition which takes place soon does away everything like monopoly, and by degrees reduces the price of the article to the minimum of a reasonable profit on the capital employed.[46]

The American Protectionists did not deny that the price of protected domestic goods would initially be higher than imported articles. However, these costs were seen as a short-term sacrifice for a long-term gain. As industries expand under protection, the price of protected articles will have a tendency to fall below the price of competing imports. This position is well captured by Calvin Colton, who explains that experience "demonstrate the general truth, that home products of manufacture, under Protection, tend invariably and uniformly to reduce the prices of the articles."[47] Or as Daniel Webster declares, "the fact undoubtedly is that, under the process of protection, the common price, or cost of goods has become less."[48]

This tendency would be later explained by American Protectionists with reference to Henry Carey's reproduction cost theory of value. As production expands, reproduction costs have a tendency to fall, and this represents a real saving to consumers. John L. Hayes thus explains that:

> No economical law is more capable of demonstration than this; that manufactured commodities are invariably cheapened in the cost of production and in the prices at which they are afforded to consumers, as home demand enlarges them. Mr. Carey lays down this

law [of declining reproduction costs] with great emphasis. This cheapening under this law applies most of all to the necessaries of life, the commodities in universal demand.

This demand justifies production at vast scale, diminishing to the lowest point the portion of the general expenses of a manufacturing establishment which each article produced bears... The large scale of production leads to the constant introduction of machinery and labor-saving machines. Finally competition between rival establishments, encouraged by the universal demand, prevent monopolies of production... and furnishes to consumers commodities at the lowest possible price at which they could be afforded at the period of consumption.[49]

Indeed, the tendency for prices to be lower in the long-run under protective tariffs was also explained via reference to the different pricing strategies undertaken by foreign producers. Some American Protectionists observed that foreign producers would temporarily lower prices to crush domestic producers who would enter the market, only to raise them back up again. Tariffs could thus be used to ensure that prices are consistently lower through the emergence of domestic competition. In the words of Joseph Wharton:

> The real effect of import duty on prices is about this:... In the case of articles produced both at home and abroad, home competition, which is at first made possible by the duty preventing foreigners from crushing it in the bud through temporary lowering of prices, or even by its causing an absolutely higher price, soon forces the foreigner to abate his price or totally lose his market. Later, it constantly obliges the foreigner to accept not what he would wish to charge, but the home producer is willing or able to sell at. Finally, in many cases, after quite driving the foreigner out of the field, domestic establishments competing among themselves force prices down to a lower point than foreigners could deliver at free of duty.[50]

In either case, the reason for the price of domestic articles being lower in the long run as opposed to simply matching the price of imports, is explained by the fact that imports have the added cost of transportation.[51] In the case of the domestic article, however there is no, or at least, very limited transportation costs involved. This means that once domestic production expands to the point that production costs are at parity with foreign producers, domestic articles will be cheaper than foreign articles due to the foregone transportation costs. In the final stage, protective tariffs would thus be more than compensatory. This means that free trade is far more costly to the consumer in the long run because the cost of transportation will continue to persist and will ultimately be borne by the consumer. Nathanial A. Ware thus explains that through protection "the price and quality of the goods... are so low and good that the difference much more than pays back the tax paid for the protection the first few years."[52]

It is for this reason that American Protectionists labelled the transportation cost associated with international trade as the "tax of transportation." It is thus on this basis that some American Protectionists, such as Calvin Colton, argued "that protective duties are not taxes, but a rescue from taxation."[53] In fact, Colton went so far as to argue that if the economy develops domestic substitutes and thus foregoes imports, they also forego any foreign taxes (which would presumably be higher than that levied in a low taxing economy such as the United States) that may be shifted onto the price of imports. He thus explains that protective tariffs "will rescue us from a grievous system of foreign taxation."[54] In any event, it is clear that the American Protectionists developed a thorough explanation for how protective tariffs have a tendency to erode away their own burden with eventual net benefits. These net benefits included not only the cultivation of new industries and avenues of production, but also the reduction in the cost of articles.

Theory of Tax Incidence

The American Protectionists did not believe that the burden or incidence of taxation could be calculated with any high degree of certainty. Still, they developed a theory which would account for the direction which incidence tended to move. This analysis could be thought of as a competition theory of tax incidence. According to the American Protectionists, it is the interplay of competitive forces in the real world which influences the proportion of incidence shouldered by each party involved. This is markedly different from the modern Neoclassical approach which treats the issue of tax incidence from the standpoint of an economy suspended in equilibrium. Before proceeding, however, it is important to note that the theory discussed in this section is a theory of incidence specifically for indirect taxation, and does not purport to determine the incidence of direct taxes.

The American Protectionists argued that the burden of taxation would be divided between the buyer and the seller. What proportion of the burden falls upon each is determined by the intensity of demand relative to the intensity of supply in the market, and this is ultimately conditioned by competitive forces. This theory also has its origins in Alexander Hamilton's early economic writings. In the words of Hamilton:

> The maxim, that the consumer pays the duty has been admitted in theory with too little reserve; frequently contradicted in practice. It is true, the merchant will be unwilling to let the duty be a deduction from his profits, if the state of the market will permit him to incorporate it with the price of his commodity. But this is often not practicable. It turns upon the quantity of goods at market in proportion to the demand. When the latter exceeds the former, and the competition is among the buyers, the merchant can easily increase his price and make his customers pay the duty. When the reverse is the case, and the competition is among the sellers, he must then content himself with smaller profits, and lose the value of the duty or at least of a part of it. Where a nation has a flourishing and well settled trade this more commonly happens than may be imagined, and it will, many times, be found that the duty is divided between the merchant and the consumer.[55]

In other words, if the level of demand exceeds the quantity of goods supplied, competition within the market will be among the consumers for the purchase of commodities. In this situation, the producer or merchant will tend to shift a higher portion of the tax burden onto the consumer. When supply exceeds demand within the market, then competition will be among the producers for the sale of commodities. In this case, producers will decide to pay a higher proportion of the tax burden, lest they lose sales to competitors.

This means that the exact proportion of incidence borne by the consumer, producer, and merchant will depend on the degree of competition within the market. Ultimately, however, the incidence will be indeterminately shared by the consumer and producers with these competitive forces only influencing the direction which incidence tends to fall. The above, of course, represents a simple case between a buyer and a seller. In practice, the incidence would be proportioned through the line of exchange by the interplay of competitive forces. Hamilton explains, for instance, that "there is strong reciprocal influence between the prices of all commodities in a state, by which they, sooner or later, attain a pretty exact ballance and proportion to each other."[56]

It must be said, however, that this theory was never intended to be viewed as a purely static explanation of tax incidence. Instead, there is a tendency for the incidence to change over the long run since producers and entrepreneurs behave in a reactive manner to changes in legislation and changes in the marketplace. This adds a crucial dimension to the theory, particularly with respect to the incidence of import duties over the long run. Because tariffs tend to stimulate domestic production, this necessarily means that the cost of the tariff will tend to diminish as production expands and prices fall. There is, however, a separate yet similar effect when it comes to the question of who bears the incidence of the import duty.

When duties are first imposed on foreign articles which compete with infant industries, this results in a temporary scarcity of goods. This means, as Hamilton shows, that the bulk of the incidence of the import duty will be shifted to the domestic consumer since there is competition for the purchase of goods. However, because the import duty creates both a scarcity and shifts the incidence to the consumer, this means that the market will be more profitable to domestic producers. Van Buren Denslow, thus explains, that "in the case of every really protective duty, therefore, there is a domestic production which the duty is constantly stimulating into a condition more nearly approximating to that of fully supplying the demand."[57] As domestic production, and thus competition from domestic producers, increases, this has the effect of shifting the incidence of the import duty away from domestic consumers. Since import duties, however, are only levied on foreign goods, as opposed to domestic production, this means that foreign producers will be compelled to shoulder the bulk of the incidence, especially since they are trying to compete with domestic producers. Denslow thus concludes that:

> When the American supply is wholly or nearly adequate to the American demand [i.e., the industry becomes mature] it may nevertheless happen that the article will be imported, notwithstanding [that] the American price is no higher than the foreign. In every such case the foreigner either divides the duty with the American consumer or pays it all… [When] our customs revenue are in this manner paid by foreigners, [they] are not a tax on the American consumer at all.[58]

This not only reinforces the view that protective tariffs represent the ideal standard of taxation posited earlier (since at least some of the burden can be shifted to foreign producers), more significantly, it underscores an important time dimension when analyzing the incidence of import duties. In short, tariffs or duties on foreign articles which compete with infant industries will tend to be shouldered more by the domestic consumer, whereas tariffs on articles competing with established industries will tend to be shouldered more by foreign producers. Incidence will thus shift between the two according to the degree of development of the particular industry in question. This incidence shifting mechanism embedded in the protective tariff is important since it means that tariffs are naturally more protective in the early stages of an industry's development when protection is needed the most. Tariffs will thus always be protective in nature, but the degree of protection will be stronger for infant industries. It also means that the burden of the tariff for the domestic consumer will gradually reduce as development progresses. This view is well expressed by Ellis H. Roberts, who explains that:

> The tendency is first to charge every impost to the final consumer of the commodity affected; thus, in articles which enter into new modifications, the tendency is to throw the charge forward upon the last purchaser. But against this tendency acts any increase of supply relative to demand… [The] operation [of the tariff] magnifies the profits in the branch of trade so affected, and when those [profits] are carried above the average, competition enters… any considerable increase in profits in one branch immediately increases the competition in it and leads soon to such an augmentation of supply that the consumer gets the benefit [due to the foreign producer burdening the tax].[59]

This also demonstrates another superiority of a protective tariff over tariff for revenue only (and to a lesser extent a simple revenue tariff). Since tariffs for revenue only are those levied on non-competing imports, there is no stimulus to domestic production, and thus no mechanism to shift incidence away from domestic consumers to foreign producers. Tariffs for revenue only would thus be paid chiefly by domestic consumers. Although perhaps exaggerating the full amount shouldered by consumers, William McKinley captures this view:

> If the duty is put upon the non-competing foreign products, the consumers in the United States will pay every dollar of that tax, because, as there is no competition at home, the price of such foreign products to the American consumer will be the foreign price with the duty added. We would secure the revenue, but we would pay it wholly ourselves. A revenue tariff is always paid by the consumer. We would secure the revenue for a time, but, in placing the duty upon the non-competing foreign product, we would give no encouragement or protection to any home industry.[60]

The American Protectionists thus developed a clear and dynamic analysis of tax incidence. This theory also clearly articulates the incidence shifting mechanism inherent to protective tariffs, and, in doing so, it controverts the popular notion that the domestic consumer pays all of the incidence of a tariff. Unlike internal taxes which are shouldered fully by the nation's citizens, tariffs are shouldered by both the domestic consumer and foreign producer, with the exact amount conditioned by competition and the level of development of the industry in question.

Theory of Governmental Restraint in Taxation

An important feature in the American Protectionists' treatment of taxation concerns the issue of governmental restraint in the formulation and imposition of taxes. American Protectionists were conscious of the possibility that excessive taxation would create burdens for domestic industry and private enterprise. In other words, the need for a well-functioning government to oversee the development and the expansion of industry needs to be checked by a policy of moderation when it comes to the imposition of taxes, so as not to stifle the expansion of private enterprise. In light of this, American Protectionists saw that indirect taxation, and especially import duties, would exhibit a tendency toward self-restraint. Of course, this theory was formulated with the view of revenue in mind, and thus only relates to revenue and revenue-only tariffs as well as internal consumption taxes, as opposed protective tariffs.

The view that indirect taxation, and particularly import duties, exhibits a tendency to impose self-restraint on the taxing authority was first expressed by Alexander Hamilton in the *Continentalist*, and elaborated upon later, in the *Federalist*. The argument, in short, assumes that if the rate of taxation is excessive, this would discourage consumption and would also encourage tax avoidance, and would thereby limit the revenue raised by the tax. In the *Continentalist*, Hamilton attributes this to the increase in smuggling and customs evasion that arises from excessive rates of duties, and also from the reduction in demand from the higher prices that accompanies an increase in indirect taxes. Both would serve as a restraint against excess. In Hamilton's words:

> They [the State] can have no temptation to abuse this power, because the motive of revenue will check its own extremes. Experience has shown that moderate duties are more productive than high ones. When they are low, a nation can trade abroad on better terms— its imports and exports will be larger—the duties will be regularly paid, and arising on a greater quantity of commodities, will yield more in the aggregate, than when they are so high as to operate either as a prohibition, or as an inducement to evade them by illicit practices.[61]

Writing later in *Federalist* 21, however, Hamilton would offer a more sophisticated and improved analysis:

> It is a signal advantage of taxes on articles of consumption [indirect taxes] that they contain in their own nature a security against excess. They prescribe their own limit, which cannot be exceeded without defeating the end proposed—that is, an extension of the revenue. When applied to this object, the saying is as just as it is witty that, 'in political arithmetic, two and two do not always make four'. If duties are too high, they lessen the consumption; the collection is eluded; and the product to the treasury is not so great as when they are confined within proper and moderate bounds. This forms a complete barrier against any material oppression of the citizens by taxes of this class [indirect taxes], and is itself a natural limitation of the power of imposing them.[62]

What Hamilton is referring to when he speaks of consumption taxes "prescribing their own limit" is the role that the price elasticity of demand plays in determining the optimal rate of revenue when levying taxes on articles of consumption. According to this view, when applying such taxes, there will be a revenue-optimizing rate of taxation, and any increase of the tax rate beyond this point will lead to a decrease in the amount of revenue raised, as consumers forego or reduce their consumption due to the excessive rate of taxation. The revenue optimizing rate will depend, of course, upon the particular price elasticity of demand for the good in question.

This represents an important distinction between consumption taxes and taxes on income. The rule of apportionment is clearly identifiable when levying or adjusting a consumption tax since the influence on revenue will be clear and explicit to the taxing authority. In contrast, when it comes to the imposition of income tax, Hamilton explains, that "no limits to the discretion of the government are to be found in the nature of things."[63] This is to say, that the taxing authority has no simple means of deciphering the revenue maximizing point of taxes on income because of the complex array of factors influencing the revenue generated from such taxes, and also because of the indeterminate nature of how the tax itself affects income.

A concern closely related to this is the secondary welfare effects produced by the tax itself. This line of thought suggests that because taxation is burdensome, it will reduce economic welfare and thus limit the amount of revenue collected from the nation's citizens by lowering consumption. Hamilton's rule of apportionment meant that indirect taxation tended not to reach excessive and burdensome levels, and it is for this reason that Hamilton opted for lower tariff rates than those advocated by later American Protectionists. Later American Protectionists did, of course, continue to affirm Hamilton's position with respect to revenue duties and other consumption taxes. Writing with respect to revenue tariffs and other indirect taxes, for instance, William McKinley explains that "it is for this reason that revenues are assured with the smallest tax; for these revenues will always be measured by the demand of our people for such foreign articles as we cannot produce [such articles] at home, [and thus consumption is] limited only by our ability to buy."[64] Protective duties, however, were seen as an exception to this rule because they have the unique effect of stimulating domestic production which enhances economic welfare. As Henry Carey explains:

> The power of the people to pay taxes for the support of government is dependent upon their power to consume commodities that are taxed, and if protection diminished wages, it must of course diminish revenue; but when we examine the facts, it is shown that, notwithstanding a great increase of the free-list, the revenue increased under the [high] tariff of 1828, and fell off [after its repeal] so much afterwards that the government was compelled almost to beg for loans in the markets of Europe.[65]

Since protection stimulates production, and since the production of commodities constitutes the demand for other commodities, many of which may be subject to taxation, it follows that high protective tariffs will tend to enhance the capacity to raise revenue, as opposed to diminishing it.

The basic idea behind this theory of governmental restraint underpins a more general argument against high tax rates. Since, for any extended period of time, taxes must necessarily be paid out of net income, it follows that if taxation exceeds the net income of an industry or individual producer, it must necessarily detract from capital accumulation and will thus leave the industry or enterprise in a paralyzed and precarious situation. Excessive tax rates would therefore ultimately reduce the revenue-raising capacity of the economy over the long run. In the words of Stephen Colwell.

> Something more than mere hard work is needful to give industry the power to endure taxation… People may work hard and long, and spare for taxes. It is needful that, in other words, that labor should not only be productive of great results and abundant commodities, but should be productive of net income, for out of such income only can taxes be paid for any protracted period… If taxes do not come from net income, they must ultimately crush the industry upon which they are levied.[66]

These same arguments would be later employed by the likes of Andrew Mellon and Calvin Coolidge in the 1920s to justify the Mellon tax cuts, demonstrating the enduring influence of American Protectionist tax theory within Republican economic policy. Anticipating the logic behind the Laffer curve, Andrew Mellon put forth the case that higher rates of taxation do not necessarily result in increased revenue. By suppressing production, higher taxes may well lower the taxable income of businesses and individuals. Mellon thus explains that:

> The history of taxation shows that taxes which are inherently excessive are not paid. The high rates inevitably put pressure upon the taxpayer to withdraw his capital from productive business… or to find other lawful methods of avoiding the realization of taxable income.[67]

Likewise, Calvin Coolidge declared in his State of the Union:

> Four times we have made a drastic revision of our internal revenue system, abolishing many taxes and substantially reducing almost all others. Each time the resulting stimulation to business has so increased taxable incomes and profits that a surplus has been produced… It has been a method which has performed the seeming miracle of leaving a much greater percentage of earnings in the hands of the taxpayers with scarcely any diminution of the Government revenue.[68]

The central idea behind this view is that high taxes, particularly of the direct kind, have the tendency to stifle initiative, enterprise, and wealth creation. Indeed, "the vital defect in our present system [of taxation]," explains Mellon, "is that the tax burden is borne by wealth in the making… We place a tax on energy and initiative."[69] In short, by cutting taxes, industry can proceed unencumbered, and the ensuing increase in production may well lead to an increase in government revenue by increasing the overall amount of taxable wealth. While this result is not guaranteed, it demonstrates that the relationship between tax rates and revenue is far from linear. This principle was well understood by the American Protectionists' analysis of indirect taxation, and it is a principle that would find echoes in later supply-side economics. To sum up, the American Protectionists understood, in the words of Ellis H. Roberts, that "every revenue system must bear upon production either with friendly or hostile hand," and the American Protectionists opted for a system that prioritized the former.[70]

Notes

1. Minority View, "General Statement," B2.
2. Roberts, *Treasury and Taxes,* 8.
3. Hamilton, "Federalist 21," 401.
4. Coxe, *Observations*, 87.
5. Thompson, *Home Industry,* 104.
6. Elder, *Questions*, 208.
7. Colton, *Public Economy*, 504.
8. Elder, *Questions*, 204.
9. Hamilton, *Report on Manufactures,* 33.
10. Thompson, *Elements*, 183.
11. Hamilton, "Spirits," 76.
12. O'Brien, *Classical Economists*, 229.
13. Ely, *Problems,* 46.
14. Roberts, *Treasury and Taxes*, 20–21.
15. Roberts, "Great Surplus," 578, 582.
16. Denslow to Carey, March 23, 1870, box 12, folder 6, *HCCP.*
17. Kelley, 'Internal Taxes', 14.
18. Hamilton, "Federalist 21," 401.
19. Blaine, *Twenty Years*, 1:188.
20. Lincoln, "Campaign Circular," 304.
21. Roberts, *Government Revenue,* 163.
22. Thompson, *Elements*, 187.
23. Bigelow, *Tariff Question*, 1.
24. Hamilton, *Report on Manufactures*, 41.
25. Hamilton, *Report on Manufactures*, 42.
26. Roberts, *Treasury and Taxes*, 19.
27. Hamilton, "Impost," 189.
28. Raymond, *Constitutional Law*, 255.
29. Stewart, *American System*, 9, emphasis in original.
30. Roberts, *Government Revenue*, 137.
31. Thompson, *Tariff Laws*, 449.
32. Raymond, "President's Message," 388, emphasis in original.
33. Hamilton, "Impost," 180–181.
34. Smith, *Wealth of Nations*, 2:425.
35. Denslow, *Principles*, 467.
36. It was not entirely clear what 'ability to pay' meant, as Denslow points out that "Dr. Smith holds that taxation should be equal according to the ability of each to pay. But who shall define ability to pay?". The American Protectionists interpreted it to mean a taxes on capital and income. Denslow, *Principles*, 463.
37. Denslow, *Principles*, 463.
38. Mill, "Property Tax," 552.
39. Denslow, *Principles*, 467.
40. Thompson, *Elements*, 182.
41. Denslow, *Principles*, 467.
42. Denslow, *Principles*, 467–468.
43. Hamilton, *Report on Manufactures*, 41.
44. Phillips, *Manual*, 273.
45. Greeley, *Essays,* 271–272.
46. Hamilton, *Report on Manufactures,* 27.
47. Colton, *Public Economy*, 368.
48. Webster, "General Effect," 534.

49. Hayes, "Customs Duties," 117.
50. Wharton, *Self-Protection*, 26–27.
51. Hamilton, *Report on Manufactures,* 27.
52. Ware, *Notes*, 66.
53. Colton, *Public Economy*, 374.
54. Colton, *Public Economy*, 505.
55. Hamilton, "Continentalist 5," 79–80.
56. Hamilton, "Continentalist 5," 80.
57. Denslow, *Logic*, 8.
58. Denslow, *Logic,* 10.
59. Roberts, *Government Revenue*, 157–158.
60. McKinley, "Value," 742.
61. Hamilton, "Continentalist 5," 78–79.
62. Hamilton, "Federalist 21," 401.
63. Hamilton, "Federalist 21," 401.
64. McKinley, 'Value, 742.
65. Carey, *Harmony,* 42.
66. Colwell, "Report," 276.
67. Mellon, *Taxation*, 13.
68. Coolidge, 'Annual Message', 20.
69. Mellon, *Taxation,* 94.
70. Roberts, *Government Revenue*, 328.

CONCLUSION

In the late nineteenth century, Alfred Marshall described the American Protectionists as "an important school of thinkers."[1] Yet, in spite of their significance being recognized at the time by no less an authority than Marshall, the American Protectionists have largely faded from our intellectual memory, and this comes despite the contemporary resurgence of protectionist policies. In essence, this book represents an intellectual recovery of America's neglected protectionist tradition. From Hamilton and Coxe's founding vision through to the twentieth century, it was their ideas that provided the intellectual foundations for American economic growth and development. Indeed, when looking back at nineteenth-century America one can only but agree with the famous statement of John Maynard Keynes that "the ideas of economists and political philosophers… are more powerful than commonly understood."[2] Not only have the ideas of the American Protectionists been poorly understood, so too has the power of their ideas in forging the economic destiny of America.

This book provides a distillation of ideas and theories of the nearly 70 economists and statesmen that made up the American Protectionist School. These were the same ideas avowed by great American statesmen ranging from Alexander Hamilton to Henry Clay, Abraham Lincoln, William McKinley, and Calvin Coolidge. Now modern readers can access these ideas and theories without having to identify, locate, and trawl through the voluminous number of texts written by the individual writers who made up the School. Whilst it would be ideal if others are now motivated to explore the writings of the American Protectionists for themselves, it is, of course, a reality that time and energy are not resources available in unlimited abundance. At the very least, this book provides a much-needed correction to the historical record and returns the system of the American Protectionists to its rightful place as a legitimate and sophisticated doctrine of economic thought.

Was There an American Protectionist School?

For the centennial of American independence, the Harvard economist Charles Franklin Dunbar was commissioned to write the first dedicated history of American economic thought. In the subsequent article, Dunbar concluded that "not only has no American school of writers on political economy been established… the United States have, thus far, done nothing towards developing the theory of political economy."[3] For over a century, this assessment has been recycled and repeated, becoming the standard interpretation of American economic thought. The implication is that there is thus no such thing as the American Protectionist School.

As this book has clearly shown, there can now be no doubt that the American Protectionists did indeed represent their own distinct school of economic thought replete with unique principles, an integrated system of economic laws, and even their own specialized language. The fact that this has been disputed only serves to demonstrate the extent to which the School has been sorely misunderstood by economists. This book thus has freed the American Protectionists from the shadow cast upon them by past scholarship. Not only did the American Protectionists secure economic independence for America, their writings are a mark of intellectual independence. Yet, even though it can be firmly concluded that the American Protectionists represent their own distinct school of thought, it raises the question of what exactly was the American Protectionist School?

The American Protectionist School can be seen as a progressive refinement and systematization of the original ideas presented by Alexander Hamilton and Tench Coxe in *The Report on Manufactures*, their other economic texts, as well as those texts by William Barton. The role of the *Report on Manufactures* as the virtual starting point of American Protectionist economics is undeniable, but American Protectionist thought was truly a collective effort of a great many thinkers. Indeed, the "great men" approach to the history of economic thought does not fit well with the development of American Protectionist thought—or perhaps it does, if one considers the nearly 70 "great men" who made up this intellectual tradition. Nevertheless, the standard depiction of American Protectionist thought as comprising a small handful of thinkers does not do justice to this deep and intellectually rich tradition of political economy.

Being such a large tradition, there is, of course, a variety and distinctiveness among its individual thinkers. Yet, despite such variety, what is truly remarkable is the sheer degree of consistency and coherence that emerged among the different thinkers who made up the tradition. Whereas mercantilism and other economic nationalist ideologies are frequently derided as a loose collection of *ad hoc* and contradictory notions than a systematic approach to economic theory, this simply cannot be said about the American Protectionists. The degree of consistency and coherence in their approach to political economy fully reflects the fact that they built their theories systematically upon a common set of principles and foundations. They were not special interest pleaders nor propagandists, but consistent and systemic thinkers. And this consistency in their approach lends further credence to the view that they were indeed a distinct and systematic school of thought, as opposed to a loose collection of arguments.

To appreciate exactly what is American Protectionist economics and how the different aspects of thought fit into their overall system, an overview of this system is provided below. After all, the American Protectionists saw their ideas as representing a complete system of interlocking laws and principles, as opposed to a few isolated ideas. In other words, their system can be considered a general theory of economy, as opposed to a partial one.

At its most basic, American Protectionist thought starts with a view of mankind as inherently flawed, but one innately capable of improvement through the use of intellect and moral reasoning. Man, according to the American Protectionists, is thus a tool-making and social creature, and one marked by a high degree of difference in individual talents, aptitudes, and dispositions. Yet, in spite of these individual differences, the American Protectionists still conceived of fundamental and natural laws of human conduct, and it is these laws of human conduct which give rise to general laws of economics. However, because Man is a social creature, these natural laws are subject, within certain limits, to modification by social and cultural institutions. Perhaps the most universal of these natural laws is the law of the endless circulation of matter and force, that is, that matter and energy cannot be created or destroyed, but only changed in form. This led to the view that economic activity fundamentally concerns Man transforming nature into instruments fit for human use. According to the American Protectionists, God bestowed Man with intellectual faculties through which he could seek out and obtain mastery over the hidden treasures of nature. This emphasis on Man's ingenuity and inventive genius led the American Protectionists to distinguish between what they saw as inventive and accumulative growth. In doing so, the American Protectionists extended their analysis beyond the confines of Classical economics by analyzing the role of invention and technology. Although the American Protectionists stressed the importance of both the inventive and accumulative in unlocking the wealth of nations, primacy was always placed upon the inventive.

Central to American Protectionist thought is also the distinction between individual and national wealth. National wealth, according to the American Protectionists, cannot simply be viewed as the aggregation of individual wealth. Instead, national wealth is defined in terms of productive power, or Man's ability to harness the forces of nature. This connects intimately with the concept of inventive growth. Since invention permanently alters the productive power of the economy through its tendency toward diffusion, and because it is permanently absorbed into the nation's technological base, the American Protectionist saw that the social benefits of invention often eclipses the private benefits it affords to the individual entrepreneur bringing it into existence. This means that it is in the national interest to promote conditions conducive to invention and entrepreneurship. This emphasis on entrepreneurship also relates to their conception of Man. Because Man is conceived as a tool-making creature, there is a natural propensity in Man to better his condition through discoveries and invention. The entrepreneur is viewed in this light and is thus depicted as a discoverer of new industrial pursuits. This entrepreneurial discovery function also relates to another crucial aspect of Man, namely the immense variety of unique talents and capabilities possessed by different individuals. Although an individual may possess an ability to be a successful entrepreneur in a particular industry, it does not necessarily follow that the individual can be successful in all industries. Thus, in order to maximize the inventive and entrepreneurial capacity of the economy, economic diversification is necessary so that the full scope of society's individual talents and inventive genius can be exercised.

This emphasis on invention and Man's mastery of nature also underpins the American Protectionist theory of value. The American Protectionists conceived value in terms of utility and resistance to be overcome. Whereas new industrial uses for commodities give rise to utility and establishes value; productivity-enhancing improvements, inventions, and processes of production will tend to press down upon value by reducing the resistance imposed by nature to acquiring such commodities. This means that there is a general tendency for reproduction costs to decline over time as industries become more productive. This led to the profound insight that wealth and value are inversely related.

In other words, as reproduction costs fall and values diminish, national wealth actually increases. Thus, for the American Protectionists, true economic progress meant that the same or even greater utility could be obtained with ever-decreasing effort. This means that low prices combined with high utility is a sign of societal enrichment rather than impoverishment.

This reproduction cost theory of value also represents one of the starting points of the American Protectionist theory of distribution. Noting the tendency for reproduction costs to fall and for productivity to increase through invention, the application of labor-saving machines, and the accumulation of intellectual capital, the American Protectionists rejected the subsistence theory of wages espoused by the Classical School. They saw instead that there would be a tendency for real wages to rise over time. This then translated into an analysis of social mobility. With the law of declining reproduction costs applying to the production of capital goods, the growth in wages combined with this cheapening of capital goods over time means that there is a gradual expansion in the opportunities for workers to become capitalists themselves. This expansion in the number of capitalists then places upward pressure on wages as there is now more competition for the purchase of workers. The American Protectionist thus espoused a harmony of interests between workers and capitalists. Indeed, because all economic activity involves Man's exploitation of nature, distribution is necessarily a positive-sum game with workers and capitalists receiving a gratuitous gift from nature.

The concept that all wealth creation involves Man's transformation of nature also extends to their analysis of land. Since all economic activity involves adapting nature to human use, the American Protectionists considered productive land to be a form of capital. Like any other form of capital investment, land requires significant outlay to render it productive and upkeep is also required to maintain its productivity. When this conception of land as capital is viewed in light of the law of the endless circulation of matter and force, it also means that in order for farming land to remain as productive capital, it is necessary to replenish nutrients lost in cultivation. This need to replenish the soil holds implications for international trade. Since agricultural exports effectively result in the exportation of productive soil, it means that agricultural exporting nations will tend to witness a perpetual deterioration in trade performance over time. Thus, the creation and preservation of a home market, in addition to providing a market for agricultural commodities, is necessary to maintain the productivity of land, so as to allow for nutrients to be returned to the soil in the form of manure.

This conception of land as capital also led to an explicit defense of land ownership, for if it holds that all economic creation involves Man's transformation of nature, it follows that private property rights must also extend to the ownership of land. In this respect, the American Protectionists were far more ardent and far more consistent in their defense of private property rights than members of the English Classical School, who often held landlords and land ownership in contempt. Whilst the American Protectionists supported intervention in the form of tariff protection, they fundamentally supported capitalism and market institutions. Indeed, American Protectionist thought considered the market system as vital and necessary for the coordination of economic activity. In the case of entrepreneurial discovery, for instance, the onset of lower profit rates in stagnant industries is seen as an endogenous and migratory force which compels entrepreneurs to seek out new industrial pursuits and sources of invention. This market coordination also extends to the geographical distribution of industry and population. In this case, the American Protectionists viewed rent as a dispersive force which causes the population to leave more densely populated centers, and to go forth and establish new towns and cities.

The view of Man as a social creature characterized by individual differences also has important implications in the formation of towns and cities. Since Man is a social creature, he has a need to associate with his fellowman, and because Man is also marked by individual differences, he is also dependent upon the services of others and thus has a need to associate with them. This process of association was seen as both the cause and the effect of individuality. Association, by allowing a greater diversity of pursuits, allows for the expression of an individual's unique characteristics. It follows from this that concentrating the population within cities and towns can allow for greater association and greater expression of Man's individuality. In addition to allowing greater association and individuality, other beneficial effects on productivity, ranging from technological spillovers to lower transportation costs, also arises from this process of concentration. These benefits would inform the views of the American Protectionists concerning population. With the process of concentration and rising population density contributing positively to productivity growth, this led the American Protectionists to reject the Malthusian theory of population. Instead of population growth outstripping the food supply and creating scarcity, the productivity growth generated from a growing population tends to produce abundance.

The emphasis which American Protectionist thought places upon invention and technological change also informs their analysis of the business cycle. In rejecting the view that aggregate demand deficiency can be the cause of recession, American Protectionist thought posits that the overproduction of specific commodities can temporarily occur through productivity-enhancing inventions and improvements. Through the presence of linkages, the overproduction of specific commodities could unravel into an economy-wide recession. Yet, the cure to the overproduction of specific commodities is not to boost aggregate demand, but to increase the production of commodities in undersupply, particularly new commodities. Diversification is therefore a means of mitigating against recessions, as well as a means of stabilizing economies experiencing recessions. The need for economic diversification also ties into an analysis of international trade, and the American Protectionists' conception of the individual. Against Classical trade theory which emphasizes the need for specialization in trade, the American Protectionists expounded the virtues of diversification. Whereas specialization means that individuals will be locked into uncongenial pursuits, fostering a more diverse array of industries would create greater scope for individuals to exercise their unique talents, aptitudes, and dispositions.

With respect to economic policy, the American Protectionists accepted a significant role for government, but they also saw that this role should be limited in scope. The basis of government policy was to create conditions conducive to entrepreneurship, the expansion of private enterprise, and the diversity of employments and economic pursuits. The American Protectionists therefore affirmed the view that government had a fundamental duty to secure and protect private property rights and to enforce contracts. Whilst they advocated a policy of free internal markets and low domestic taxation, they also advanced the view that government has the right and the duty to protect domestic industry through the imposition of protective tariffs, and to aid business through the provision of infrastructure. The revenue from the tariffs would be used to defray the general operations of government and the cost of the infrastructure. This significant role, yet limited scope, for government also related to the American Protectionist conception of economic freedom. In contrast to freedom of trade, the American Protectionists emphasized industrial freedom or the freedom of production. Industrial freedom means freedom for domestic producers to engage in entrepreneurial and economic activities, but perhaps most importantly, it means freedom for individuals to maximize their individuality by having the widest choice of diverse industrial pursuits.

This overview, of course, cannot fully capture all the individual elements that make up the American Protectionist system of thought, but it does give a general picture of what the School represents. It is thus abundantly clear that the American Protectionists indeed represented a systematic and distinct school of thought that held its own against other nineteenth century schools of economics.

America's Protectionist Tradition in Comparative Perspective

To fully appreciate the distinctiveness of the American Protectionist School within nineteenth-century economic thought, it is useful to compare their positions with those of their contemporaries. The following table presents a comparative analysis across several key theoretical and policy dimensions. It contrasts the approach of the American Protectionists with the English Classical School, Marxist economics, the French Liberal School, and the German Historical and Progressive tradition. This comparison reveals not only the comprehensiveness of American Protectionist thought, that they developed positions on virtually all major domains of economic analysis, it also highlights the uniqueness of their approach which sets them apart from other schools of thought. Indeed, where the Classical economists emphasized capital accumulation, Marxists focused on class struggle, the French emphasized market exchange, and the Germans and Progressives emphasized institutions, the American Protectionists built their entire theoretical system on the foundations of human ingenuity, individuality, and the diversity of talents.

Of course, it should go without saying that this represents a broad birds-eye view of the different nineteenth-century schools, and thus cannot capture the full variety of ideas within each tradition. It will nevertheless, however, help to situate the approach of the American Protectionists within the broader picture of nineteenth century economic thought (Table 1).

Table 1. Comparison of Nineteenth-Century Schools of Economic Thought

Category	American Protectionist	English Classical	Marxist	French Liberal	German Historical / Progressive
Main driver of growth	Human ingenuity and invention	Capital accumulation (savings & investment)	Capital accumulation driven by the extraction of surplus value (workers are responsible for all value)	Capital accumulation embedded in individual choice	Institutional and cultural factors
View of human nature	A social and toolmaking creature. Inherently flawed but possesses a capacity for invention and improvement	Self-interested. Capitalists are rational accumulators, workers are short-sighted consumers, and landlords are rent seekers.	Under capitalism: capitalists pursue profit maximization, workers become alienated from their labor and true nature	Rational, self-interested, and naturally inclined toward beneficial exchange	Culturally and institutionally shaped beings who evolve through historical processes
View of the individual	Characterized by a high degree of difference in individual talents, aptitudes, and disposition	Uniform within their respective class	Uniform within their respective class.	Characterized by differences in subjective preference	Culturally and institutionally conditioned
Treatment of technology	Endogenous: explains what augments the technological base of society	Exogenous	Exogenous: emphasis on effect rather than cause. Technology drives socioeconomic relations but emerges exogenously.	Exogenous	Endogenous: technology emerges from institutional and cultural development

Continued

Table 1. (*Continued*)

Category	American Protectionist	English Classical	Marxist	French Liberal	German Historical / Progressive
Economic methodology	Induction to uncover natural laws	Deduction from given assumptions (abstract model building)	Deduction: use of dialectical logic	Deduction from assumptions, but less emphasis on abstract models than Ricardo	Induction to uncover institutional influences and relations
Nature of economic laws	Natural and general but modified somewhat by institutions	Natural and fixed ("iron-laws")	Scientific and dialectical	Natural and general	Relative and institutionally determined (rejection of general laws)
Origin of the division of labor	Invention—creates a diversity of production	Propensity to truck, barter, and exchange (following Smith)	Emerges through historical process of alienation and capitalist control of production	Propensity to truck, barter, and exchange	Evolution of institutions: extension of primitive tribal division of labor
Price determination	Utility and productivity but emphasis is placed on productivity (reproduction cost)	Embodied labor (labor theory of value)	Socially necessary amount of embodied labor	Utility and subjective preference	Institutions, rules, and routines
Wage determination	Diverse and approximates productivity (multicausal)	Uniform and gravitates towards subsistence	Uniform and fixed at subsistence	Diverse and reflects the supply and demand for labor	Institutionally determined. Emphasis is placed on bargaining
Nature of rent	Difference between profit and rent is nominal. Rent also represents a coordinating force in the process of agglomeration	Unearned surplus from land's "original and indestructible powers," appropriated by landlords	Similar to profit, as both are an unearned surplus exacted through exploitation of tenants and workers	Legitimate return to land as factor of production, determined by supply and demand	Product of social arrangements. Progressives viewed it as unearned increment to be taxed or minimized through rent controls

	income from production and captures a reward for invention paid to the entrepreneur. Also represents a migratory force that guides entrepreneurs into new pursuits	residue surplus leftover after rent is paid. Has an inverse relationship with wages	through exploitation	Capitalist share of income from production and captures a brokerage fee paid to the entrepreneur	Varies by institutional context—may be earned return or unproductive surplus
Role of entrepreneur	Undertakes industry and discovers new industrial pursuits	Not applicable	Not applicable	Serves as a broker between sellers and buyers	Organizes production
Class relations	Harmonious: capital and labor exploit nature together. Emphasis on social mobility limits the importance of class	Implicitly antagonistic: distribution is zero-sum between classes	Explicitly antagonistic and exploitative: capitalists exploit workers	Harmonious: based on voluntary exchange and mutual benefit	State is necessary to resolve class conflict and to foster harmony
Population Growth…	Raises productivity and is self-regulative	Pushes cultivation to less fertile land which leads to diminishing returns	Adds to the reserve army of unemployed which places downward pressure on wages	No systematic population theory, but assumes market adjustment	Determined by institutional factors and cultural development
Profit rate trends	No general tendency to fall. Creation of new industries means the creation of new sources of profit. A falling rate of profit guides entrepreneurs to seek out new profits	Tendency to fall due to rising food costs and diminishing returns	A general tendency to fall. The result of an irrational overaccumulation of capital and the reduction in worker's purchasing power from the extraction of surplus value	No strong view on long-term trends. Focus on competition preventing excessive profits.	No strong view (rejection of general laws suggests no general trend)

Continued

Table 1. *(Continued)*

Category	American Protectionist	English Classical	Marxist	French Liberal	German Historical / Progressive
Cause of recessions	Temporary overproduction of specific commodities resulting from technological improvements. Diversification mitigates against recessions	Miscalculations in the structure of supply versus the structure of demand Malthus emphasized demand deficiency.	Generalized overproduction combined with restricted purchasing power of workers resulting from capitalist extraction of surplus value	Miscalculations in the structure of supply versus the structure of demand (emphasis on Say's law)	Institutional failures and inadequate social coordination of economic activity
Government's role	Significant, but limited in scope	Significant, but limited in scope. Wider scope under J. S. Mill	All encompassing (dictatorship of the proletariat)	Limited	Significant in both involvement and scope
Policy recommendations	Tariff protection, internal improvements, free internal markets, and limited domestic taxation	Free trade, limited government intervention, primarily for public goods and enabling market efficiency More emphasis on social programmes and reforms under Mill	Socialism and abolition of private property	Laissez-faire with minimal government intervention, strong anti-monopoly stance	Active government role in economic planning and social welfare.

Resurrecting a Lost Paradigm?

It should be recalled from earlier that economics rarely progresses in an onward and upward march toward a pinnacle of ever-increasing truth. Economic paradigms can be shunted aside, not because they are lacking, but due to factors unrelated to the paradigm itself. Of course, the American Protectionists were never truly the dominant paradigm, at least not within academia. But they were the clear alternative in American economics for the vast bulk of the nineteenth century, and within the political domain, their policy prescriptions received near universal assent among Whig and Republican statesmen.

Although a detailed examination of the School's decline is better suited for a more complete intellectual history, it is apparent that rhetorical and institutional factors played no small part in the School fading from intellectual prominence. The Progressive School takeover of the Wharton School and the ousting of Robert Ellis Thompson can be seen as a microcosm of this broader sweeping aside of the American Protectionists, and the fact that the School was more generally precluded from academia adds further weight to this view. Indeed, by the late nineteenth and early twentieth centuries, American economics increasingly became a contest between Progressive and the free market-oriented schools. The rise of credentialism in economics departments, combined with the American Protectionists' outsider status within academia, meant they could be easily dismissed by both camps. It also meant that the American Protectionists were starved of fresh recruits as economics graduates would be taught only Progressive and Neoclassical economics, and were thus unacquainted with ideas of the American Protectionists. Indeed, the decline of the American Protectionists need not be the result of some coordinated conspiracy but rather a predictable outcome of institutional dynamics that excluded them from the academic mainstream.

In any event, what is abundantly clear is that the system of the American Protectionist School did not collapse due to objective and scientific dismantling of their economic system. On the issue of trade theory alone, the American Protectionists had thoroughly dismantled the theory of comparative advantage, yet these refutations were simply ignored, and the theory of comparative advantage remained as economic orthodoxy well into the twentieth century, and arguably remains so until this day. Indeed, it seems far more apparent that the American Protectionists were dismissed because their ideas were considered too heretical within the economics discipline. To the economics establishment, it would be unthinkable that such ardent and consistent champions of protective tariffs could possibly have anything valuable to contribute to economic science.

The sophistication of the American Protectionists is demonstrated by the fact that they pioneered the way in fields that would reemerge independently within modern economics. Such examples include endogenous growth theory, agglomeration economics, and new trade theory, and what is more is that it is unclear whether these modern renderings have surpassed those originally put forth by the American

Protectionists. Whereas the American Protectionists integrated these domains of economic analysis into a clear and unified system of economic relations, it is difficult to claim that those independent rediscoveries made by modern economists have achieved this. Their theories are at best fragmentary, whereas the American Protectionists' approach is theoretically coherent, comprehensive, and systematic. The modern approaches are also often predicated on unrealistic assumptions that prioritize mathematical cleanness and elegance over the complexities of the real world, whereas the American Protectionists better capture real-world economic realities and processes. One only needs to look at modern models which assume that individuals are generic and devoid of all individuality versus the American Protectionist conception which takes into account the natural diversity in individual talents, aptitudes, and dispositions. Similarly, where modern endogenous growth models treat innovation as a presupposed mechanical output of R&D expenditure, the American Protectionists understood that it emerges from human ingenuity, real-world entrepreneurial discovery, the diffusive tendency of inventions, and the interaction between human individuality and the diversity of economic pursuits.

The need for an intellectually robust and historically informed approach to protectionism is more important than ever. In the political sphere, the free trade consensus has crumbled, and protectionism has re-emerged as a serious alternative. This is particularly true in the United States—the birthplace of the American Protectionist School. The ideas and policies of the American Protectionists were once responsible for forging the United States into the largest economy in the world, and this should serve as a testament to their system of economic thought.[4] It therefore stands to reason that there is much which policy makers can learn from this rich economic tradition. If protectionism is here to stay then it is only prudent to be informed by the ideas and theories of its most successful theorists and practitioners.

Of course, the above is not to suggest that the system of the American Protectionists were more correct by every measure and on every domain of economic analysis. No school of economic thought has achieved such a feat, and this is all the more unsurprising for the American Protectionists given how they faded from intellectual prominence prematurely. Rather, what is clear is that the American Protectionist School developed an understanding of economic development that deserves serious reconsideration, not as a historical curiosity, but as a theoretical framework that can offer insights into how economies actually grow and transform through human ingenuity, the diversity of talents, innovation, and industrial diversification.

This book therefore concludes by echoing the sentiments put forth by Robert Ellis Thompson and George B. Dixwell in the opening of the book. They were correct that we have no reason to be ashamed of the long series of writers and orators that have upheld that policy of protection. Those of able mind should review their conclusions and read with candid spirit, what has been urged by those who have written in favor of protection. We have every reason to recover the insights of the American Protectionists. These were the economic ideas that built America.

Notes

1. Marshall, "Foreign Trade," 34f.
2. Keynes, *General Theory*, 383.
3. Dunbar, "Economic Science," 489–490.
4. The combination of correlation data and case studies (e.g., Chang, *Kicking Away the Ladder*, 24–32; Bairoch, *Economics*, 30–43; Fasteau and Fletcher, *Industrial Policy*, 278–310) and the causal mechanisms articulated by the American Protectionists provides a sound basis for inferring causality. This same evidentiary standard is widely adopted by economists who argue for free trade.

REFERENCES

American Iron and Steel Institute Records (AISIR). Hagley Museum and Library. Wilmington, DE.

General Administration Collection Post 1820 (GACP1). University Archives and Records Centre. University of Pennsylvania. Philadelphia, PA.

Henry Charles Carey Papers (HCCP). Edward Carey Gardiner Collection. Historical Society of Pennsylvania. Philadelphia, PA.

Joseph Wharton Papers (JWP). Friends Historical Library, Swarthmore College, Swarthmore, PA.

[Gunton, George?]. "Is the Tariff an Issue?" *Gunton's Magazine* 26, no. 6 (1904): 479–486.

American Iron and Steel Association. "The New Campaign for Protection." *Bulletin of the American Iron and Steel Association* 20, no. 1 (1886): 4.

American Protective Tariff League. "Principles of the American Protective Tariff League." *The American Economist* 3, no. 6 (1889): 80.

Baird, Henry Carey. *Protection of Home Labor and Home Productions Necessary to the Prosperity of the American Farmer.* Philadelphia: Henry Carey Baird, 1860.

———. *The Rights of American Producers.* Philadelphia: Collins, 1872.

Bairoch, Paul. *Economics and World History: Myths and Paradoxes.* University of Chicago, 1995.

Barber, William J. "American Economics to 1900." In *A Companion to the History of Economic Thought,* edited by Warren J. Samuels, Jeff E. Biddle, and John B. Davis, 231–245. Malden: Blackwell Publishing, 2003.

Barton, William. "The True Interest of the United States, and Particularly of Pennsylvania, Considered." *American Museum* 2, no. 1 (1787): 23–36.

———. *Observations on the Progress of Population, and the Probabilities of the Duration of Human Life, in the United States of America.* Philadelphia: R. Aitken & Son, 1791.

Bancroft, George. *The Necessity, the Reality and the Promise of the Progress of the Human Race.* New York: The New York Historical Society, 1854.

Bastiat, Frederic. *Harmonies of Political Economy.* London: John Murray, 1860.

Beecher, Lyman. "Means of National Prosperity." In Mathew Carey, *Addresses of the Philadelphia Society for the Promotion of National Industry,* 5th ed., 263–286. Philadelphia: James Maxwell, 1820.

Belko, William S. "A Tax on the Many to Enrich a Few": Jacksonian Democrats vs. the Protective Tariff." *Journal of the History of Economic Thought,* 37, no. 2 (2015): 277–289.

Bigelow, Erastus B. "The Relations of Labor and Capital" *The Atlantic* 43, no. 252 (1878): 475–487.

———. *The Tariff Question Considered in Regard to the Policy of England and the Interests of the United States.* Boston: Little, Brown, and Company, 1862.

Bishop, John Leander. *A History of American Manufactures from 1608–1860.* Philadelphia: Edward Young & Co., 1864.

Bowen, Francis. *American Political Economy; Including Strictures on the Management of the Currency and the Finances since 1861.* New York: Scribner, Armstrong & Co., 1877.

Blaine, James G. *Twenty Years of Congress,* vols. 1–2. Norwich: Henry Bill Publishing House, 1884.

Blaug, Mark. *Economic Theory in Retrospect.* Revised Edition. Homewood: Richard D. Irwin, 1985.

Boritt, Gabor S. *Lincoln and the Economics of the American Dream.* Chicago: University of Illinois Press, 1994.

Browning, Andrew H. *The Panic of 1819: The First Great Depression.* Columbia: University of Missouri Press, 2019.

Byrdsall, Fitzwilliam. *The History of the Loco–Foco, or Equal Rights Party*. New York: Clement & Packard, 1842.
Cairnes, John Elliot. "Political Economy and *Laissez-faire*." *The Fortnightly Review* 10, no. 55 (1871): 80–97.
Calvo, Christopher W. *The Emergence of Capitalism in Early America*. Gainesville: University of Florida Press, 2020.
Cannan, Edwin. *A History of the Theories of Production and Distribution in English Political Economy from 1776 to 1848*. 3rd ed. London: P. S. King and Son, 1917.
Carey, Henry Charles. *Financial Crises: Their Causes and Effects*. Philadelphia, H. C. Baird, 1864.
———. *The Harmony of Interests: Agricultural, Manufacturing and Commercial*. Philadelphia: J. S. Skinner, 1851.
———. *Manual of Social Science*, edited by Kate McKean. Philadelphia: Henry Carey Barid, 1866.
———. *Review of an Address of the Joint Board of Directors of Delaware and Raritan Canal and Camden and Amboy Railroad Companies*. Philadelphia: C. Sherman, Printer, 1848.
———. *The Past, the Present, and the Future*. Philadelphia: Carey & Hart, 1847.
———. *Principles of Political Economy*. Vols. 1–3. Philadelphia: Carey, Lea & Blanchard, 1837.
———. *Principles of Social Science*. Vols. 1–3. Philadelphia: J. B. Lippincott & Co, 1858–1859.
———. *The Unity of Law*. Philadelphia: Henry Carey Baird, 1872.
Carey, Mathew. *An Appeal to the Common Sense and Common Justice*. 3rd Edition. Philadelphia: H. C. Carey & Lea, 1822.
———. *Autobiographical Sketches: In A Series of Letters Addressed to a Friend*. Philadelphia: John Clarke, 1839.
———. *Essays on Political Economy*. Philadelphia: H. C. Carey & I Lea, 1822.
Chang, Ha–Joon. *Kicking Away the Ladder: Development Strategy in Historical Perspective*. London: Anthem Press, 2002.
Choate, Rufus. "Value of Mechanical Industry." *The American Magazine* 1, no. 3 (1851):127–128.
———. *Speech Upon the Subject of Protecting American Labor by Duties on Imports*. Washington: Gales and Seaton, 1844.
Clarke, Albert. "Trust Insanity." *The Protectionist* 11, no. 12 (1899): 1–4.
Clay, Henry. "On Abolition." In *The Works of Henry Clay*, vol. 6, edited by Calvin Colton, 139-159. New York: Henry Clay Publishing Company, 1896.
———. "On American Industry." In *The Works of Henry Clay*. Vol. 5, edited by Calvin Colton, 496–538. New York: Henry Clay Publishing Company, 1896.
———. "On the American System." In *The Works of Henry Clay*. Vol. 5, edited by Calvin Colton, 438–486. New York: Henry Clay Publishing Company, 1896.
———. "On Domestic Manufactures." In *The Works of Henry Clay*. Vol. 5, edited by Calvin Colton, 7–11. New York: Henry Clay Publishing Company, 1896.
———. "On Internal Improvements." In *The Works of Henry Clay*. Vol. 5, edited by Calvin Colton, 166–235. New York: Henry Clay Publishing Company, 1896.
———. "On Nullification and Other Topics." In *The Works of Henry Clay*. Vol. 5, edited by Calvin Colton, 392–415. New York: Henry Clay Publishing Company, 1896.
Colton, Calvin. "Labor and Capital." *The Junius Tracts* no. 7 (1844): 97–112.
———. *Public Economy for the United States*. New York: A. S. Barnes & Co., 1848.
———. *The Rights of Labor*. New York: A. S. Barnes & Co., 1847.
Colwell, Stephen. *A Preliminary Essay Prefixed to the American Edition of List's National System of Political Economy*. Philadelphia: J. B. Lippincott & Co, 1867.
———. *The Claims of Labor and Their Precedence to the Claims of Free Trade*. Philadelphia: C. Sherman & Son, 1861.
———. "Report upon the Relations of Foreign Trade to Domestic Industry and Internal Revenue." In *Reports of a Commission Appointed for a Revision of the Revenue System of the United States 1865–66*, by David A. Wells, Stephen Colwell, and Samuel S. Hayes, 276–294. Washington: Government Printing Office, 1866.

———. *The Relative Position in Our System of Industry of Foreign Commerce, Domestic Production, and Internal Trade*. Philadelphia: Lindsey and Blakiston, 1850.

Colston, Raleigh Edward. "The Problem of Free Society." *Southern Literary Messenger* 26, no. 1 (1858): 1–18.

Conkin, Paul K. *Prophets of Prosperity*. Bloomington: Indiana University Press, 1980.

Cooke, Jacob E. *Tench Coxe and the Early Republic*. Chapel Hill: University of North Carolina Press, 1978.

Coolidge, Calvin. "Our Heritage from Hamilton." Address on the Anniversary of the Birthday of Alexander Hamilton, Before the Hamilton Club, Chicago, January 11, 1922. In *The Price of Freedom: Speeches and Addresses*, 101–116. New York: Charles Scribner's Sons, 1924.

———. "President's Annual Message." In *Congressional Record*. Vol. 70, pt. 1, 20–25. Washington: U.S. Government Printing Office, 1929.

Cooper, Thomas. *Lectures on the Elements of Political Economy*. Columbia: Doyle E. Sweeny, 1826.

Coxe, Tench. *An Essay on the Manufacturing Interest of the United States*. Philadelphia: Graves, 1804.

———. "An Inquiry into the Cause of the Disorders in the Private Business of the Civilized World, with a Particular View to the Cause of the United States, and Especially of the Manufacturing Branch of its National Industry." *Enclosed in Tench Coxe to James Monroe*, November 27, 1819. James Monroe Papers, 1723–1859. Library of Congress, Washington, DC.

———. *Memorial of the Artists and Manufacturers of Philadelphia*. Philadelphia: Graves, 1804.

———. *Observations on the Agriculture, Manufactures, and Commerce of the United States*. New York: Francis Childs & John Swaine, 1789.

———. *Report of the Committee of Commerce and Manufactures on Various Memorials and Petitions from Citizens of New York, New Jersey, Pennsylvania, and Maryland, Praying for Legislative Patronage of to Several Domestic Arts, Trades and Manufactures*. Philadelphia: Graves, 1804.

———. *A Statement of the Arts and Manufactures of the United States of America for the Year 1810*. Philadelphia: A. Cornman, 1814.

———. "Tench Coxe's Second Draft." In *The Papers of Alexander Hamilton*, vol. 26, edited by Harold C. Syrett, 632–647. New York: Columbia University Press, 1979.

———. *A View of the United States of America: In a Series of Letters; Written at Various Times Between the Years 1787 and 1794*. Philadelphia: William Hall, 1794.

Curtiss, George B. *The Industrial Development of Nations*. Vols. 1–3. Binghamton: George B. Curtiss Publisher, 1912.

———. *Protection and Prosperity*. New York: Pan-American Publishing Company, 1896.

Dallas, Alexander J. *Letter from The Secretary of the Treasury Transmitting A Report on a General Tariff of Duties Proper to Be Imposed on Imported Goods, Wares, and Merchandise: Prepared in Obedience to a Resolve of the House of Representatives of Feb. 23, 1816*. Washington: William A. Davis, 1816.

Denslow, Van Buren. "American Economics." *The North American Review* 139, no. 332 (1884): 12–29.

———. *Freedom in Trade*. Cambridge: John Wilson and Son, 1882.

———. *Modern Thinkers Principally Upon Social Science: What They Think and Why*. Chicago: Belford Clarke & Co., 1880.

———. *The Logic of Protection*. Brooklyn, NY, 1883.

———. *Principles of the Economic Philosophy of Society, Government, and Industry*. New York: Cassell & Company, 1888.

———. "Why I am a Protectionist." *Twentieth Century* 4, no. 17 (1890): 7–8.

Dixwell, George Basil. "Review of Bastiat's Sophisms of Protection." *Bulletin of the National Association of Wool Manufactures*. 11, no. 3 (1881): 233–257.

———. "Review of Perry." *Bulletin of the National Association of Wool Manufacturers* 12, no. 1 (1882): 28–43.

———. *The Premises of Free Trade Examined*. Cambridge: John Wilson and Son, 1881.

———. *"Progress and Poverty": A Review of the Doctrines of Henry George.* Cambridge: John Wilson and Son, 1882.

Dorfman, Joseph. *The Economic Mind in American Civilization, 1606–1865.* Vols. 1–2. New York: Augustus M. Kelley, 1966.

———. "The Economic Philosophy of Thomas Jefferson." *Political Science Quarterly.* 55, no. 1 (1940): 98–121.

Dudley, Thomas Haines. *The Farmer Feedeth All: How Protection Affects the Farmer.* Philadelphia: Allen, Lane & Scott's Printing House, 1882.

———.*Which is Best for Farmers, Protection or Free Trade?.* New York: The American Protective Tariff League, 1885.

Dunbar, Charles Franklin. "Economic Science in America, 1776–1876." *The North American Review* 122, no. 250 (1876): 124–154.

Elder, Cyrus. *Man and Labor: A Series of Short and Simple Studies.* Chicago & New York: Belford, Clarke, and Co, 1886.

Elder, William. *Conversations on the Principal Subjects of Political Economy.* Philadelphia: Henry Carey Baird & Co, 1882.

———. *The Doctrine and Policy of Protection.* Philadelphia: Ringwalt & Brown, 1860.

———. *A Memoir of Henry C. Carey.* Philadelphia: The American Iron and Steel Association, 1880.

———. *Questions of the Day: Economic and Social.* Philadelphia: Henry Carey Baird Publisher, 1871.

Elkins, Stanley, and Eric McKitrick. *The Age of Federalism: The Early American Republic, 1788–1800.* New York: Oxford University Press, 1993.

Ely, Richard T. *Outline of Economics.* New York: The Macmillan Company, 1914.

———. *Problems of To–Day: A Discussion of Protective Tariffs, Taxation, and Monopolies.* New York: Thomas Y. Crowell, 1888.

Everett, Alexander Hill. *British Opinions on the Protecting System.* 2nd Edition. Boston: Nathan Hale, 1830.

———. "Memorial of the New–York Convention to the Congress of the United States." In *Journal of the Proceedings of the Friends of Domestic Industry in General Convention at New York*, edited by Hezekiah Niles, 138–140. Baltimore, 1831.

———. *New Ideas on Population: With Remarks on the Theories of Malthus and Godwin.* Boston: Oliver Everett, 1823.

Fasteau, Mark; and Ian Fletcher. *Industrial Policy for the United States: Winning the Competition for Goods Jobs and High–Value Industries.* Cambridge University Press, 2024.

Feyerabend, Paul. *Against Method.* London: Verso, 1975.

Foner, Eric. *Free Soil, Free Labor, Free Men: The Ideology of the Republican Party before the Civil War.* Oxford: Oxford University Press, 1995.

Frith, Mathew A. "Alexander Hamilton, Tench Coxe, and the Diversity of Talents: A Neglected Argument in Early American Protectionist Thought." *History of Economics Review* (in press) https://doi.org/10.1080/10370196.2026.2657703.

———. "American Protectionist Thought: The Economic Philosophy and Theory of the 19th Century American Protectionists." PhD Dissertation, Federation University Australia, 2024.

———. "An Outline of 'American Protectionist Thought: The Economic Philosophy and Theory of the 19th Century American Protectionists.'" *History of Economics Review* 89 no. 1 (2024): 31–39.

———. "Van Buren Denslow and the Migratory Theory of Profit." Paper presented at the 52nd Annual Meeting of the History of Economics Society, University of Richmond, Richmond, Virginia, June 27–30, 2025.

Fletcher, Ian. *Free Trade Doesn't Work: What Should Replace it and Why.* Washington, D. C.: US Business & Industry Council, 2010.

Furner, Mary. *Advocacy and Objectivity: A Crisis in the Professionalization of American Social Science 1865–1905.* Lexington: University Press of Kentucky, 1975.

Galbraith, John Kenneth. *The Affluent Society*. New York: Houghton Mifflin Company, 1998.

Gerring, John. *Party Ideologies in America, 1828–1996*. Cambridge: Cambridge University Press, 1998.

Greeley, Horace. *Essays Designed to Elucidate the Science of Political Economy*. Boston: Fields, Osgood, & Co, 1870.

———. "The Return of Prosperity." *The Nashville Union*. April 28, 1838.

———."The Tariff Question," *American Whig Review*, 2, no. 2 (1845): 111–115.

Griswold, Rufus. "Henry C. Carey: The Apostle of the American School of Political Economy." *American Whig Review*, 37 (January 1851): 79–86.

Groenewegen, Peter. *Eighteenth–Century Economics: Turgot, Beccaria and Smith and Their Contemporaries*. London: Routledge, 2002.

Gunton, George. *Principles of Social Economics*. New York: G. P. Putnam's Sons, 1891.

Hamilton, Alexander. *Alexander Hamilton's Famous Report on Manufactures*. Boston: Home Market Club, 1892.

———. "Alexander Hamilton's Fourth Draft of the Report on the Subject of Manufactures, 1791." In *The Papers of Alexander Hamilton*. Vol. 10, edited by Harold C. Syrett, 124–230. New York: Columbia University Press, 1962.

———. "Constitutional Convention. Remarks on the Term of Office for Members of the Second Branch of the Legislature." In *The Papers of Alexander Hamilton*. Vol. 4, edited by Harold C. Syrett. 218–220. New York: Columbia University Press, 1962.

———. "The Continentalist No. 5." In *The Papers of Alexander Hamilton*. Vol. 3, edited by Harold C. Syrett, 75–82. New York: Columbia University Press, 1962.

———. "The Defence No. 1." In *The Papers of Alexander Hamilton*. Vol. 13, edited by Harold C. Syrett, 393–395. New York: Columbia University Press, 1967.

———. "Defence of the Funding System." In *The Papers of Alexander Hamilton*. Vol. 19, edited by Harold C. Syrett, 1–73. New York: Columbia University Press, 1973.

———. "The Examination Number III." In *The Papers of Alexander Hamilton*. Vol. 25, edited by Harold C. Syrett, 464–468. New York: Columbia University Press, 1977.

———. "The Farmer Refuted." In *The Papers of Alexander Hamilton*. Vol. 1, edited by Harold C. Syrett, 81–165. New York: Columbia University Press, 1961.

———. "The Federalist No. 21." In *The Papers of Alexander Hamilton*. Vol. 4, edited by Harold C. Syrett, 386–401. New York: Columbia University Press, 1962.

———. "The Federalist No. 35." In *The Papers of Alexander Hamilton*. Vol. 4, edited by Harold C. Syrett, 476–482. New York: Columbia University Press, 1962.

———. "The Report on the Impost Duty." In *The Works of Alexander Hamilton*. Vol. 2, edited by Henry Cabot Lodge, 179–192. New York: G. P, Putnam's Sons, 1904.

———. *The Report of the Secretary of the Treasury of the United States on the Subject of Manufactures*. Philadelphia: Childs and Swain, 1791.

———. "Spirits, Foreign, and Domestic." In *The Works of Alexander Hamilton*. Vol. 2, edited by Henry Cabot Lodge, 368–408. New York: G. P. Putnam's Sons, 1904.

Harcourt, Geoff C., and Peter Kriesler. "On Ricardo and Cambridge." In *Reclaiming Pluralism in Economics*, edited by Jerry Courvisanos, Jamie Doughney, and Alex Millmow, 150–167. London and New York: Routledge, 2016.

Harding, Warren G. "Inaugural Address to Congress." March 04, 1921.

Hayes, John L. "Carey's Unity of Law." *Bulletin of the National Association of Wool Manufacturers* 4, no. 3 (1873): 288–316.

———. "Customs Duties on the Necessaries of Life and Their Relations to the National Industry." *Bulletin of the National Association of Wool Manufacturers*. 14, no. 2 (1884): 113–144.

———. "The Nationalistic and Cosmopolitan Schools of Political Economy'." *Bulletin of the National Association of Wool Manufacturers*. 14, no. 2 (1884): 145–154.

———. *The Protective Question Abroad and Remarks at the Indianapolis Convention*. Cambridge: John Wilson and Son, 1870.

———. "The Solidarity of the Industries." In *Thirty–First Annual Report of the American Institute of the City of New York, 1870–71*, 115–136. Albany: The Argue Company Printers, 1871.

———. *The Woollen Tariff Defended and Explained*. Cambridge: John Wilson & Son, 1885.

Helleiner, Eric. *The Neomercantilists: A Global Intellectual History*. Ithaca: Cornell University Press, 2021.

Hodgson, Dennis. "Malthus' Essay on Population and the American Debate over Slavery." *Comparative Studies in Society and History*. 51 no. 4 (2009): 742–770.

Holt, Michael F. *The Rise and Fall of the American Whig Party: Jacksonian Politics and the Onset of the Civil War,* Oxford: Oxford University Press, 2003.

The Home Market Club. "Champions of Protection: Van Buren Denslow." *The Protectionist*. 11, no. 128 (1899): 441–464.

Horr, Roswell G. "Are Taxes Ever a Blessing?" *The New York Tribune*. May 25, 1891.

Hoyt, Henry M. *Protection versus Free Trade*. New York: D. Appleton & Company, 1886.

Hudson, Michael. *America's Protectionist Takeoff*. Baskerville: ISLET, 2010.

———."E. Peshine Smith: A Study in Protectionist Growth Theory and American Sectionalism." Unpublished PhD Dissertation. New York University. 1968.

Irwin, Douglas A. "The Aftermath of Hamilton's 'Report on Manufactures'." *The Journal of Economic History*, 64, no. 3 (2004): 800–821.

———. *Clashing Over Commerce: A History of US Trade Policy*. Chicago: The University of Chicago Press, 2017.

Jarvis, William Charles. *The Republican*. Pittsfield: Phineas Allen, 1820.

Jefferson, Thomas. Thomas Jefferson to James Madison, October 28, 1785. In *The Papers of Thomas Jefferson*. Vol. 8, edited by Julian P. Boyd, 681–683. Princeton: Princeton University Press, 1953.

Jennison, William. *An Outline of Political Economy*. Philadelphia: 1828.

Jevons, William Stanley. *Methods of Social Reform and Other Papers*. London: Macmillan and Co., 1883.

Joseph, Richard T. *The Origins of the American Income Tax: The Revenue Act of 1894 and Its Aftermath*. Syracuse: Syracuse University Press, 2004.

Kaldor, Nicholas. "Alternative Theories of Distribution." *The Review of Economic Studies*. 23, no. 2 (1955–1956): 83–100.

Kates, Steven. *Classical Economic Theory and the Modern Economy*. Cheltenham: Edward Elgar Publishing, 2020.

———. *Say's Law and the Keynesian Revolution: How Macroeconomics Lost its Way*. Cheltenham: Edward Elgar, 1998.

Kelley, William D. *Reduction of Internal Taxes*. Philadelphia: The Industrial League, 1887.

———. "A Science Based Upon Assumptions." *The International Review* 12 (1882): 285–298.

Keynes, John Maynard. *The General Theory of Employment, Interest, and Money*. London: MacMillan and Co., 1936.

Kuhn, Thomas. *Structure of Scientific Revolutions*. Chicago: University of Chicago, 1962.

Lakatos, Imre. *The Methodology of Scientific Research Programmes*. Cambridge: Cambridge University Press, 1980.

Lee, Arthur M. "Henry C. Carey and the Republican Tariff." *The Pennsylvania Magazine of History and Biography* 81, no. 3 (1957): 280–302.

Leonard, Thomas C. *Illiberal Reformers: Race, Eugenics, and American Economics in the Progressive Era*. Princeton: Princeton University Press, 2017.

Lincoln, Abraham. "Campaign Circular from Whig Committee." In *Complete Works of Abraham Lincoln*. Vol. 1, edited by John G. Nicolay and John Hay, 72–79. New and enlarged ed. New York: Lincoln Memorial University, 1894.

———. "First Lecture on Discoveries and Inventions." In *Collected Works of Abraham Lincoln*. Vol. 2, edited by Roy P. Basley, 437–442. New Brunswick: Rutgers University Press, 2001.

———. "I Am Humble Abraham Lincoln." In *Life and Works of Abraham Lincoln*. Vol. 1, edited Marion Mills Miller, 1–2. New York: Lincoln Centenary Association, 1907.

Lind, Michael. *Land of Promise: An Economic History of the United States*. New York: HarperCollins, 2012.

List, Friedrich. *Outlines of American Political Economy*. Philadelphia: Samuel Parker, 1827.

———. *The National System of Political Economy*. Translated by G. A. Matile, edited by Stephen Colwell. Philadelphia: J. B. Lippincott & Co., 1856.

———. *The Natural System of Political Economy*, translated and edited by W. O. Henderson. New York: Routledge, 1983.

Lodge, Henry Cabot. "The Tariff." In *Speeches and Addresses, 1884–1909*, 87–152. Boston and New York: Houghton Mifflin Co., 1909.

Lui, Glory M. 2022. *Adam Smith's America: How a Scottish Philosopher Became an Icon of American Capitalism*. Princeton: Princeton University Press.

Maclay, William. *Sketches of Debate in the First Senate of the United States, in 1789–90–91*. Harrisburg: Lane S. Hart, 1880.

Marshall, Alfred. Letter to Unknown Correspondent, 6 June 1907. In *The Correspondence of Alfred Marshall, Economist*. Vol. 3, edited by John K. Whitaker, 160–161. Cambridge: Cambridge University Press, 1996.

———. "The Theory of Foreign Trade and Other Portions of Economic Science Bearing on the Principle of Laissez Faire, 1873–7." In *The Early Economic Writings of Alfred Marshall, 1867–1890*. Vol. 2, edited by J. K. Whitaker, 3–212. London: Macmillan Press, 1975.

Mason, David H. *How Western Farmers Are Benefited by Protection*. Chicago: David H. Mason, 1875.

———. *The Impending Crisis: Protection Must Be Maintained, or Past Better Experiences of Depression Will be Repeated*. Philadelphia: Henry Carey Baird & Co, 1887.

———. "Protection's Natural Law." *The Protectionist* 11, no. 123 (1899): 118–125.

McCloskey, Deidre. *The Rhetoric of Economics*. Madison: University of Wisconsin Press, 1985.

McKinley, William. "The Value of Protection." *The North American Review*. 150, no. 403 (1890): 740–748.

Meardon, Stephen. "'A Reciprocity of Advantages': Carey, Hamilton, and the American Protective Doctrine." *Early American Studies: An Interdisciplinary Journal* 11, no. 3 (2013): 431–454.

———. "Richard Cobden's American Quandary: Negotiating Peace, Free Trade, and Anti–Slavery." In *Rethinking Nineteenth–Century Liberalism*, edited by Anthony Howe and Simon Morgan, 208–228. Aldershot: Ashgate Publishing Limited, 2006.

———. "Yankee Ingenuity in Theories of American Economic Development, from the Founding to the Closing of the Frontier." *History of Political Economy* 50, no. S1 (2018): 41–58.

Melish, John. *A Geographical Description of the World: Intended as an Accompaniment to the Map of the World on Mercator's Projection*. Philadelphia: J. Melish & S. Harrison, 1818.

———. *Travels through the United States of America in the Years 1806 & 1807 and 1808, 1810 & 1811*. Philadelphia: John Melish, 1818.

Mellon, Andrew. *Taxation: The People's Business*. New York: The Macmillan Company, 1924.

Mill, John Stuart. "Errors and Truths on a Property Tax." In *Collected Works of John Stuart Mill*. Vol. 23, edited by Ann P. Robson and John M. Robson, 549–554. Toronto: University of Toronto Press, 1968.

———. *Essays on Some Unsettled Questions of Political Economy*. London: John W. Parker, 1844.

Minority View of the Joint Committee on Revenue. "Minority Views—General Statement." In *Subcommittee on Administration of the Internal Revenue Laws, Internal Revenue Investigation*. Washington: Government Printing Office, 1953. B1–B24.

Morrill, Justin Smith. *A Protective Tariff or Free Trade*. Washington: F. & J. Rives & Geo. A. Bailey, 1870.

National Association of Wool Manufacturers. *Objects and Plan of the National Association of Wool Manufacturers: Its Organization, Articles of Association, and By–Laws*. Boston: John Wilson & Son, 1865.

Niles, Hezekiah. *Journal of the Proceedings of the Friends of Domestic Industry in General Convention at New York*. Baltimore, 1831.

O'Brien, Denis. *The Classical Economists Revisited*. Revised Edition. Princeton: Princeton University Press, 2004.

O'Connor, Michael J. L. *Origins of Academic Economics in the United States*. New York: Columbia University Press, 1944.

Patten, Simon. *The Reconstruction of Economic Theory*. Philadelphia: The American Academy of Political and Social Science, 1912.

Patton, Jacob Harris. *Our Tariff: Why Levied and Why Continued. The Reasons why the American People Wish to Pay Better Wages than are Paid in Europe; Also a Sketch of the Cobden Club*. New York: The American Protective Tariff League, 1887.

———. *Political Economy for American Youth*. New York: A. Lovell & Co, 1892.

Perry, Arthur Latham. *Principles of Political Economy*. New York: Charles Scribner's Sons, 1891.

Peskin, Lawrence. "How the Republicans Learned to Love Manufacturing: The First Parties and the 'New Economy.'" *Journal of the Early Republic*, 22, no. 2 (2002): 235–262.

———. *Manufacturing Revolution: The Intellectual Origins of Early American Industry*. Baltimore: John Hopkins University Press, 2003.

Phillips, Willard. *A Manual of Political Economy*. Boston: Hilliard, Grey, Little, and Wilkins, 1828

———. *Propositions Concerning Protection and Free Trade*. Boston: Charles C. Little and James Brown, 1850.

Porter, Robert Percival. *Protection and Free Trade To–Day: At Home and Abroad, In Field and Workshop* Boston: James R. Osgood and Company, 1884.

Putnam, Oliver. *Tracts on Sundry Topics of Political Economy*. Boston: Russell, Odiorne, and Company, 1834.

Rae, John. "Genius and its Application." In *John Rae: Political Economist*. Vol. 1, edited by R Warren James, 320–326. Toronto: University of Toronto Press, 1965.

———. John Rae to John Stuart Mill, c. 1854. In *John Rae: Political Economist*. Vol. 1, edited by R Warren James, 430–437. Toronto: University of Toronto Press, 1965.

———. "Sketches of the Origin and Progress of Manufactures and of the Policy which had Regulated their Legislative Encouragement in Great Britain and in Other Countries." In *John Rae: Political Economist*. Vol. 1, edited by R. Warren James, 195–196. Toronto: University of Toronto Press, 1965.

———. *The Sociological Theory of Capital: Being a Complete Reprint of the New Principles of Political Economy*. New York: The Macmillan Company, 1905.

———. *Statement of Some New Principles on the Subject of Political Economy*. Boston: Hillard, Gray and Co., 1834.

Raymond, Daniel. *The Elements of Constitutional Law and Political Economy*. Baltimore: Cushing & Brother, 1840.

———. *The Elements of Political Economy*. Vols. 1–2. Baltimore: F. Lucas, Jr., and E. J. Coale 1823–1826.

———. "The President's Message, and the Report of the Secretary of the Treasury." *The American Whig Review*, 1, no. 6 (1848), 384–396.

———. *Thoughts on Political Economy*. Baltimore: Fielding Lucas Jr., 1820.

Reed, Thomas Brackett. *Reed on the Tariff*. Washington: 1896.

———. *The Tariff*. Washington: Gray & Clarkson, 1888.

———. "What Shall we do With the Tariff?" *The North American Review* 175, no. 553 (1902) 746–755.

Reinert, Erik. *How Rich Countries Got Rich and Why Poor Countries Stay Poor*. London: Constable 2007.

Republican National Convention. "Republican Platform, 1936." In *Factual Campaign Information* edited by Edwin A. Halsey, 29–36. Washington: Government Printing Office, 1939.

Ricardo, David. David Ricardo to Thomas Robert Malthus, October 10, 1820. In *Letters of David Ricardo to Thomas Malthus, 1810–1823*, edited by James Bonar, 173–177. Oxford: Clarendon Press, 1887.

———. *On the Principles of Political Economy and Taxation.* 3rd ed. London: John Murray, 1821.

Rice, David Hall. *Protective Philosophy: A Discussion of the Principles of the American Protective System as Embodied in the McKinley Bill.* Boston: George B. Reed, 1890.

Roberts, Ellis H. *Government Revenue, Especially the American System. An Argument for Industrial Freedom Against the Fallacies of Free Trade.* Cambridge: The Riverside Press, 1884.

———. *The Revenue and American Labor: Necessity and Growth of Home Production.* Washington: F. & J. Rives & Geo. A. Bailey, 1872.

———. *The Treasury and the Taxes.* Washington: Government Printing Office, 1874

———. "The Wrong of the Great Surplus." *The North American Review* 185, no. 619 (1907): 577–586.

Roncaglia, Alessandro. *The Wealth of Ideas: A History of Economic Thought.* Cambridge: Cambridge University Press, 2005.

Roscher, Wilhelm. *Principles of Political Economy with Additional Chapters on Paper Money, International Trade, and the Protective System.* Vol. 2. Translated by John L. Lalor. New York: Henry Holt & Co, 1878.

Rossi, Matteo. "Protecting America: Order, Nation and Exception in Henry Carey's Social Science." *USAbroad: Journal of American History and Politics.* 2 (2019): 1–16.

Rothbard, Murray N. *An Austrian Perspective on the History of Economic Thought.* Vols. 1–2. Cheltenham: Edward Elgar Publishing, 2006.

Salerno, Joseph T. "The Neglect of the French Liberal School in Anglo–American Economics: A Critique of Received Explanations." *The Review of Austrian Economics.* 2, no. 1, 1988: 112–156.

Samuels, Warren J. *The Classical Theory of Economic Policy.* Cleveland: The World Publishing Company, 1966.

Sass, Steven A. *The Pragmatic Imagination: A History of the Wharton School, 1881–1918.* Philadelphia: University of Pennsylvania Press, 1982.

Say, Jean Baptiste. *A Treatise on Political Economy; or the Production, Distribution, and Consumption of Wealth.* Translated by Clement C. Biddle. Edited by New American. Philadelphia: Lippincott, Grambo & Co., 1851.

Schlesinger, Arthur M., Jr. *The Age of Jackson.* Boston: Little, Brown, and Company, 1945.

Schumpeter, Joseph. *The History of Economic Analysis.* New York: Routledge, 2006.

Seaman, Ezra. *Essays on the Progress of Nations.* New York: Charles Scribner, 1852.

———. "Human Progress: Its Elements, Impediments, and Limits." *Hunt's Merchants' Magazine* 28, no. 4 (1858): 407–416.

Seligman, Edwin. *Essays in Economics.* New York: Macmillan, 1925.

Skinner, Orrin. *The Issues of American Politics.* Philadelphia: J. B. Lippincott & Co., 1873.

Skousen, Mark. *The Making of Modern Economics: The Lives and Ideas of the Great Economists.* Armonk: M.E. Sharpe, 2015.

Smith, Adam. *An Inquiry into the Nature and Causes of the Wealth of Nations.* Vols. 1–2. London: W. Strahan and T. Cadell, 1776–1778.

Smith, Adam. *Lectures on Jurisprudence (1762–1766).* Edited by David M. Hart. Digital Library of Liberty and Power, 2023. http://davidmhart.com/liberty/Books/1766–Smith_LecturesJurisprudence/Smith_LecturesJurisprudence1766–ebook.pdf.

Smith, E. Peshine. "Protection versus Free Trade: The Law of Progress in the Relations of Capital and Labor." *Hunt's Merchant Magazine and Commercial Review* 26, no. 1 (1852): 31–44.

———. *A Manual of Political Economy.* New York: George P. Putnam & Co, 1853.

———. "Notes on Political Economy Designed Chiefly for Japanese Readers: Chapter 1." *The Tokio Time* 1, no. 7 (February 17, 1877): 80.

———. "Notes on Political Economy Designed Chiefly for Japanese Readers: Chapter 3." *The Tokio Time,* 1, no. 8 (February 24, 1877): 88–89.

———. "Notes on Political Economy Designed Chiefly for Japanese Readers: Chapter 7." *The Tokio Times,* 11, no. 6 (1877): 79–80.

Stebbins, Giles B. *The American Protectionist's Manual.* Detroit: T. Nourse, 1883.

———. "No Lasting Colonial Policy." *The Protectionist* 9, no. 121 (1899): 8–9.

Steele, George M. *Outline Study of Political Economy.* New York: Chautauqua Press, 1886.

———. *Rudimentary Economics for Schools and Colleges.* Boston: Leach, Shewell, and Sanborn, 1890.

Stewart, Andrew. *The American System: Speeches on the Tariff Question, and on Internal Improvements.* Philadelphia: Henry Carey Baird, 1872.

Stone, A. B. "How Protection Protects." In *Proceedings of the Convention of Iron and Steel Manufacturers and Iron Ore Producers, at Pittsburgh, Tuesday, May 6,* 1879, 24–33. Philadelphia: American Iron and Steel Association, 1879.

Thompson, R. W. *The History of Protective Tariff Laws.* 3rd Edition. Chicago: R. S. Peale & Co., 1888.

Thompson, Robert Ellis. "Carey, Henry Charles." In *Supplement to Encyclopaedia Britannica: A Dictionary of Arts, Sciences, and General Literature.* 9th Edition. Edited by Joseph Marshall Stoddart. New York: J. M. Stoddart, 1883: 720–722.

———. *The Divine Order of Human Society.* Philadelphia: John D. Wattles, 1891.

———. "Economic Literature." *The American* 12, no. 324 (1886): 9–10.

———. "Economic Literature." *The American* 16 no. 415 (1888): 214–215.

———. *Elements of Political Economy with Especial Reference to the Industrial History of Nations.* Philadelphia: Porter & Coates. 1882.

———. "Henry Charles Carey." *The Penn Monthly.* 10 [November] (1879): 816–834.

———. "Laveleye and the Kathedersocialism." *The Penn Monthly.* (May 1876): 378–394.

———. "Pennsylvania Protectionists." *The Protectionist.* 11, no. 131 (1900): 648–649.

———. "Points on National Policy: We Have Manufactures Because We Have Had a Protective Tariff—Trusts and Shipping Questions." *The Protectionist* 14, no. 159 (1902): 146–149.

———. *Political Economy for High Schools and Academies.* Boston: Ginn & Company, 1895.

———. "Protection." In *Johnson's Universal Dictionary.* Vol. 6, edited by Charles Kendall Adams, 817–822. New York: D. Appleton and Company, 1897.

———. *Protection to Home Industry.* New York: D. Appleton & Company, 1886.

———. "Review of Protection Versus Free Trade." *The American.* 11, no. 286 (1886): 234–235.

———. "Social Reform and the Socialists." *The Chautauquan* 13, no. 6. (1891): 731–735.

———. "The Tariff a Live Issue." *The Protectionist.* 32(6): 1920, 269.

Tibbits, George. *Essay on the Expediency and Practicability, of Improving or Creating Home Markets for the Sale of Agricultural Production and Raw Materials, by the Introduction or Growth of Artizans and Manufacturers.* Philadelphia: Clark & Raser, 1829.

———. *Memoir on the Expediency and Practicability, of Improving or Creating Home Markets for the Sale of Agricultural Production and Raw Materials, by the Introduction or Growth of Artizans and Manufacturers.* 3rd Edition. Philadelphia: J. R. A. Skerrett, 1827.

Valeonti, Sofia. "Henry C. Carey's Monetary Thought and American Industrialization in the Greenback Debate." *History of Political Economy.* 54, no. 2 (2022): 189–216.

Walker, Robert J. "Report from the Secretary of the Treasury on the Subject of the Finances, etc." In *State Papers and Speeches on the Tariff.* edited by Frank W. Taussig. 214–251. Cambridge: Harvard University, 1892.

Walters, Raymond, Jr. *Alexander James Dallas: Lawyer—Politician—Financier, 1759–1817.* Philadelphia: University of Pennsylvania Press, 1944.

Ware, Nathaniel A. *Notes on Political Economy.* New York: Leavitt, Trow, and Co., 1844.

Webster, Daniel. "Convention at Andover." In *The Works of Daniel Webster.* Vol. 2. 18th ed, 155–200. Boston: Little, Brown, and Company, 1881.

———. "General Effects of Protection." In *The Works of Daniel* Webster. Vol. 4. 18th ed, 528–539. Boston: Little, Brown, and Company, 1881.

———. "Lecture Before the Society for the Diffusion of Useful Knowledge." In *The Writings and Speeches of Daniel Webster.* Vol. 13, 63–78. Boston: Little, Brown, & Company, 1902.

———. "Speech at the Whig Convention of Philadelphia." In *The Works of Daniel Webster.* Vol. 2, 18th ed., 249–275. Boston: Little, Brown, and Company, 1881.

———. "The Tariff." In *The Works of Daniel Webster.* Vol. 3, 18th ed., 94–149. Boston: Little, Brown, and Company, 1881.

Wharton, Joseph. *National Self–Protection.* Philadelphia: The American Iron and Steel Association, 1875.

Wilson, William D. *First Principles of Political Economy.* Ithaca: Finch & Apgar, 1875.

Young, Andrew W. *National Economy: A History of the American Protective System, and Its Effects Upon the Several Branches of Domestic Industry.* New York: J. C. Derby & N. C. Miller, 1866.

Young, John Philip. "Economic Aspects of Reciprocity." *The Protectionist* 13, no. 146 (1901): 80–91.

———. *Protection and Progress: The Study of the Economic Bases of the American Protective System.* Chicago: Rand, McNally & Company, 1900.

INDEX

www.ingramcontent.com/pod-product-compliance
Ingram Content Group UK Ltd.
Pitfield, Milton Keynes, MK11 3LW, UK
UKHW041830100926
8556IPUK00002B/108

9 781839 99926